THE COLD CANYON
FIRE JOURNALS

3 years & 9 months since
the start of the Wragg Fire

THE COLD CANYON FIRE JOURNALS

Green Shoots and
Silver Linings in the Ashes

Written and Illustrated by

ROBIN LEE CARLSON

Heyday
Berkeley, California

The publisher is grateful to the Moore Family Foundation
for their generous support of this project.

Library of Congress Cataloging-in-Publication Data
Names: Carlson, Robin Lee, author, illustrator.
Title: The Cold Canyon Fire journals : green shoots and silver linings in
    the ashes / written and illustrated by Robin Lee Carlson.
Description: Berkeley, California : Heyday, [2022] | Includes
    bibliographical references.
Identifiers: LCCN 2021060772 | ISBN 9781597145848 (paperback)
Subjects: LCSH: Carlson, Robin Lee--Travel--California--Stebbins Cold
    Canyon Reserve. | Wildfires--Environmental aspects--California--Stebbins
    Cold Canyon Reserve. | Fire ecology--California--Stebbins Cold Canyon
    Reserve. | Restoration ecology--California--Stebbins Cold Canyon
    Reserve. | Stebbins Cold Canyon Reserve (Calif.)--Environmental
    conditions--21st century.
Classification: LCC SD421.32.C2 C395 2022 | DDC
    363.37/909794--dc23/eng/20220121
LC record available at https://lccn.loc.gov/2021060772

Cover Art: Robin Lee Carlson
Cover Design: Ashley Ingram
Interior Design/Typesetting: Ashley Ingram

Published by Heyday
P.O. Box 9145, Berkeley, California 94709
(510) 549-3564
heydaybooks.com

Printed in East Peoria, Illinois, by Versa Press, Inc.

10 9 8 7 6 5 4 3 2 1

FSC
www.fsc.org
MIX
Paper from
responsible sources
FSC® C005010

To Jacob and Isaac,
storytellers

fruits on Parry manzanita
Arctostaphylos parryi

carpenter ant (Camponotus sp)
wandering on muddy trickle
running across the trail

TABLE OF CONTENTS

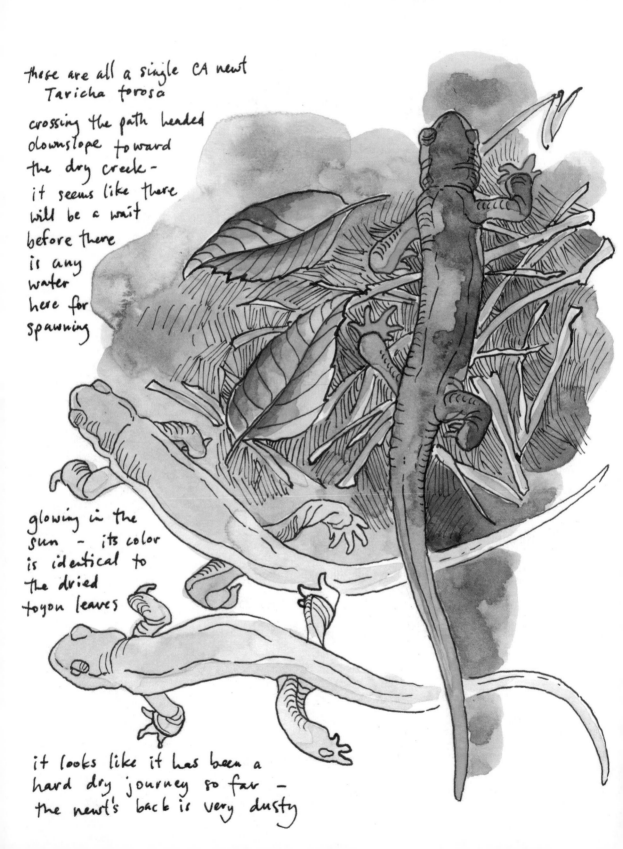

these are all a single CA newt
    Taricha torosa

crossing the path headed
downslope toward
the dry creek -
it seems like there
will be a wait
before there
is any
water
here for
spawning

glowing in the
sun - its color
is identical to
the dried
toyon leaves

it looks like it has been a
hard dry journey so far -
the newt's back is very dusty

INTRODUCTION

A small, leathery form moves slowly over the bare ground. Its brown back is almost gray with dirt and ash, caked in rivulets along its sides. Its belly, normally a flaming orange, is also muted. In color and shape it is indistinguishable from the dried toyon leaves it walks past. Its every wrinkle and fold stands out, the grooves outlined in dirt. The California newt is heading slowly, unerringly downhill toward the creek bed. In its clumsy-looking way, it climbs steadily over twigs and under branches. It is coming from its burrow somewhere on the hill above us down to the creek to mate, making its way through a vastly different world than the one from which it retreated early last summer.

When the newt crawled underground to begin its long hibernation, the shrubs were full and green, and the scattered oaks and pines spread their canopies over the hillsides and the canyon floor. Ample shade was broken by occasional sun-dappled clearings. Even in the hot summer, there were plenty of cool shadows in which to shelter. But now, after a wildfire, almost all of that is gone. I am hiking along a dusty trail in early January. Midmorning, the light slanting down into the canyon casts my shadow far ahead, and it precedes me down the path. The gentle winter sunlight falls on starkly exposed earth. Almost no leaves remain to block it. What the light exposes are the signs of recent fire—blackened stumps and twisting branches, alternating swaths of black and white ash, vivid spots of sienna where the soil is freshly exposed. The leaves of resprouting plants, coming up in flashes of green here and there amid the brown and black, remain very low to the ground, just getting started.

The newt's movement just off the trail catches my eye. Its journey looks arduous and far more uncomfortable than it would be in a normal year. Everything is dry and bright, with nowhere for a moisture-loving amphibian to find relief. Is the newt surprised to find the world so changed? I worry for it, because the drought means that the creek is still dry in this part of the canyon. I wonder how long the newt will need to wait for the creek to flow, or whether it will find water sources I do not know about.

I watch the newt and think:

Here is an empty landscape, a blasted wasteland with a solitary survivor making its lonely way to an uncertain fate.

Here is a bustling landscape, full of life in unexpected places, emerging from nooks and crannies and underground refuges to revel in the new vistas.

I wonder which of these the newt experiences. Is this a still and silent place or a place full of the calls and songs of birds, the beat of wings, the buzz of bees, and the rustle of small bodies in the underbrush? Is it a place of grim survival or of new opportunities?

In 2015, in the middle of a hot California summer, I was keeping my usual watch on the sky to see what the dry weather held in store. I was not surprised on July 23 to see a heavy band of smoke over the western hills. The day before, the Wragg Fire had ignited in Napa County near Lake Berryessa and quickly spread east into Solano County and through the rugged terrain of Stebbins Cold Canyon Reserve, part of the University of California Natural Reserve System. This is a place I know well, having hiked there for decades. Its steep hillsides and boulder-filled, shady creek harbor a diverse world of plants and animals, fungi and lichen that are both familiar and wild.

Though my mind understood fire's importance in the ecosystem, my heart did not. After the Wragg Fire, I was devastated: what a calamity to befall this beautiful place! In this, I am a product of my time. Despite abundant evidence of regeneration, the modern view of fire remains stubbornly one-dimensional. It is difficult to see beyond the harsh and desolate landscape of a recent burn, and my anxiety about the changing climate only makes this harder. While once I started to hold my breath at the beginning of summer, now I do all year. I'm waiting to smell smoke and see the sun turn red. Here in California, frequent and severe drought and the new climate conditions have stretched our fire season year-round—the question is not whether there will be devastating wildfires but when and how many. Understandably, this is the primary image of fire that we see in the news and all around us. Its human toll and destructive power are the beginning and end of the story.

These images have particular resonance for me, fire having lain at the heart of all my childhood nightmares. I dreamed of flames hidden in walls or behind doors. Flames creeping into view, leaving me with nowhere to run or hide. I would wake with a jolt, often in tears, and the dreams stayed with me into the daylight hours. I wouldn't let my parents light candles in our house until I was older than I like to admit. In our built-up lives of wooden structures and hoarded belongings, fire is wildness and uncertainty and danger.

With so much to lose in a fire and so much to fear from modern infernos, it is nearly impossible to comprehend that fire could be anything but unmitigated and all-consuming calamity. Modern humans assemble our homes and possessions at great expense, and we know that the mature, leafy habitats we see in nature are also the result of long years of

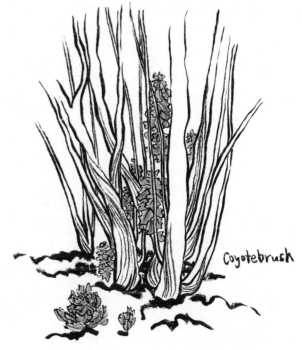

Coyotebrush

investment. We think about losing everything around us—our homes, belongings, and even lives—and conclude that the same must be true in nature. The full-grown habitat—full of large shady trees, soft mats of leaves on the ground, thickets of shrubs—seems irreplaceable. But this is a very narrow perspective of nature as a pretty, static backdrop—the idea that the land here is "supposed" to look like this forever, with shoulder-height, dense chaparral shrubs, tall green oaks in the woodlands, and a picturesque shady stream running through. All seeding and leafing and flowering and foraging seem to have built up to this habitat, and to lose it feels like a terrible tragedy.

But what if we take that linear progression and tie it head to tail, like ouroboros, the world-eating snake who forms a circle without end? The mature ecosystem would be just one point on the circle, no more or less important than any of the other stages. Is it possible to understand that a newly burned landscape is just as valuable an environment as a landscape full of large shady trees and shrubs?

And so I wondered what it would actually be like after the fire. By forging a personal connection to the habitats at Cold Canyon, I hoped to develop a more nuanced understanding of fire's impact on the canyon and everything that calls it home. I sought a more intimate knowledge of what happens after fire, knowledge that could only be gained by spending considerable time in a place that had burned, visiting regularly over the years. I was moved by the otherworldly landscape I saw when I first visited shortly after the fire and was eager to watch the new face of the landscape emerge. Cold Canyon is not far from my home, and I began hiking there monthly.

A full understanding of fire's role in shaping the natural world cannot just be told but must also be felt in the passage of time and season. I am a biologist by education and early career, and I spent summer internships and my graduate studies hunting spiders and millipedes and learning their ecology. My firsthand participation in fieldwork taught me that experiencing the burned landscape directly was essential to understanding it. To watch annual plants come and go, burned and

blue oak
Quercus
douglasii

heat-scorched shrubs and trees resprout, and seeds germinate after being activated by fire and smoke. To watch animals as they returned to burned areas and made use of new resources revealed by fire. To learn all I could about the science of fire and how it has evolved in tight embrace with the species in these habitats. And as a lifelong artist and now science illustrator, I needed to draw what I saw. It would be an act of discovery, a way to ensure that I looked more deeply and more thoroughly—under leaves, into cracks, beneath the surface—over and over again with passing time, to see and feel what is around me with eyes and heart focused on recording both the extraordinary and the mundane. But it would also be an act of consolation, memorializing the fire, marking this point in time with all its simultaneous loss and potential.

My sketchbooks, pens, and paint are my tools for experiencing the world and thinking through all of my discoveries. Translating what I am seeing, hearing, and feeling into images on a page is a way to find correlations and connections between all the different parts of the narrative I am watching unfold over time. It is also a way to share the story. Drawings made in the field are more spontaneous and full of life, and I use this immediacy to connect with other people and share my insights.

I felt dizzy reimagining a recently burned area as a vital habitat in its own right, but that thought grew slowly as the evidence accumulated before my eyes and on the pages of my sketchbook. Plants, animals, fungi—all have species that thrive in a burned landscape, and sometimes they find better opportunities here than in any other habitat. I expected to learn a lot from my visits. I did not expect to have my perspectives so fundamentally altered. Exploring Cold Canyon in the years after the Wragg Fire gave me a chance to see the world from some wildly unfamiliar viewpoints and to turn my understanding of a healthy habitat on its head.

Although this book is about a very specific place and time, what I have been watching at Cold Canyon is happening all over the western US. The details change, but the principles of fire ecology and the integral role of fire in many western habitats remain the same. Many important western ecosystems are found at Cold Canyon—chaparral, riparian woodland, oak woodland, savanna, and grassland, even if that grassland is now dominated by introduced species. It is a teeming, diverse world folded into a single small canyon in the California Coast Ranges. Over the course of this project, my direct observations have been a springboard to learn about the fire cycle across western landscapes, and I have met many wonderful scientists, restoration ecologists, and land managers in the process. I have asked how my local observations relate to climate change and recent trends in fire behavior, as large conflagrations replace smaller, less intense fires throughout the West. These changes have widespread repercussions, and I have viewed them through the lens of my personal investigations; being grounded in deep understanding of a single place has been an invaluable starting point for understanding patterns of ecological change in the broader world.

I started this project focused on the aftermath of a single event in time, but in fact I have watched as Cold Canyon falls victim to the ever more compressed cycle of modern wildfires. The canyon burned again in August 2020, just over five years after the fire that touched off my journey. Cold Canyon's story is an increasingly common one in the West. I have been a closer witness to these dramatic changes than I ever expected, and I constantly wonder what we are losing and what we have already lost. I have stood in absolute stillness and quiet after fire, and in its opposite, too—the dance and cacophony of birds overhead and insects nearby, the green shoots rising and pollen falling. Contemplating changes to the climate set in motion long ago and accelerating to this day, I think of destruction and ruin and time, while all around me there still are hearts beating, lungs breathing, buds swelling, and life continuing.

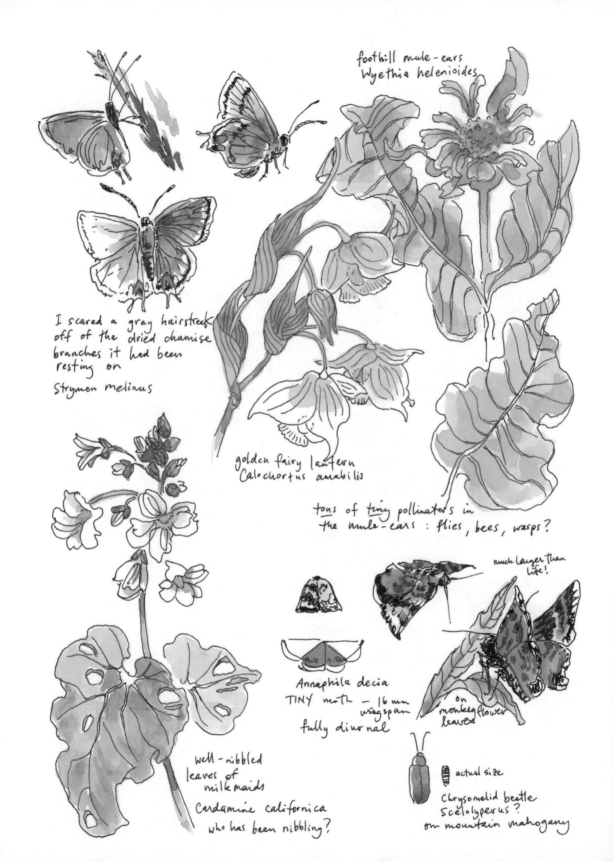

foothill mule-ears
Wyethia helenioides

I scared a gray hairstreak
off of the dried chamise
branches it had been
resting on

Strymon melinus

golden fairy lantern
Calochortus amabilis

tons of tiny pollinators in
the mule-ears : flies, bees, wasps?

much larger than
life!

Annaphila decia
TINY moth — 16 mm
wingspan
fully diurnal

on
monkey flower
leaves

well-nibbled
leaves of
milkmaids

Cardamine californica
who has been nibbling?

actual size

Chrysomelid beetle
Scelolyperus ?
on mountain mahogany

If we are to comprehend the global climate crisis, it is more essential than ever to be rooted in a place. I started studying Cold Canyon to more fully understand what is happening in my own backyard, knowing that this was the first step toward adapting to the new realities of our rapidly changing world. As I deepened my connection to my local landscape, links between the different parts of the ecosystem were revealed, opening my eyes to worlds I had not previously imagined. These worlds sometimes felt suddenly illuminated, much as the fire tearing through the canyon burned away the vegetation and peeled back layer after layer of the landscape, leaving behind the land's bare skeleton. During my first visits after the fire, I felt as though I had x-ray vision as I peered into the wide-open vistas of exposed earth and denuded branches. It was a revelatory glimpse into what had been there all along: the shapes of the rocks and hills, the patterns of trees, and the paths of the tiny tributaries to Cold Creek etched into the slopes.

My perspective shifted again and again, as I developed a new appreciation for what constitutes a rich and healthy life. Just as a chaparral shrub is transformed by fire, looking dead to human eyes but actually still fully alive, I have come to see that things that look like loss are actually hope. Looking at the charred canyon and slopes from the perspective of a flower, insect, or bird, I see that this is not a wasteland but a landscape brimming with potential. My hope is not absolute—climate change and suburban development are kindling an acceleration of fire cycles and fire intensity, which has critical implications for biodiversity and resilience. But when fire comes at healthy intervals, far from being an unnatural cataclysm, it is an essential part of western habitats' normal life. That normal life is change, continuous change, and fire should fit seamlessly into the pattern. The damage and destruction of fire are essential for the vigorous flowering to come.

Chapter One

FIRE IN THE CANYON

The Wragg Fire and What Came Next

The Wragg Fire burned through Cold Canyon in 2015, a seeming tragedy that became a chance to see the world from new perspectives and to understand that there is still abundant life in a burned landscape.

A car pulls off the road on a summer day. The afternoon is scorching hot, and the clear blue sky is beautiful but oppressive in its promise of continuing brutal temperatures. The car's passengers have been traveling through the winding curves of the eastern Coast Ranges near Lake Berryessa and are at this point paralleling the farthest eastern arm of the lake. Perhaps they have pulled over to take a look at the view. The hillsides are covered in parched yellow vegetation, and the ground is baked to porcelain brittleness. Underneath the car, hot metal touches dry grass and ignites. This is not an uncommon story in the American West, nor is what happens next. The flames leap free and hurry through the dry brush. Stopped by the waters of Lake Berryessa on one side, they spread east. Up the first ridge they run, fanning out to north and south and cresting Blue Ridge. After that they are down into the next canyon—Cold Canyon—burning hot and fierce, where the wind encourages them to spend a while at the base of the canyon, swirling and gusting around and around, burning more thoroughly the vegetation aboveground and also sending heat more deeply into the soil than if they had simply raced through.

Eventually, the flames dash east out of Cold Canyon and over Pleasants Ridge. Voracious, they will consume over six thousand acres in the first twenty-four hours. On July 23, 2015, the day after the fire starts, I am out for a walk near my

stopped & got out of the car to see the smoke - looks like the Wragg fire is still burning (burning again?)

home in Davis and see smoke over the western hills. Smoke in the evening sky is unsurprising during a California summer, but always worth noting, so I draw it quickly in my pocket sketchbook and walk on. Three days later, riding in the passenger seat of a car, I draw the burned hills and note the line where the fire ended to the north. There are still smoking spots near the ridgeline, but the fire is largely contained.

Then on July 28, returning home from an afternoon errand, I notice a large new plume of smoke hanging over the hills. My son is in the car with me, so we pull over to take a longer look. One of the great revelations of having a young child is the close attention we pay to so many things that have become common-place to me as an adult: emergency vehicles, airplanes overhead, every insect we pass on a walk, and smoke in any place or form. We park on the shoulder of the country road and get out of the car to stand at the edge of a field. The smoke rises in a thick black column and spreads south, fading to brown, then dull white. As we wonder whether this is still the Wragg Fire or whether a new fire has started, our ears tell us to look up. The bulky form of an air tanker rumbles overhead on its way to the blaze. All the excitement that a three-year-old could hope for! Sitting in the car before heading home, I quickly draw the smoke and the tanker, with Isaac making sure I do not leave out the telephone poles.

This is indeed a flare-up of the Wragg Fire, which continues to burn for another week before it is finally extinguished. In the end, the fire burns a further eight thousand acres, with no loss of life, but seven structures damaged or destroyed. By the time of the flare-up, I have heard that the entirety of Cold Canyon burned in the early part of the fire. Although there were no human tragedies, I feel a different kind of sadness. This is a wild area close to home and familiar, a place I have assumed would always be there for me. The oak woodlands, chaparral, and riparian habitats are full and mature. I have just begun to take my son to Cold Canyon to introduce him to all the rocks, plants, and animals I love.

DC 10 Tanker Air Carrier
flew directly overhead leaving fire

In the coming days, the local newspaper and the UC Davis website publish photos of the stark new landscape, full of blackened limbs reaching up into the sky. I see alternating patches of white and black ash and little rivulets of mud running down the hillside into the sludgy black creek bed. I see a nighttime trail-camera photo of what is suspected to be the last dusky-footed woodrat remaining in the canyon after the fire, because the dens of all the others were incinerated. The images are deeply affecting. I feel just as I did after the 1995 Mount Vision Fire burned over twelve thousand acres in Point Reyes. I grew up hiking there, too, and it was always a coastal oasis of cooler temperatures and fog, distinctively gnarled Bishop pines, and stunning fields of yellow and purple lupine. Or after the 2013 Morgan Fire consumed over three thousand acres on Mount Diablo, where I have long hiked and hunted tarantulas in the fall. In both places, the forests were replaced by jagged black trunks and emptiness, and both times I thought: something I love is now gone. Wildfire feels like loss, like a hole in our heart where a beautiful, mature ecosystem used to be. I am stuck in the idea of Cold Canyon as a place full of natural architecture, made of the trees and shrubs that define its character. With those gone, I try to picture navigating the canyon, and think it must be like making my way through a familiar town where the buildings have been torn down: disorienting and confusing and unspeakably sad.

On a sunny day in April 1990, the piercing blue sky expanding around us forever in all directions, I walked with my ninth-grade biology class along the trail at Cold Canyon. It was a day of bright colors. I remember listening to stories about the resin-covered leaves of bush monkeyflower, with its glowing orange flowers, and how those flowers attract bees, moths, hummingbirds, and other pollinators. We learned about the vivid blue of scrub jay feathers. Our teacher demonstrated that the blue is an optical illusion. When not catching the light, the feather is dull brown. In a shaft of sunlight, though, the light is scattered by pockets of air in the jay's feather, which act like a prism. The jay feather is a powerful lesson in perspective that I have always associated with Cold Canyon: a reminder to look more closely and not take first sights and impressions for granted.

in bright sun
CA pitcher sage
Lepechinia calycina
growing intermingled
with
bush monkey flower
Diplacus aurantiacus

& poison oak underneath
them
Toxicodendron diversilobum

Another lesson in perspective took much longer to appreciate. Our teacher loved lichens and happily pointed them out to us here and there. I am not sure that any of my classmates shared her enthusiasm—I, for one, was mystified by how such a seemingly boring subject could fascinate her. I loved hawks and falcons best then. I had spent a blissful couple of months earlier that school year documenting their activity at a hawk and owl preserve across from the county landfill. The project combined all of my favorite activities both then and now: careful observation, getting to know new species, note-taking, and drawing. Now that I am an adult, returning to Cold Canyon to learn all I can about fire ecology, I find myself drawn back to those moments with my teacher. With many years' more thought about ecosystems and how all of the pieces in them fit together— the large and charismatic along with the small and easily overlooked—I too understand the rewards to be found in slowing down, crouching beside a boulder, pulling out a hand lens, and peering closely at lichens.

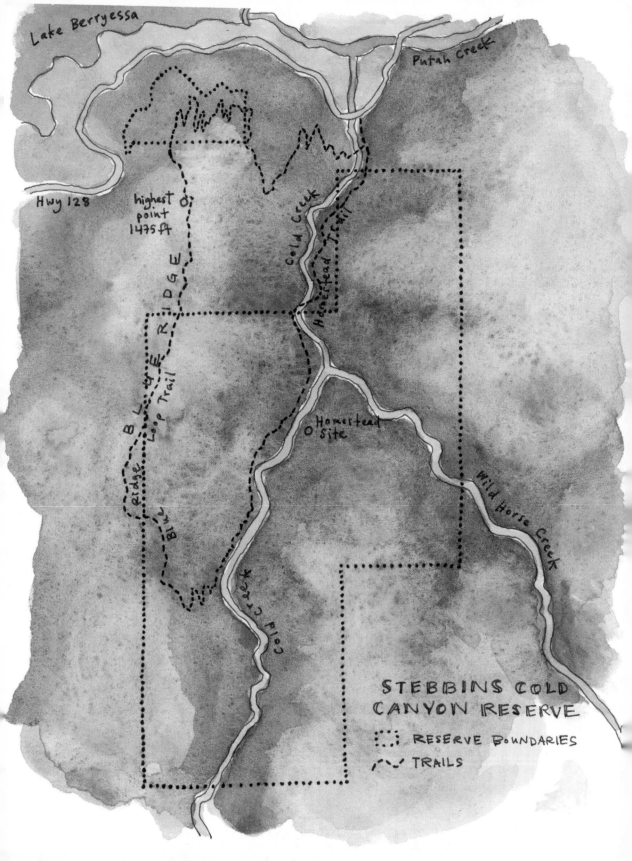

Lake Berryessa

Putah Creek

Hwy 128

highest
point
1475ft

Cold Creek

Homestead Trail

B L U E   R I D G E

Blue Ridge Loop Trail

Homestead
Site

Wild Horse Creek

Cold Creek

STEBBINS COLD
CANYON RESERVE

RESERVE BOUNDARIES

TRAILS

Cold Canyon became a perfect refuge during my teen and early adult years, a leafy green riparian habitat below golden California hills. It was close to home and always there whether I needed an energizing hike or a trip to linger in the shade beside the rocky pools in the creek. On a weekday morning in the spring of 2015, four months before the fire will charge through the canyon, I am looking forward to both.

Driving to Cold Canyon from Davis is a journey from flatlands to hills, starting in the Sacramento Valley with its expanses of dusty sky and lines of hills on the horizon. As I head west, my wheels hum along the highway through the agriculture that fills the valley. These are the fields I knew best in my childhood, once full of alfalfa and tomato and now mostly almond orchards. The valley gently gives way to hills as I enter the eastern edge of the Coast Ranges. I am now in Putah Creek Canyon, a portal into the Blue Ridge Range, traveling through sedimentary rocks that have come from ocean deposits, sandstones and shales alternatingly lifted and eroded to form layered ridges in colorful striations of ochre, sienna, carbon, sepia. Putah Creek was dammed in 1957 to create Lake Berryessa, but it continues below the Monticello Dam, and after years of farmers' diverting too much water for irrigation, Chinook salmon are spawning once again in its waters. At a spot near Putah Creek just below the dam, I stop the car and get out. This is where Stebbins Cold Canyon Reserve begins.

I walk on the trail into Cold Canyon, and the sporadic noise of cars and trucks on the highway fades away quickly. Unaware that this is the last time I will see the canyon looking the way I have known it for the past several decades, I take a deep breath under the dusty-green oak leaves that filter the bright sun into a mellow checkerboard of light and shade. To my left, east, is Pleasants Ridge. Blue

Ridge is to my right. Both sides of the canyon are formed of sandstone from the long-ago marine sediments that compose this entire portion of the Coast Ranges. The floor of the canyon is softer shale, worn down by the creek to form the valley. Landslides and erosion have sharpened Cold Canyon's steep sides and changing topography, creating many different habitats in a relatively small area.

I quickly reach the right turn to head straight up the hillside to the top of Blue Ridge before making the full loop, which continues along the ridge, down into the canyon, and back along Cold Creek. The trail immediately crosses the creek. There are large boulders strewn along the canyon floor here, not far from the highway, remnants of long-ago landslides. They make the creek bed an appealing place to stop and sit for a while. The water is running briskly. By the middle of the coming summer, though, the creek here will be dry, having moved entirely underground as it does every year when rain is a distant memory. I cross by stepping from rock to rock, stopping in the middle to peer into the water for interesting signs of life. I see a few freshwater snails clinging to the underside of a submerged stone.

As I continue uphill, the trail travels steeply up switchbacks, through patches of shrubs and trees. The clusters of interior live oaks provide welcome shade, in which I pause to admire the trees' profuse collections of lichens on trunk and branch. Climbing higher, I emerge from the trees and out into an expanse of chaparral. Here, as in many places in Cold Canyon, the terrain is dominated by chamise, whose long, thin branches are covered in tiny, almost scale-like leaves. They are flowering now, tiny white sprays of petals along their branches. The effect is feathery and almost ethereal as I look out over the hillside. In this spot, I particularly love where pink-orange sandstone boulders are visible between the chamise, the smooth, flat surfaces of the rock inviting for sitting and sketching.

Habitats alternate frequently on this side of the canyon. Continuing up toward Blue Ridge, I travel through a microcosm of some of California's more common ones. Through chaparral shrubs—mountain mahogany, coyotebrush,

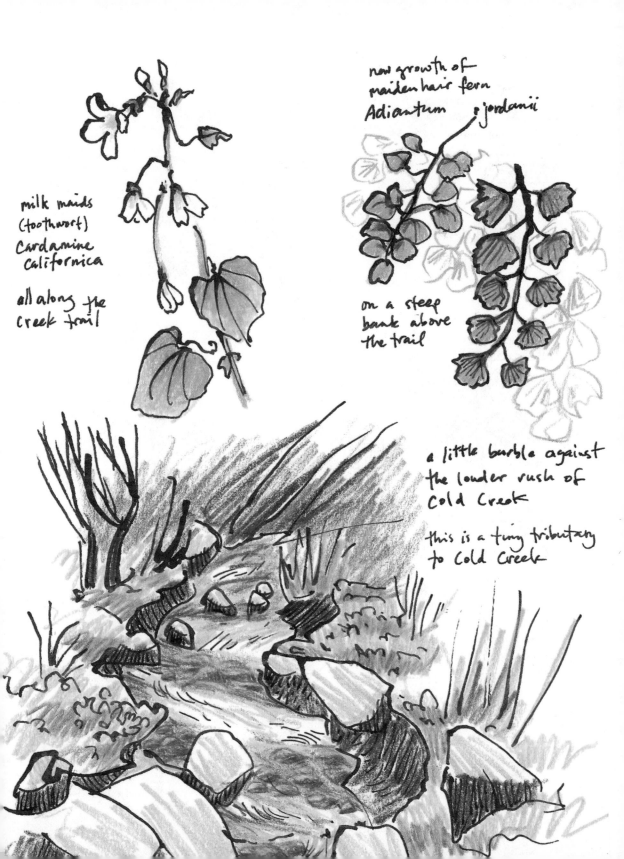

milk maids
(toothwort)
Cardamine
californica

all along the
creek trail

new growth of
maiden hair fern
Adiantum   jordanii

on a steep
bank above
the trail

a little burble against
the louder rush of
Cold Creek

this is a tiny tributary
to Cold Creek

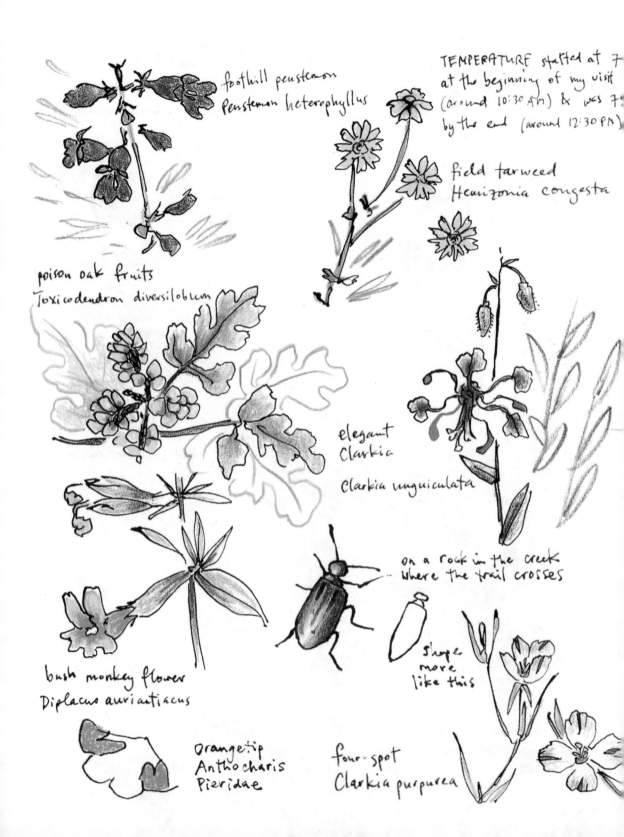

foothill penstemon
Penstemon heterophyllus

TEMPERATURE started at 7~
at the beginning of my visit
(around 10:30 AM) & was 7~
by the end (around 12:30 PM)

field tarweed
Hemizonia congesta

poison oak fruits
Toxicodendron diversilobum

elegant
Clarkia

Clarkia unguiculata

on a rock in the creek
where the trail crosses

shape
more
like this

bush monkey flower
Diplacus auriantiacus

orangetip
Anthocharis
Pieridae

four-spot
Clarkia purpurea

California lilac, and scrub oak. Past little groves of redbud that glow shockingly pink in the early spring. Under leafy branches of interior live oaks. Across small grasslands with scattered patches of miniature lupine, purple sanicle, and other wildflowers. When I reach the top of the ridge, the whole panorama is laid out before me—Cold Canyon far below, Lake Berryessa to the west, and the foothills down to the Sacramento Valley to the east. I can see the gap in the hills cleaved by the road I will travel home. It is only a thirty-minute drive, and it seems as though my town is almost visible from here.

On the far side of the canyon, the hillsides of Pleasants Ridge undulate, their slopes strikingly marked in alternating bands of color, a dark forest green and a bright yellow-green. The colors follow distinct ridge and valley folds, marking the alternating habitats on each side. The north-facing slopes, which receive less direct sunlight, are cooler and moister. They are covered in dark-green chaparral: toyon, manzanita, California lilac, chamise, and other shrubs. The south-facing slopes, with more direct sun, are hotter and drier and covered in grasses. Right now, they are bright green, though they will turn golden yellow in the summer and fall.

These grasses that change from green to gold, plus some herbaceous wild-flowers, dominate the grasslands and savannas on Pleasants Ridge. The savannas also have scattered blue oaks and gray pines, trees that are hardy and able to tolerate the dry conditions on these parched south-facing slopes. As in the rest of the California foothills, the grassland and savanna habitats at Cold Canyon are now full of nonnative annual grasses such as oats, foxtails, and bromes, whose takeover has been encouraged by grazing and plowing. Native grasses are not completely gone from the area, though, and Cold Canyon still has, for example, purple needlegrass, California melic, and blue wildrye.

In between the folds of Pleasants Ridge, it is easy to see where tiny tributaries to Cold Creek cut down the hillsides, their paths marked by greener and more abundant vegetation. The rivulets of green meet up with the riparian habitat at the bottom of the canyon, where there are even more trees than up on the hills.

Turning back to the trail, I walk along the narrow spine of Blue Ridge. It is bright up here, with no trees and only small, sparse shrubs. Sometimes scrambling over and between boulders, I briefly stop in the shade of the larger rocks to peer at a woolly paintbrush flower or to see a fence lizard basking on the warm rock above. A little less than a mile south along the ridge, the trail begins to head downhill. California lilacs are on either side of me, buzzing with insect life: bumblebees, honeybees, metallic green bees, flies, a wasp, and many others I see or hear too quickly to identify. A series of steep switchbacks takes me back down to the canyon bottom, where it is cooler, moister, and more wooded. I find shooting stars and large-leaved hound's tongue here, along with checker lily and foothill delphinium. I smell the distinctive perfume of California foothills coming from the bay laurels lining the canyon.

The trail turns north and then follows the creek, sometimes close to its stony bed and sometimes a little way up the slope. There are interior live oaks here, growing where it is wetter and avoiding the higher slopes where their more drought-tolerant blue oak cousins are comfortable. Willows, Fremont cottonwoods, and California black walnuts want their feet wet as often as possible and tend to grow in the creek bed itself or right at its edges. The trail meanders through stands of extremely dense shrubs, toyons, and California lilacs high enough to turn the trail into a tunnel at times. Their shade is pleasant now and has been a deep relief on summer hikes. I hear a Bewick's wren close by, a metallic trill followed by a very clearly enunciated and almost exaggerated *tweet tweet tweet tweet tweet*.

I make one more creek crossing on this sunny spring day, hopping across on the large rocks. Just upstream of the crossing, there are pools that always have water, even during the summer when much of the rest of the creek is dry.

Especially in the spring, the sound of the rushing water mingles with the susurration of leaves in the creek-side trees. I always stop at this crossing to watch the water striders, mesmerized by the shadows cast by the dimples of water where each of their feet touches the water, cast down on the rocks at the bottom of the pools. It is just after noon. When I start walking again, I am preceded along the trail by a Sara orangetip butterfly, mostly white with vibrant wedges of orange lined in black at the front of its forewings. Every once in a while it pauses on the ground, but my footsteps make it startle up again and continue its flutter-and-dip, flutter-and-dip flight pattern along ahead.

The canyon is quite narrow at the bottom, and even here the trail climbs and drops, following stair steps up the steeper sections, going around shady, sharp curves and descending again into tiny meadows lit by sunlight. When I come to stretches of California buckeye growing along the trail, I am almost bowled over by their flowers' aggressively sweet fragrance. They, like the lilacs, are full of insects, and these scenes of busy living—blooming and feeding and pollination—buoy me happily along the final stretch of trail.

A few short months later, in the days after I learn that the canyon has burned, I pull out my sketchbook and with trepidation turn to the pages from that last trip. There are the orangetip butterflies, the metallic green bees, the flowering buckeyes, and the woolly paintbrush. When I drew them, idling in the spring sunshine, in no way did I expect my sketches to become memorials. I was doing as I usually do when on a hike or even a walk in my neighborhood, making small sketches of some of the things that catch my eye. Staring at my drawings and notes now, I wonder whether anything I recorded is still alive, and I mourn for the emptiness that I think will surely have replaced all the life I saw around me on that verdant spring hike.

Lake Berryessa

Hwy 128

Cold Creek

Wild Horse Creek

Putah Creek

Hwy 128

Putah Creek Rd

Pleasants Valley Rd

WRAGG FIRE AREA
July 22 - August 5, 2015
STEBBINS COLD
CANYON RESERVE

On a warm, sunny day with wispy clouds in September 2015, fifty-one days since the Wragg Fire started and thirty-six days since it was fully contained, I drive to the entrance to Cold Canyon to see what I can see. Paper and pen in hand, I stand at the fence hastily erected to keep people out of the still possibly dangerous landscape, and stare at the panorama in front of me. The ground is black with ash, and the gnarled fingers of charred branches poke eerily out of the barren earth. My nostrils fill with the sharp tang of burned wood. The hills in front of me are smoothed to a wash of similar colors—dark brown, lighter brown, brownish orange—as if I were looking at the scene through the gauze of a used tea bag, stained with tannins.

I think, oh, everything has burned, and the trees that I see still standing must all be dead. As my eyes adjust to the landscape and I start to let go of my initial impressions, I can see that there is still some green in the branches of the tall oaks just a little way into the canyon. The green is pale and dusty, but a firm reminder that the trees are not dead and there is more to see here than I first thought. Standing guard at the entrance into the canyon just past the highway, a tall blue oak has not burned, except for some charred bark around its lower trunk, and it still has plenty of leaves. Many were killed by the fire and are brittle and orange, but I see patches of olive green.

Seeing all of this in front of me, I anxiously wonder how long it will take for things to grow back. How long until it looks the way I remember? The words often used to describe fires and their aftermath assume a return to a perfect state: the mature ecosystem that was there just before the fire. The leafy trees and full shrubs are the habitat many of us like the most. It is also the way we think the landscape ought to look. In current American culture, we think about the long process of *recovery*, and we talk about *regrowth*, *restoration*, and *rehabilitation*. These words all emphasize the *re*-turn to a standard, to normality, to the final goal. And I use the same words when I see those photos. This is exactly how I think about Cold Canyon in those first months after it burned, as a place that has been taken apart and will slowly grow back into itself. Language both reflects and drives our understanding of natural cycles.

Although the fire continues to feel like a tragedy, over the next couple of months I also begin to recognize an opportunity. Here is a chance to watch what happens immediately after a wild area has burned. More and more, I have felt driven to visually document the world altering around me, a response both to my fears and to my fascination with the accelerating impacts of climate change. I have been looking for ways to study the daily, monthly, yearly details of eco-system change on an intimately observable level, and what better example than a landscape responding to fire? This is how I can feel those changes myself, through sight, sound, touch, and smell. I believe that art created in direct obser-vation of the natural world creates an emotional connection between the artist, the place, and the audience. Recording my experiences in drawings captures not only the facts of what happens but also the emotions that come with those facts. I use art to communicate the *life* around me and the importance of what I am observing. I start to think about all the things I want to explore: What it feels like to walk through a burned area. What signs of life I see. Which species regrow or return quickly and which take a long time. Whether some will never return. How the observations change me and how I share that experience with other people.

Because Cold Canyon is a UC Natural Reserve, it will be left alone after the fire; there will be no intentional human interference with its habitats' responses, no clearing or replanting. The only work will be to rebuild trails and prevent trail-side erosion. Of course, the absence of human intervention is in some ways an illusion. The popularity of the canyon means that we are always present as hikers, runners, and wanderers, so we will all be influencing the course of fire response. In this important natural laboratory and place for recreation and nature exploration, human visitors are constant and were an integral part of the prefire status quo as well. Every step we take at Cold Canyon alters the environment, and by making my own regular visits to the canyon, I am a part of the story too. I am adding my own presence to the always-changing landscape, becoming one more witness to the drama that will unfold after the fire.

On an overcast winter day, slowly clearing to cloudy skies, I wait at the entrance to Cold Canyon along with a dozen or so other hikers. It is the end of December 2015, five months after the fire. Striding up to the group comes Jeffrey Clary, and he unlocks the padlock on the temporary chain-link gate across the entrance to the trail. "It's great to see you all here," he says as he checks our names off his list. Cold Canyon is still closed to the public, but Jeffrey has been bringing interested community members to the canyon on guided walks to look around and learn about the fire's impacts. "Let me tell you a little bit about the fire and what we've been seeing here since then." We gather up and enter through the gate, following Jeffrey up the trail.

At the time of this hike, Jeffrey is the Reserve director for Cold Canyon, though he will later go on to become the associate director for the entire UC Natural Reserve System and its forty-one reserves. He is tall and slender, a calm presence, speaking knowledgeably and with deep consideration about things both seen and unseen along the way. There are also several UC Davis professors and researchers in the group, whose questions and insights add new dimensions to the discussion. I scribble notes and sketch furiously at every stop.

There are big questions about what the fire will mean for Cold Canyon. Although it has been nearly thirty years since the last fire here, those years have been a time of rapid climate change, and the warming and drying that have occurred may have grave implications for the ability of the ecosystem to recover from the fire. The intensity with which the fire raged in the canyon makes Jeffrey worry that the heat

On a hike with Jeffrey Clary looking at the new landscape, all blackened limbs, blackened ground and heat dried leaves

penetrated the soil deeply enough to damage the seeds stored within. Jeffrey is also concerned about blue oaks, which have been suffering throughout California as the climate changes. In the Wragg Fire, they have been blackened, toppled, or reduced entirely to white ash. It may be a while before we know how many of them are still alive, though charred, and how many are truly killed.

The hills we walk past are highly unstable. Large expanses of land are exposed to the sky, and gone are the plants that once held the soil in place. When the fire churned across the canyon from one ridge to the next, the living plants were burned, reduced partly or fully to ash. So too all of the plant material that was already dead: fallen leaves, branches, logs. The same went for nonplants—lichens, fungi, and the animals that did not escape. This absence we can see. Not immediately apparent are the consequences of removing all of this organic material. Before the fire, the rich layer of living and decomposing material on and just below the soil surface was a luxurious blanket, keeping the soil protected and regulating the effects of the elements. The blanket was an insulator, keeping the soil from becoming too hot during the day and too cold at night. Seeds, roots, insects, millipedes, worms, fungi—all were able to make a life in the soil thanks to the regulating effects of this organic blanket. This layer was also a filter, distributing air and water throughout the soil and helping capture and store water for plants and other organisms. Now the blanket is gone, and the soil is no longer held in place or protected from rain and wind.

Burning plant material creates hydrocarbons. Although plant metabolism produces these organic chemicals naturally, combustion releases much greater amounts into the ecosystem in a shorter time. The hydrocarbons accumulate just below the soil surface to make a waxy, water-repellent layer that further reduces the ability of the hillsides to absorb any rain that falls. Before this December visit, there have only been a few light rains. But even these have washed soil, ash, and hydrocarbons down the slopes, depositing all into Cold Creek at the bottom. The thick, black sludge in the creek bed looks oily, and Jeffrey points out that it easily captures the prints of every animal that walks across it. We see the small prints of a bird that walked briefly along the edge of the muddy expanse. I picture it testing the surface and perhaps leaving again after finding it so sticky.

Jeffrey is relieved that the first rains of the season have been light. Although they have washed sediment into the stream, they have been gentler on the soil than harder downpours would have been. Their small drops have percolated down, beginning to open up the soil again, making it fluffier, in Jeffrey's words, and better able to hold the rain that we hope is coming later this winter.

Water is a potent, landscape-sculpting force, and wildfire reveals this in spectacular ways. Several times along the trail, we pass boulders that are split open as if dropped from a great height by a passing giant. Jeffery explains that during a fire, moisture trapped within rocks can boil, and as the water turns into gas, it expands and can force the rock apart. These fresh rock faces—bright, barren surfaces that contrast starkly with the older, weathered, lichen-covered sides of each boulder—become a symbol for me of the landscape laid bare and turned inside out by fire.

The rains have hastened a happy sight: the fresh green leaves of soap plants bursting from the blackened earth, their wildly wavy edges a particularly charismatic sign of life. They are a common sight after wildfire, growing back quickly from their bulbs. They are not the only green—we see new sprouts of chamise, toyon, coyotebrush, and California spicebush. We also see nonnative species enjoying the open space and sunlight. Redstem filaree, yellow starthistle, and several annual grasses are usually shaded out in Cold Canyon, and will be again, but for now are enjoying their opportunity to claim space in the ecosystem.

the streambed 5 months after the fire
all silted/sedimented, black & thick

a month later - moving water

WAVY LEAF
SOAP PLANT
Chlorogalum pomeridianum

its greens glow
against the black
soil

brand new rock faces —
the fire boiled the moisture
inside & its expansion
cracked the rock open

By the end of the hike, the sky has cleared to warm and blue. As I walk back down the trail toward the highway, my gaze rises with the slashes of black that are slowly, lazily circling Blue Ridge. The oblique Vs, almost straight lines, with delicate fringe at their tips, waver slightly as they make tiny adjustments to maintain their spirals, around and around. Heat from the exposed rocks at the top of the ridge quivers into the sky and holds these turkey vultures aloft. I see my own earthbound path reflected there. Each of my visits to Cold Canyon will be a loop in the spiral, and by coming here again and again I will watch the seasons change and life respond to the fire. Each incremental change will build over years to reveal the larger pattern of an ecosystem in full.

On my first postfire visits to Cold Canyon on my own, I feel keenly how little context I have for what I see. I want to document changes after the fire, but where do I start? As I walk into Cold Canyon after the fire, I try to exist on two levels at once. The first is to be fully present in the act of observation—to see, hear, feel, and smell all the different parts of the world around me right now. The second is to extend my imagination around me in time and space, more through questions than answers: What was here right before the fire? What happened to it during the fire? Where is it now if it still exists at all? What is below me and around me that I cannot sense, but is there nonetheless?

I know that many lives were simply destroyed in the fire. Animals that could not flee quickly enough, caught unaware or trapped. Plants and fungi that were not deeply rooted enough for their underground parts to survive.

What survives? Birds, mammals, insects: any animal that is mobile might escape, with enough time and sufficient energy to flee beyond the fire's reach before becoming exhausted. Anything that burrows—rodents, amphibians,

turkey vultures
above Blue Ridge

reptiles, insects, arachnids—has a good chance of escaping the heat underground, as long as the fire is not too intense. Soil's insulation can keep trapdoor spiders safe and cool in burrows that are only five to eight inches deep. From Jeffrey, I learn that California newts, California slender salamanders, and western pond turtles were likely buried deep enough to survive.

Walking in the canyon, I can see another mode of survival. There is a ribbon of green that snakes through the bottom of the canyon, with smaller threads joining occasionally from the slopes. Trees and other plants with wet feet were much better able to resist the heat and flame, and the burned landscape makes this apparent, with the greenery tracing the lines of tiny streamlets down the slopes and along the main creek through the canyon. Many of the plants appear unscathed, having been protected by the flames in two ways. First, the cool moisture of the streambed itself ensured that wet areas did not burn and the fire hurried past. Second, the plants along the streams had more moisture in their own tissue, providing resistance to burning or drying out from the heat.

Cold Creek is a seasonal stream. In some parts of the canyon, its water is aboveground for only a portion of the year. At the lower end of the creek, the stream generally runs aboveground between December and June, though there is quite a bit of variation depending on when the rains start and end each year. That section of the creek is reliably dry by midsummer, which means there was no water aboveground in the lower part of the canyon when the fire tore through. But the dry creek bed and yellow, arid hills can be deceptive. Even at the height of summer, the earth just below the gravel in the creek bed is still wet. The sheer quantity of green, leafy plants in the dry creek bed is a powerful testament to how much water remains underground even when we can see none of it ourselves. The veins of green foliage throughout the canyon are the invisible made visible by the fire.

After the fire, the moisture that gathers in the lowest parts of the slopes—in the trickles, the seeps, and the creek itself—drives the fastest regrowth. Those plants that did burn, wholly or partially, are using stored resources in their roots to send up new shoots. If they are also in wet soil, they are able to regrow even faster. California spicebush grows close to the stream courses and has broad green leaves that release a peppery, sweet fragrance when I crease them in my fingers. I am amazed at how lush its regrowth is in these places where it has ample access to water.

And it is not only plants that are protected by the watercourses in the landscape. There are so many forms of life that I cannot see and must use my imagination to picture in their homes and shelters below the ground on which I stand. Even with the flow underground, the wet soil in the creek bed shelters abundant animal life. Insects, amphibians, mollusks—all are used to surviving the hot, dry summer underground. In a fire, the survival method they used seasonally every year becomes an important strategy for avoiding the flames.

Wonders of survival: Foaming newts

Given the timing of the Wragg Fire, the California newts living in the canyon were probably all underground in their summer burrows. The adults spend the dry months in and under moist logs or in holes in the ground that they happen upon—they are not diggers themselves. In the winter, they emerge and make their way down the hill to the creek, where they undergo a second metamorphosis, regaining gills and seeing their tails change from thin and tapered to a paddle shape for swimming. Once mating and egg laying are complete, the adults become terrestrial again and return to the hillsides and their burrows. Their eggs hatch and live as aquatic larvae for several months, metamorphosing into adults as the creek begins to dry at the beginning of the summer. These youngsters also migrate upslope to find their own burrows to wait out the long, dry summer. Newts will make this journey and metamorphosis annually throughout their relatively long lives—up to fifteen years.

But what happens to animals that cannot flee fire when they are caught aboveground by the flames? It is exceptionally difficult to study animal behavior during wildfires or to replicate wildfire conditions experimentally, so much of what we know about the subject comes from chance observations. A surprising discovery during a prescribed burn in 1996 offers a glimpse into what may be a world of interesting survival strategies we have only just begun to guess at. Mark Stromberg, then the resident Reserve director of the Hastings Natural History Reservation in Carmel Valley, was participating in a burn there when he watched two newts approach and then walk directly into a small flame front. As they entered the flames, their naturally slimy skin coating foamed up in the heat. The foam appeared to act as a fire retardant, protecting them by dissipating heat over the foamy surface until they emerged from the flames again. The white coating came off easily as they walked through the ashy leaf litter, and their skin appeared undamaged. Mark has examined many, many newts over the course of his career and was certain that the newts emerged unscathed from the experience. It is a truly wondrous trait to carry around your own fire-retardant foam with you at all times.

People have long known something about this creature's ability to withstand flame. Newts are a kind of salamander, and the ancient Greeks believed that salamanders, especially the aptly named fire salamander found in Europe, had an intimate association with fire. It was thought that they were born in fire and retained the ability to put out fires using their own body's frigidity. Mark watched the newts intentionally walk into the flames, which is interestingly concordant with ancient Greek claims that salamanders seek fire. The mythology around salamanders and fire was not limited to Greece, either. The word *salamander* is itself derived from the Persian word *samandar*, meaning "fire within." In China, fireproof garments woven from asbestos were said to have been made from salamander hair, a strange twist for an inarguably hairless beast.

Although there has been some acknowledgment in modern herpetology that the mucus secreted by newts' skin to keep them moist may afford them protection against heat, Mark's rare opportunity to observe that their skin secretions foamed up in the fire gives a new dimension to the mythological association of salamanders with fire. I boggle at the thought of all the other adaptations to fire that we are unaware of and how rich the world must be to contain so many still-unseen wonders.

After surviving the fire, either in subterranean safety or by walking right through, newts must also navigate the burned landscape and all the new perils it brings. The streambed, though sometimes a haven during wildfire, may become an unlivable wasteland for amphibians for a year or two afterward. The sediment washed down from the hillsides fills the streambed and obliterates pools that are necessary for newt reproduction. This is a problem for other

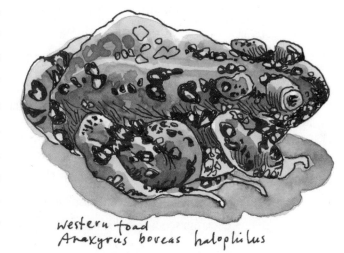

western toad
Anaxyrus boreas halophilus

amphibians too, such as foothill yellow-legged frogs, which studies have shown experience population declines after wildfires, likely due to stream sedimentation. But it all depends on the timing of the fire and the amount of rainfall that year. Except in the driest years, newts will usually find enough water to meet and mate. Pacific chorus frogs, whose loud *kreek-eek* follows me from the vicinity of the creek all along my spring hikes, have certainly seemed to weather this wildfire well.

Recently burned areas also are apparently attractive to western toads, which have been found to be more numerous in burned areas than in nearby unburned areas for the first three years after a fire, perhaps because they face less competition from other amphibians. They are drawn to disturbed landscapes, and this is a source of ongoing fascination to me as I slowly explore the burned canyon. Fire is a destroyer, an occasional annoyance, and a bringer of opportunities—all of these at once, even within a related group of animals like these amphibians.

Moments in the sun: Lizards

Because Cold Creek runs south to north, mornings along the creek are cool and shady, with the rising sun blocked by Pleasants Ridge to the east. After the fire, my hikes at Cold Canyon usually start early enough that few cold-blooded animals are visibly active when I start walking. By the end of the hikes, though, the sun has risen far enough to reach to the bottom of the canyon, and it is starting to warm up. By then, I can count on seeing at least the quick flash of a lizard's tail as it slips into a crack in the rocks at my approach. Or if the day is warmer and the lizards are loath to leave their basking spots, I can watch them for a bit as they soak up the heat. I mostly see western fence lizards, abundant and less shy than the alligator lizards and western skinks that I see occasionally and usually briefly. The fence lizards seem to be doing well after the fire, and I am happy to see them

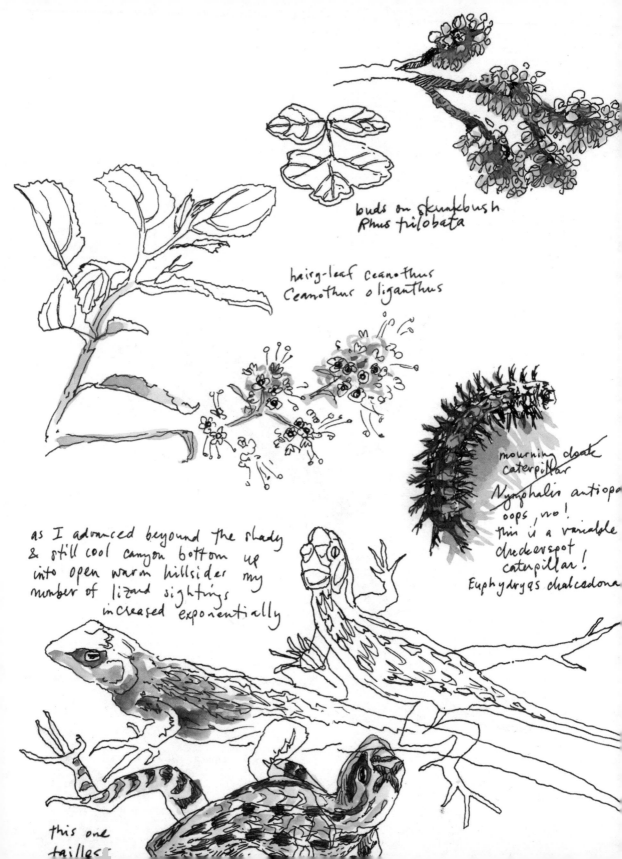

buds on skunkbush
Rhus trilobata

hairy-leaf ceanothus
Ceanothus oliganthus

mourning cloak
caterpillar
Nymphalis antiopa
oops, no!
this is a variable
checkerspot
caterpillar!
Euphydryas chalcedona

as I advanced beyound the shady
& still cool canyon bottom up
into open warm hillsides my
number of lizard sightings
increased exponentially

this one
tailless

this juvenile alligator lizard was
found at the base of a burned
clump of deergrass - the grass
was damp enough at the base to
stay cool while the top of the
bunch burned, so the lizard
remained safe & comfortable

thriving. It is comforting to know they are here in this environment, these friends from my childhood.

On long, lazy afternoons while the grown-ups were talking and cooking inside, I spent happy hours with my cousins looking for fence lizards on my father's family farm in the San Joaquin Valley. The lizards were everywhere, and it required only a little practice to snatch them from their basking spots in the sun and hold them upside down to stroke their brilliant blue bellies. On one charmed visit, there seemed to be lizards everywhere we looked, and we must have picked up dozens of them, one at a time. We spent a while with each one, marveling at this small piece of the wild suddenly becalmed in our hands, giving us the illusion of happy surrender to our ministrations.

The lizards, of course, were not happy at all, but rather exhibiting a fear response: immobility to make a predator lose interest. But it made us love them. Fence lizards are common in the West, and their willingness to live in close proximity to people—hence their name—makes them very familiar and even relatable. Many of us have had experiences with lizards in our hands, maybe even soothing them to "sleep." To a lizard, a burned landscape is something very different than it is to me. What is it like to crawl out of a burrow into this world of bare branches and unrelenting sun exposure?

Like newts, many lizards survive fire underground or in protected places under rocks or roots. While observing a controlled burn not far from Cold Canyon, I saw the wonders of survival in tiny niches strikingly demonstrated. A juvenile alligator lizard had remained safely tucked away at the base of a deer-grass bunch that burned. The grass stems burned nearly to the ground, leaving a charred lump. But at the base of that lump, the stems were still moist and cool, and it was from this haven that the lizard wandered out, unharmed and healthy.

The burned grass and the lizard are what I can see and feel. What about all that I can't sense but a lizard can? Thinking about Cold Canyon, especially, I

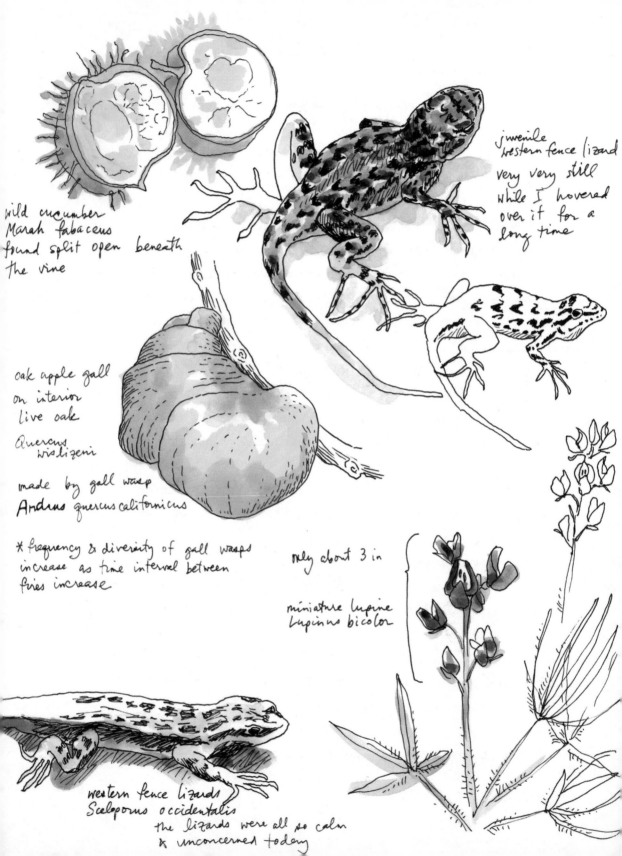

wild cucumber
Marah fabaceus
found split open beneath
the vine

juvenile
western fence lizard
very very still
while I hovered
over it for a
long time

oak apple gall
on interior
live oak

Quercus
wislizeni

made by gall wasp
Andrus quercuscalifornicus

* frequency & diversity of gall wasps
increase as time interval between
fires increase

rely about 3 in

miniature lupine
Lupinus bicolor

western fence lizards
Sceloporus occidentalis
the lizards were all so calm
& unconcerned today

wonder what is it like to suddenly find your home warmed by the sun earlier in the day, and later, too, with all the vegetation that usually shades the ground gone. To emerge into the bright sunlight, crawl out along an exposed branch, and feel the heat begin to course through your body. To gorge on some of the new insects traveling through the canyon, drawn by the dead and dying trees and shrubs.

This is how I enter the canyon now, on my hikes in the constantly changing world after the fire. I tie the things I can observe to those that I cannot but instead experience vicariously through another. Although there is life in abundance right before my eyes, the limits of scale, time, and my senses prevent me from directly experiencing all the things that remain hidden. Through fence lizards and alligator lizards, I extend my understanding beyond my own physical presence. It is very much an act of imagination, but it is empathy based in scientific observations and anchored by my own experiences. I am not ascribing any human traits to the lizard, just walking a little while in its footsteps. I know all along that the lizard's own perspective is beyond my ken, and I never make the mistake of believing that just because I haven't thought of something, it cannot be true. My imaginative sympathy for the lizard's view is a way to start to understand a world that runs so counter to my own deep associations with health and beauty.

The lizards at Cold Canyon have emerged into a world full of fabulous new basking opportunities and plentiful insects and spiders to eat. This is not a landscape of fear or disappointment or hardship. Nor is fire a regrettable disaster that must be endured on the way to reaching the *real* habitat. It is when I start to walk the trails regularly and start to think like the lizards that cracks appear in my certainty that this is a path from nothingness to fullness. My view changes as I watch plants and animals thriving in what is for them clearly not a hostile environment but a rich and healthy place, still full of resources.

Chapter Two

FIRST RESPONDERS

Life Comes Rushing to the Flames

Although the thought of it goes against everything our human instincts tell us, some animals are drawn to fire. Fire is a place to feast, to mate, to begin a new generation. Rather than cataclysm, they find health and new life.

To many humans, wildfire is synonymous with flight. We assume that anything that can get out, get away, get ahead of the onrushing flames will do so. It is an image engrained in the minds of anyone who watched *Bambi* as a child: forest fire means danger, running, and fear. Sure, some things burrow, but the overarching imperative is to flee. But. I have seen it once myself. Not everything is hurrying away from the fire. There are some that rush *toward* it. Winging through the air they come, drawn by the heat of the flames, drawn by the smoke, or drawn by the chemicals emitted by injured and dying trees and shrubs.

Reaching the site of the fire, males and females find each other amid the smoke, ash, and sometimes even the flames themselves. Within this seeming apocalypse, new life is created. They mate, and the females lay their eggs into wood that is still hot, sometimes so hot that with her life's mission complete, the female literally melts into the wood. The eggs hatch, and the larvae spend about a year within the fallen wood, growing and feeding and encountering none of the defenses that the tree or shrub would have been able to mount had it been alive.

Many of these fire-followers are beetles. *Tragidion annulatum* is a longhorn beetle that though showy in its brown and bright-orange garb, is not well enough known to have a common name. Its body, dark with vivid orange wing coverings, is just over an inch long, though its long, striped antennae more than double its length. Observers of chaparral fires have watched *T. annulatum* flying into fires and laying eggs on burned shrubs. Its larvae, also just over an inch long, have been found in the burned branches of these shrubs, having mined galleries throughout the dead wood. After a year, they pupate in a chamber at the end of a gallery, emerging finally to seek out a new conflagration.

How do the adults find new fires? We do not yet know how *T. annulatum* senses burning fires, but there is a beetle that is better understood. In Berkeley in the 1940s, when smoking cigarettes during football games was permitted and the stands were cloudy with smoke, hordes of beetles would sometime descend on the crowd. Known as charcoal beetles for their predilection for active fires, they came to the stadium expecting to find charred wood in which to lay their eggs. Instead, finding only people, they bit some fans in their scramble to find egg repositories. This strange phenomenon led scientists to investigate and eventually discover that charcoal beetles have an infrared-sensing organ just under their wings. So sensitive is this organ that it allows them to detect heat from a fire up to an astounding eighty miles away. A fire burning at the UC Berkeley football stadium could be sensed by a charcoal beetle as far away as Sacramento.

Charcoal beetles are partial to pine trees and have been found mostly in conifer forests in the Sierra, but they were observed on Mount Diablo in 2013 after the Morgan Fire, attracted to the pines there. Perhaps they were drawn to the pines in Cold Canyon after the Wragg Fire, too.

In June 2016, nearly a year after the fire, I find a mating pair of California elderberry borers, picturesque with their orange-rimmed wing coverings. Not all wood-boring beetles require fire-weakened wood for their larvae, but the rapid regrowth after fire opens up opportunities for beetles like these that appreciate soft, green, young wood. The two are atop a cluster of creamy-white elderberry flowers. These are bushes that have regrown since the fire. I observe these beetles

Klamathweed
Hypericum
perforatum

coyote mint
Monardella
Villosa

blue elderberry
Sambucus mexicana

with a longhorn beetle
mating pair

approx. shape
of the one
that landed
on my sketchbook
very black
approx. 1.5 in
long, maybe
2 in with ovipositor

Horntail — family
Siricidae
drawn to trees in
distress

might be
Urocerus
Californicus
this one is
more common

or Urocerus
albicornis

toward the very end of their mating season. Soon the females will finish laying their eggs in the bark of the young elderberry plant, and the larvae will begin to hatch and burrow into the plant's stems. The larvae, less than an inch long, may feast within the stems for up to two years before emerging from a tiny exit hole to pupate. Charred wood and green, both are abundant in the days and years after fire, and both supply fine castles and rich banquets to searching beetles.

While many of the insects that come to fires are beetles, they are not the only ones. In the fall of 2019, four years into observing fire ecology at Cold Canyon, I participate in a controlled burn in the Klamath Mountains of Northern California. I am one in a group of field artists and nature journalers who are attending the event to document our observations in drawings, paintings, and notes. While intently focused on drawing the movements of flame, smoke, and fire crew, I hear another field artist say, "Ooh! There's one on your back!" I try to catch a glimpse of whatever it is, but it is gone before I see it. Before I can be too sad about the missed opportunity, something large and dark lands clumsily on my sketchbook page. It flies away again quickly, but once it is gone, I draw its general size and shape from memory, so that I have a record of its presence. I see many more after this, finding their way through the billowing smoke to the charred trees that are their final destination.

These are wasps in the horntail family, and they lay their eggs in wood much like the fire-following beetles. Horntails are marvelous creatures, inch-and-a-half-long solitary wasps in shiny black, rust, and gold, with a "horn" at the tip of their abdomen that they use to bore a hole into wood before inserting their ovipositor to lay eggs. Most fascinating of all is that horntails deposit more than just their eggs into the wood. They have formed symbioses with fungi that the adults carry in abdominal glands. There are a few different fungi that engage in this relationship, but each horntail species harbors only one type of fungus. When the horntail inserts her eggs into a weakened tree, she injects the fungus too. As the larvae wait to hatch for a week or more, the fungus is hard at work, digesting the wood cellulose that the larvae are unable to break down on their own. Once the larvae hatch, they follow the trails left by the fungus, eating both digested cellulose and the fungus itself. Eating the fungus ensures that it lives on in their gut and comes with them when, as adults, they fly to new fires or other sources of weakened wood.

Everyone wins, except the tree: the fungi are delivered directly into the heart of their food source by the female wasp, and the wasp larvae are provided with a ready source of nutrition when they hatch. So much of this interaction is unseen: hidden from sight, two wildly different forms of life come together. This ensures that nothing goes to waste and that life begins anew even before the flames are extinguished.

Coming to the feast: Fungi break things down

The new green shoots of trees and shrubs vividly herald the surge of life after a wildfire. As I lean in to examine the almost waxy surfaces of the fresh leaves at the bases of burned shrubs, I catch sight of other life, too: tiny shelf fungi starting to emerge along the length of the charred branches. Less assuming than the greenery that first catches my attention, the fungi appearing on dead and dying wood aboveground show just how much life is happening out of view. Looking closely at a recently burned landscape opens up brand-new worlds of discovery. Below our feet in the soil, life is already bustling. Although the fire's heat kills some of the fungi living in the soil, many are left unaffected. In fact, some fungi are stimulated by fire—perhaps by high temperatures or by increases in soil carbon—and grow faster underground and reproduce more rapidly. These are often found in higher numbers after fires than at any other time. Amazingly, recent research has

speckled greenshield
lichen
Flavopunctelia sp.

followed a California tortoiseshell
butterfly (Nymphalis californica)
down the trail
their caterpillars feed on Ceanothus

resprouting pitcher sage
Lepechinia calycina
with at least three different
fungi growing on the
dead branches ⟶

pitcher sage leaves
& dry seed pods

discovered that these fire-loving, or pyrophilous, fungi survive between fires by living inside mosses and lichens. The fire burns away their host, cuing the fungi to grow and reproduce.

Mossy maze polypore, a kind of fungus carried by horntails, is but one of many species of fungi that grow on wood and other weakened plant material. These fungi consume the wood and then enrich the soil with all the nutrients once contained in the tree, now made available for other plants to absorb into their own tissue. They are prodigious recyclers, without which new plants would be unable to find enough nutrition to grow.

Other fungi grow directly in the soil, and many of these support plants in an even more intimate way. Deep in the soil, they attach to plant roots. From these anchors grow their mycelia, the thin structures that function much like a plant's roots. And indeed these mycelia act as extra roots for the plant to which the fungus is attached, taking in more water and nutrients than the plant would be able to on its own. The mycelia do even more for the plants, facilitating water and nutrient exchange between the roots of individual plants. This interaction greatly enriches the plants' ability to survive difficult conditions and ensures that the entire ecosystem makes the most of the resources within.

At Cold Canyon, I marvel at the fungal diversity that I directly observe and know that it represents just a tiny fraction of the fungi stitched into my surroundings, the threads of their mycelia uniting the landscape. There are delicate new yellow fieldcap mushrooms beside the trail in February 2016, six months after the fire. I first find hare's foot inkcaps in November 2016. The fieldcap and inkcap mushrooms—the reproductive parts of fungi—are extremely

yellow field cap
just one in new
green grass

Bolbitius titubans

a little bracket fungus - looks like it is
growing on the charred portions of
the trunk

short lived. Mushrooms usually last only one day for the yellow field caps and a few days for the ink caps. Such ephemeral structures aboveground belie the true body of the fungus underground, where its mycelium does the day-to-day work of digestion and growth and lives for years or decades.

I find a rich diversity of wood-eating fungi too, from the well-known turkey tail, its striped fans of orange, brown, and purple sticking out like ledges along a tree trunk, to purplepore bracket fungus, with warm-violet pores underneath and mossy green on top. They appear on the ends of stumps, many the remains of trees that were weakened by the fire and eventually fell. I am so happy to see this vitality, even on a dead tree. We often think of fungi as markers of death and decay, which of course they are, but they are also the harbingers of all the new life that arises from the basic materials of the dead stump and from their own hard work. They are the vigorous life force that keeps the cycle turning.

So let us celebrate the decomposers, hidden and hard at work, keeping the ecosystem thriving through periods of calm as well as disturbance. Let us remember the sprawling lattice beneath us, especially after fire, as fungi rebuild the soil with their mycelia, hold it in place against erosion, and help plants reach their full potential as they regrow and stretch upward into the sunlight.

More connections: Birds in the burned landscape

Overhead, small forms zip past. Some come in low, just above my head, but most are higher, winging from one side of the canyon to the other. I look up and catch striking black and white against the glowing sapphire sky. Walking along in an ashy, barren landscape, I sometimes sense little activity at ground level, but the air is alive with movement and sound. The metallic *pit . . . pit . . . preeeeeeeeet* of Nuttall's woodpeckers alerts me to their presence even before I spot them.

Nuttall's
woodpecker
*Dryobates
nuttalli*

acorn
woodpecker
*Melanerpes
formicivorous*

Nuttall's

acorn & Nuttall's both species
dashing back & forth across
the canyon from one snag
to another

In the postfire world at Cold Canyon, a web of relationships radiates outward from each organism in the ecosystem. The insects that hasten to the flames come for a feast, some of them even bearing fungi that will also find a rich repast, but these insects will become the feast in turn. Insect-eating birds such as woodpeckers take advantage of these new riches of insect larvae burrowing through the dead wood. The unseen fungi and beetle larvae, hidden under the rough bark of their host trees, become seen—excavated and devoured by hungry birds.

Not infrequently, as I walk beneath an oak, living or dead, I hear the fast patter of a woodpecker drilling above me. I know how the muscles and tendons in woodpeckers' necks act as shock absorbers, how their skulls are full of a bony matrix that cushions their brains, and how their incredibly long tongues wrap fully around the backs of their skulls to provide even more protection. But I will always be shocked at how fast their heads must move to make the rapid-fire percussion I hear. And whenever I hear it, I wonder what the drilling means this time. The bird may be boring for food, may be opening up a nest hole, or may be drumming to announce its territory and find a mate.

Nuttall's woodpeckers are closely tied to oaks. They find larvae in trees by probing cavities and just beneath bark; with a beak only about three-quarters of an inch long, they are too small to bore deeper into wood as do the larger woodpeckers. They nest in the cavities of dead trees or on dead limbs of living trees, preferring oak, willow, or alder. It may be that fire helps them, bringing more wood-boring beetle larvae and more dead wood for nesting. Fittingly, the Nuttall's woodpeckers I see so frequently are the very image of a forest on fire: their black-and-white-spotted body reminds me of a blackened tree trunk with patches of white ash, and their head is crowned with what looks like a dancing red flame. It is a flight of fancy on my part, but one that pleases me as I think of them thriving in this sometimes desolate-feeling environment.

Although Nuttall's woodpeckers are not known to be particularly attracted to burned areas—I have no reason to think there are any more of them after the fire than there were before Cold Canyon burned—other woodpeckers are. Hairy woodpeckers, though only occasionally seen at Cold Canyon, have been found in surveys elsewhere in the state to be more abundant after burns. They seem to favor the edge areas between burned and unburned areas, where they can take advantage of the new insects coming to the charred wood and the new cavities in dead trees for nesting, but can retreat to unburned areas for cover. Northern flickers, common at Cold Canyon, are like hairy woodpeckers in their taste for wood-boring beetles, and probably have similar behaviors after fire. Red-breasted sapsuckers come not for the beetles but for the sap exuded by the tree in response to the beetles. The sap is abundant in trees injured by fire and beetles, and draws these woodpecker relatives.

The darting bodies, occasional whispers of wings, and sharp calls of Nuttall's woodpeckers at Cold Canyon keep the air above me lively, while down below, amid the branches and shrubbery that survived the fire or have since sprouted, other birds find ample resources in the postfire environment. They too make tasty morsels of the insects that were drawn to the fire as well as the ones that returned to the landscape shortly afterward.

In a fire, birds enjoy the distinct advantage of being able to escape by flying away. Not all escape the flames and smoke, of course, but many reach safety in neighboring habitats. The question after fire, as far as birds are concerned, is when will they or their descendants return to the burned area?

Much depends on birds' foraging habits and their need for the safety and security of dense vegetation for cover. Birds and fire are better studied in conifer forests than in chaparral and oak woodlands—the charisma of California's extensive forests, as well as their economic value, has ensured more plentiful research funding into the effects of fire on forested lands. Wanting context for what I am seeing at Cold Canyon in the larger realm of fire studies in California, I dig a little deeper into what we know about birds in the Sierra. To broaden my perspective, I meet Lynn Schofield, an ornithologist who works for the Institute for Bird Populations in Petaluma, California. I immediately recognize in Lynn a kindred spirit when we talk about her early love for raptors. She fell in love with birds of prey as a child in Minnesota, and started working with them in a rehabilitation setting, helping care for injured and orphaned birds before their release back into the wild. Having done this as a teen myself, I know well the intensity of affection for animals that develops when you handle them and observe them up close while they are returning to health.

Talking to Lynn, I learn about the Institute's fascinating work on black-backed woodpeckers. These are just slightly larger than the Nuttall's woodpeckers I am familiar with at Cold Canyon, with a solid black back—perfect camouflage against charred tree trunks—and a jaunty yellow crown on the males. They are known for their predilection for burned habitat, sometimes arriving within hours of the fire going out. They hurry into newly burned forests to make the most of the chance to claim new spots for nesting and fresh sources of wood-boring beetles, their favorite food. Although these woodpeckers do not live in the oak and chaparral of Cold Canyon but in the conifer forests of the Sierra, it turns out that they offer powerful insights into burned landscapes.

Young adult woodpeckers establishing new nesting sites find rich opportunities in newly burned forests, and have been known for a while to prefer areas dense with dead but still standing trees—snags—killed in high-severity fire. There they find the most beetle larvae and also appealing cavities in the snags for nesting. As researchers are finding, though, there is a lot of nuance within this story. While the adults nest in areas thoroughly scorched by high-severity burns, their offspring do much better when they can move to areas that did not burn or only burned at low-to-medium severity. Fledglings need the greater cover provided by living trees that still have needles, and are more likely to survive if they can find this kind of habitat when they leave the nest. But they cannot go too far from their parents, who continue to feed them while they learn to fully provide for themselves.

Looking at black-backed woodpecker life histories in such depth has given researchers invaluable insights into the complexity of this species' relationship with fire. The picture that emerges from the research underscores the importance of pyrodiversity—diversity in burning patterns. Within this single species of fire-following bird, different life stages thrive in different types of postfire habitat. If fires burn more uniformly at high severity, adults will find plentiful nesting and foraging opportunities, but their offspring will be at a great disadvantage during the crucial time when they are ready to leave the nest but not to fully leave their parents' care. They need plenty of edge habitat between severely burned areas and less- or unburned areas so that adults and fledglings can reach each other but still spend most of their time in their preferred habitat.

This has interesting implications for other species of animal that are drawn to burns. We may find all manner of complications to the simple fact that some species benefit from fire—variations in their needs for burn severities, sizes of burned areas, frequency of burning, and more. Each study, each careful piece of research reveals another layer of understanding, and in turn raises new questions. Black-backed woodpeckers need a mosaic of burn severities to survive and continue as a species, a theme that I encounter again and again as I learn about organisms that have evolved with wildfire.

northern flicker
Colaptes auratus

Lynn is friendly and engaging, and in our far-reaching conversation, she also tells me about the work she did in Yosemite National Park after the 2013 Rim Fire, studying the effects of the fire on spotted owls. For three years, Lynn and her colleagues conducted surveys to identify where owls lived after the fire. There may be no more romantic method of studying animals than owl surveys. Scientists go out just before dusk and work into the night, walking through the area of interest and imitating owl calls. Owls are extremely territorial, so when they hear the sounds of a potential competitor, they reply to warn the intruder that the area is already taken. Usually scientists make the calls with their own voices, though they also sometimes use recorded calls. When I was a high school student and my mind was full of raptors, I participated in a survey of owls while on a backpacking trip in the Sierra. It was a warm summer night, and I remember sitting on a large boulder in the forest, staring up into tall pines silhouetted against the star-filled sky, listening to the scientists hoot and then waiting, straining my ears to hear an owl respond.

Spotted owls usually select territories full of tall trees, and it might stand to reason that fire would greatly reduce the amount of habitat that owls were willing and able to use. Lynn's research, though, suggests that fires, at least at low severity—as measured in the percentage of vegetation destroyed by the fire—may not have as great an impact on their territories as one might expect. The biggest predictor of where owls claimed territory after the fire was where the most canopy cover—the largest, tallest trees—had been *before* the fire, not where it was *after* the fire. The explanation for this preference is not entirely clear, but it may be related to the numbers of remnant large trees postfire, or perhaps prey availability both before and after the fire. The only exception was in territories where more than one-third of the area had burned at high severity. These territories had been abandoned. Just like black-backed woodpeckers, spotted owls are dependent on mosaic burning patterns, where low-severity and unburned patches are interspersed with higher-severity areas. In places where fire burns patchily and at varying intensities, life can continue, in some ways unchanged. But more homogeneous, high-severity burning, the kind that sears the land to the horizon, changes everything. Modern megafires force owls to abandon their territory and relocate to areas with more prey and tree cover, which means more competition and fewer resources to go around for an already threatened population.

Lynn explains to me that the driving question now is what the next generation of owls will do. Do younger owls, just establishing their territories for the first time, select recently burned areas like the ones where their parents have remained? Or do they find new, unburned areas to make their homes?

And I wonder about the owls at Cold Canyon. The Wragg Fire burned the canyon fairly completely, in a mixture of medium and high severities. But there were pockets of low-severity burning, too, especially along the riparian corridor —opportunities for shelter within the burned area as well as along the edges. There are so many opportunities for research among the oak woodlands and chaparral habitats of the Coast Ranges. Lynn and I talk about our hope that as fires burn more of the state and continue to remain uppermost in the public eye, the focus of fire ecology research will continue to shift to include the forests, chaparral, coastal sage scrub, and grasslands of the western side of the state. Western screech owls are common in the area of Cold Canyon, and great horned and northern pygmy owls are also present. I would love to know how the fire has affected them, whether they have continued to find what they need or have moved on, only to return some number of years later when plants and prey have regrown and returned. I suspect that there are plenty of refuges around—both in unburned areas within the fire's footprint, and outside the fire perimeter as well—so that owls will have shifted some of their nesting and hunting spots but not left the area completely.

Without more research, though, we cannot know for sure. These are the questions that animate science. They animate me too, as I notice, record, and entangle myself with the lives of the plants, animals, and fungi of Cold Canyon. While I wish we knew more—now—about fire in these habitats, I am at the same time excited by all the discoveries to come. I try to be a sponge as I walk these trails, absorbing the details around me, eyes open for the things that change from visit to visit and for all that stays the same.

Over and over on my visits, I see for myself at Cold Canyon how important habitat mosaics are. Burned areas offer new resources such as insects and fungi that themselves are drawn to dead and dying plants. Nearby, unburned or lightly burned areas offer shelter. A sparrow lights on the open, ashy hillside to use its tiny claws to expose beetle grubs. After fire, shrubby vegetation that rebounds quickly, long before trees regrow, attracts plenty of ground-foraging birds. Fox sparrows and dark-eyed juncos in particular, Lynn notes, are drawn to recently burned areas, scratching through leaf litter to reach the delectable insects beneath.

As I am learning, however, fire's consequences can be both helpful and harmful, and some birds that spend a lot of time on the ground, such as California quail, find that burned areas offer too little cover from the prying eyes of hawks. Quail tend to be scarce for a few years after fire until sufficient shrubbery has regrown. Today a family of quail crosses quickly from one patch of partly scorched but still leafy toyons to another, their dappled gray-and-tan bodies blending almost seamlessly into the dusty path, belied only by the stark black and white on the adult male's head. Hawks love burned areas, of course, for the exact reason quail hate them: fewer hiding places for prey, and bountiful hunting. Fungus–beetle–sparrow–hawk—an essential cycle. On every visit it is driven home to me, in even the smallest observations and the most seemingly insignificant of animal activities: all parts of this landscape are necessary, and all are well used.

If there are any birds I can count on as constant companions when I hike at Cold Canyon, they are towhees. I often see them on the hillside or in the shade of a shrub just a little off the trail. But just as often, they are unseen trail mates. I am alerted to their presence only by the sounds they make in the brush as I pass. Shrubs, especially in a landscape that has not been touched by fire in many, many decades, can be like armored fortresses. Even at small to medium size, they repel the curious proddings of large mammals like me with their dense, sharp branches, crackly and loud and certain to warn away any birds hiding within. And even after fire, at least a fire that did not annihilate the entire landscape, plenty of impenetrable shrubs remain.

Perhaps self-defeatingly for a biologist, I try very hard to leave other species to their own devices. As a graduate student I found it deeply uncomfortable to study the evolution of spiders and millipedes by killing my research subjects in

large family of quail
at the entrance to
the parking area
this isn't all of
them...

order to examine their otherwise inaccessible insides. I do not want to interfere with the world around me, nor disturb the routines and rituals that sustain the daily lives of the birds and insects and arachnids and myriapods and everything else on the trail. It is a delicate balance to satisfy my curiosity without too much disruption, and requires awakening all of my senses to the world. And sometimes the best choice is not knowing, enjoying all the possibilities of what creature might be in the bushes beside me without ever having an answer.

Two kinds of towhee are common at Cold Canyon. They dart across the trail at about shoulder height, from a shrub on the upslope side to one closer to the creek. The chaparral here is just what they love—thickets of dense, tangly brush with plenty of open spaces between. Places to hide, patches to forage in. Toyon, elderberry, coffeeberry, poison oak. Dry litter beneath and around the shrubs perfect for spiders, insects, and seeds.

spotted towhee
Pipilo maculatus
busily engaged in a patch of green
grass & unconcerned by my
loitering & watching

California towhees, with their soft-brown bodies and russet shading underneath the tail, are particularly fond of poison oak for nesting. When the berries appear in the summer, for food, too. I have a soft spot for them from early childhood, when I delighted in watching them gather seeds from my grandparents' brick patio. They looked so soft and fat, and I longed to scoop them up and cradle them in my hands.

With white splashed spots on their black wing feathers and vibrant orange breast feathers below, loudly patterned spotted towhees are more striking in appearance, though their habits are similar to their drabber California towhee cousins. Both kinds find seeds and insects on the ground among the leaf litter by scratching their feet backward in a characteristic hop, turning over the leaves and exposing tasty morsels underneath. Towhees occupy a similar niche to the fox sparrows that are so drawn to burned areas, and it seems there are at least as many of them around immediately after the fire, if not more.

Spotted towhees have amazing orange eyes that make their gaze hard to miss. I was once caught and held by the eyes of a spotted towhee that I frightened out of a bush. It flew onto a perch a little further down the trail and fixed me with a particularly hard stare for a few long moments before darting off again.

Perhaps the masters of the fierce gaze are the wrentits, who also require dense shrubbery and generally remain close to the ground. Like towhees, they love poison oak and eat a variety of seeds and insects. They have a taste for spiders especially. They are a small bird, with a relatively large head and a long tail often cocked straight up. It is their uncanny eye that draws me the most, though, and I often wait motionless by a shrubby laurel or buckeye in hope that the little form moving about inside the branches will come out far enough for me to catch a glimpse of that surprisingly round eye with a very pale yellow-white iris. Even without a sighting, I am reminded of the wrentits' company from a distance, for

a wrentit in an
oak just above me
Chamaea fasciata

California pipevine
appearing - it looks like
it may be suffering in this
dry winter

Aristolochia californica

they sing all year, their jaunty calls bouncing down the hillside: *pit-----pit----pit---pit--pit-prrrrrrrrrrrrrrrr*.

These birds who keep me company as they forage in the shrubs to either side of the trail count on the safety, shade, and protection they find in the vegetation that remains after the fire. Many shrubs are burned away completely or reduced to a few charred stubs, but some have survived the fire with foliage left unburned. A few have foliage that was heat-killed but still hangs on the branches. All of these provide welcome shelter to hungry birds.

I think about these little islands of sanctuary in a newly open and dangerous landscape. The only reason that towhees, sparrows, wrentits, and juncos can forage in Cold Canyon after the fire is that these islands survived the blaze. In a less flamboyant, but no less important way than the black-backed woodpeckers, these oak- and chaparral-dwelling birds are just as dependent on mosaic patterns of burning. And if I have any tiny trace of feeling that by studying fire ecology in a place of shrubs and oaks instead of pines and firs, I am missing the greater drama or mysteries, it is banished by my moments with these small brown birds. We are immersed in the same patterns of fire and life as anywhere in the western US that burns.

This recently burned land is a bright place, with light reaching where there was only shade before, now that much of the canopy and cover have been turned to gas and ash. With each visit to Cold Canyon and every month that passes, I see how vividly this landscape illuminates the secrets of fire's place in the ecosystem, a narrative usually hidden. Familiarity and deeper knowledge are the antidotes to grief. I am watching the story unfold around me, the story of this great disturbance that is actually its own form of nourishment and continuity.

Chapter Three

EMERALD AND SEPIA

New Leaves on Burned Slopes

Shoots of green appear on the black hillsides. Some of these leaves are newly emerging from seeds; others are sprouting directly from the roots on burned shrubs. These are the visible proof of life that seemed lost but was never fully extinguished by the flames.

A newly burned landscape is full of reminders of what has been lost. At the beginning of this journey, visiting the canyon the first January after the summer fire, I am still wholly consumed by these thoughts. I look around at the bare earth and can only see what is missing, and my heart presses against my ribs with shocked sadness. This is the second time I've visited since the fire, and the scenery still has raw power. Where have so many of the trees and shrubs gone? Can some truly have been reduced to only a streak of white ash? Others have left behind more than that. The twisted, blackened branches of chaparral reaching skyward impress themselves deeply into my memory. It is the very picture of death, like the rubble and ash of a ruined city. The soil is black beneath my boots, interspersed with spots of white ash where trees or shrubs were incinerated completely. The air is still and quiet.

I know that the phoenix rises from the ashes. The legends of firebird and phoenix are beautiful, their images potent. And it is easy to understand the rebirth that happens after a fire, as new plants grow and animals return—I am familiar with that story too. What is harder to see, though, is that life never ended in the burned zone. While many lives did indeed end in the heat and flames, many more survive than we can see. Plants who aboveground are blackened and dead can still be fully alive underground.

The words that we use are important. Fire is not the end of everything, no matter how true that seems when we walk along ashy trails. The burned limbs and persevering roots are just as much a part of the life cycle of some of these plants as their flowering, fruiting abundance in their mature years. And fire is in turn an integral part of the life cycle of the entire ecosystem. The cycle of organisms—through fire, sprouting, leaving, flowering, fruiting, seeding, and burning again—*is* the story. It is the underlying story of natural history in the western US, where fire and life have developed together—fire guiding the evolution of western habitats, and that fire-adapted life in turn shaping the timing, frequency, and intensity of western fires.

Stoking and damping the flames

Some plants resist fire, some burn easily, and others embrace the flames and stoke them even higher. Chamise dominates many of the chaparral hillsides at Cold Canyon, especially on the east-facing side of the canyon. Running between and above the pinky-red sandstone boulders, its long, wispy branches are covered in short, needle-like leaves. When chamise burns, the multitude of thin branches helps distribute fuel evenly throughout the canopy, transferring heat and flames from plant to plant and speeding the fire's spread. The tiny leaves are packed with waxes, resins, and oils that are full of energy and burn hot, driving up the intensity of the fire. Chamise, it seems, is made to burn.

Why would this be? Evolving methods of coping with fire is an obvious necessity for plants in climates like this one with long, dry summers where wildfire is a regular occurrence. Encouraging fire is another thing entirely. Not long after the Wragg Fire, and a couple of months before I set foot inside the burned canyon, I saw a photograph of a burned chamise plant, with its branches black and dead.

In only a few short weeks since the fire, though, new growth was appearing at the plant's base, startlingly green against the dark branches and soil. The incredible speed with which chamise sprouts again after fire offers a glimpse into a radically different life cycle. Such rapid resprouting gives chamise a head start over its competitors in gaining space and water resources in its chaparral habitat, and the fire that it encouraged is an integral part of that strategy.

As humans, we are accustomed to going where we please, but also entirely dependent on keeping almost all parts of our bodies attached throughout our lifetime, save the continuous shedding of skin, hair, and nail. What would it be like if we expected occasionally, maybe a couple of times in our life, to let go of half our body? Muscle, tendon, organ, bone? In a fire, many chaparral shrubs are killed from the ground level up—branches, leaves, fruits, and flowers. Underground,

CA bay laurel

Umbellularia californica

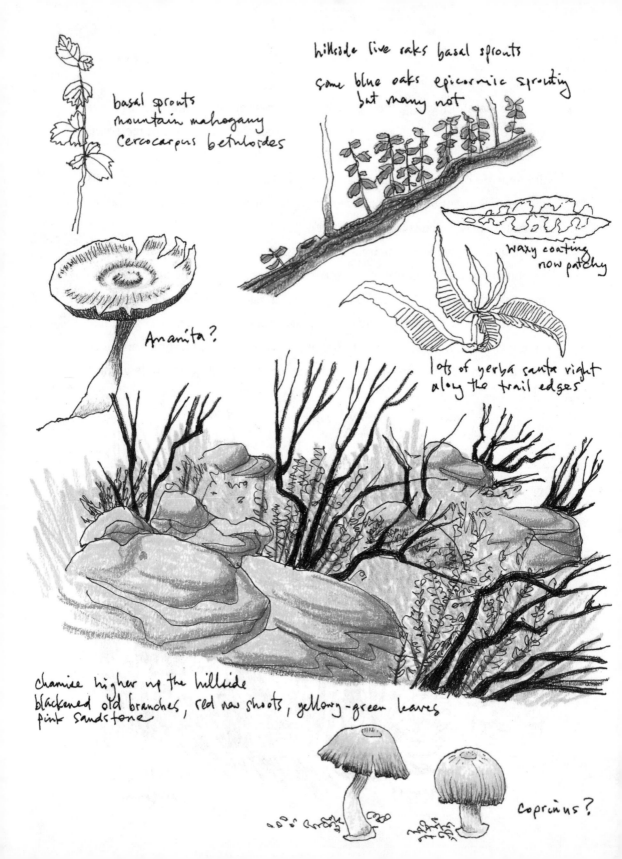

basal sprouts
mountain mahogany
Cercocarpus betuloides

hillside live oaks basal sprouts

Some blue oaks epicormic sprouting
but many not

waxy coating
now patchy

Amanita?

lots of yerba santa right
along the trail edges

chamise higher up the hillside
blackened old branches, red new shoots, yellow-green leaves
pink sandstone

Coprinus?

they go on living. To us, seeing only what is aboveground, this does not look like survival. We think that what we see are the most important parts of the plant, the beautiful foliage, the flowers, the strong branches. What is most important to the plant, though, are the roots drawing up moisture and nutrients, and the burl where the plant's reserves of carbohydrates are stored for future growth.

Chamise offers us a striking perspective on what makes a life. One in which the greater part of an organism's mass can be turned to ash, but the individual goes on. Thrives, even. Fire is an active part of this life, a necessary partner. When I first visit Cold Canyon after the fire, four months later, chamise regrowth is well under way. New sprouts make lush skirts at the base of charred branches, and by a year after the fire, the new growth has reached a quarter of the shrub's full height. In five years, the shrubs will be as tall as they were before the fire. Looking at the vigorous new sprouts of chamise, I am reminded of the vitality of the plant in the soil, out of view, and how what we see above the ground is in truth the most expendable part. Like antlers of a deer, made to be shed.

When the Wragg Fire crested Blue Ridge and raced down its eastern slope toward Cold Creek, its flames leapt higher and moved faster as it encountered chamise thickets. Mingled within and between the chamise, though, were stands of toyon, its verdant leaves and showy red berries a familiar sight in the chaparral. If chamise acts like a torch in a wildfire, toyon is a damper. Its larger leaves hold more moisture, and it is not laden with as many fire-accelerating compounds as chamise. Toyon slowed the flames in patches, part of the push and pull between plants and site conditions which ensure that fires of even moderate severity are patchy, with some areas more thoroughly burned than others. In healthy fire regimes, this patchiness ensures that there are pockets of shelter for animals to survive the fire. It also provides important habitat for species that gravitate to the edges of burns, such as hairy woodpeckers.

Coyotebrush is an underappreciated chaparral shrub. Garbed in small yellow-green leaves, its flowers are tiny, different depending on whether the bush is male, with yellow flowers scented sweet and strong, or female, with odorless white flowers that turn to fluff. It is hardy and grows well on roadsides, beside trails, and in other disturbed areas, so it is easily dismissed as weedy and scrubby. But it grows a deep root system that helps hold the hillsides together, and it too moderates wildfire. Like that of toyon, its fire resistance helps it slow fires, and coyotebrush even contains fire-retardant chemicals in its leaves.

At the bottom of the canyon, even more plants resisted the flames. With their feet in the still-moist soil of the creek bed, their water content was high, and many—including oaks, willows, California black walnuts, Fremont cottonwoods, and California buckeyes—were passed by completely. All of the ways that plants resist fire—or stoke it—are keys to understanding what the fire cycle should look like. For fire to be a healthy agent of change in the life of an ecosystem, it cannot move across a landscape as a monolithic force. In addition to offering places of escape, unburned areas ensure that as the habitat regrows after the fire, not all of the plants are the same age, providing a greater diversity of resources to other inhabitants of the canyon. If habitats lose their diversity—through development, through agriculture, through climate change—fires will also lose their diversity, becoming more uniformly intense and rushing through ecosystems burning everything. In turn, these more frequent, more intense fires reinforce the lack of habitat diversity, making it difficult for the full range of plants to return. It is a vicious cycle.

Hiking in Cold Canyon before the fire, I took far too little notice of the shrubs in the canyon. They dominate the chaparral and oak woodland habitats that make up much of the Cold Canyon landscape, and I find, in retrospect, that they were so often just the furniture in the room, easily overlooked in my search for more exciting life forms. Returning to the canyon after the fire, I see so clearly how their vitality is the scaffolding on which the rest of the ecosystem builds.

resprouting
toyon

tough-looking leaves

Heteromeles
arbutifolia

Even during a long, dry summer, new green shoots appear. I am struck by how this growth can be possible in such an arid season. Surely they must wait for new rain to begin to return to life. But of course that is just it: they *are* still alive, just not where I can see. Within their underground structures, life has never ended. I stand in awe of all the different ways that shrubs have evolved to thrive in a landscape of regular disturbance.

Deep roots: The resilience of shrubs

In California chaparral growing in this Mediterranean climate, the soil is not rich in nutrients, winter rainfall is unpredictable, summers are long and dry, and periods of drought are common. Not a place for the faint of heart, chaparral communities have cultivated resilience in the hardy souls of their plants. Easily dismissed in their generally unshowy foliage, chaparral shrubs are are hardy survival artists.

Chamise, our flame-spreading torch, sends its roots deep into the earth, as far as twelve feet beneath the surface. Here they are protected from heat and are deep enough to find moisture even in the middle of a fierce summer. At the top of its roots, where they meet the plant's stems, chamise grows a fat burl, sometimes twice the width of its trunk. The burl is a swollen woody base that sits right at ground level, sometimes partially showing above the soil, sometimes buried just below. As the plant's energy reserve, the burl stores carbohydrates that can be used to fuel growth even when the plant's green leaves are all gone and it cannot photosynthesize. Buried within the burl, buds lie dormant, ready to grow again when need arises after fire.

Many plants grow burls—technically a burl is any swelling of woody plant tissue filled with dormant buds. Burls can grow anywhere along the trunk or branches, not just at the top of the roots. The buds' growth inside the burl creates intricate swirling and folding patterns. These beautiful patterns are what make burls so desirable a raw material for carvings and furniture. In the western US, people are likely most familiar with redwood burls, which are sold as burlwood treasures in countless shops along the Northern California coast. Because burls are filled with buds, new sprouts can grow anywhere a plant grows a burl, propelled by the carbohydrates and moisture stored there. A burl at the base of a trunk is right at the plant's root crown, the place where the roots meet the stem. This is a very active part of the plant, and some shrubs and trees that do not have burls can still grow new sprouts at their root crowns.

Technically, the burls growing at the joining of root and stem, so critical for the regrowth of the plant after fire or pruning, are referred to as lignotubers: *ligno* for the lignin in the cell walls of woody plants, making them rigid, and *tuber* for the enlarged organ storing starch, similar to a potato. Because *burl* is the more commonly used word for resprouting shrubs, I prefer that term. Burls are the secret heart of fire survival in chaparral and other shrubby habitats, but not the only one.

Arctostaphylos manzanita

Deep red bark and tough, flat leaves in the shape of flames pointing up to the sky: manzanita is fire personified. Manzanitas can be roughly divided into two groups by their responses to fire. Some have burls and can resprout after burning, just like chamise. These are referred to as facultative seeders, able to both resprout from a burl and grow back from seeds. Others lack burls and are completely killed by fire. Known as obligate seeders, these must grow again from seeds that were already dispersed and are waiting in the ground. There are two species of manzanita at Cold Canyon, and they represent each of these fire responses. Eastwood manzanita has a burl and is a facultative seeder. Seedlings have a low survival rate, though, so the burl sprouts are its dominant mode of recovery. By contrast, common manzanita is an obligate seeder, unable to resprout from a burl.

The same split in fire response strategies occurs in California lilacs as well, with both obligate and facultative seeders represented in the genus. At Cold Canyon, though, the only two species present are both obligate seeders. Without burls, hairy-leaf and wedge-leaf ceanothus must grow from seed after wildfire. Because it takes much longer for a shrub to grow from seed than to resprout from a burl, no new California lilacs appear at Cold Canyon right after the fire. As a result, all of the resprouters—manzanita, chamise, toyon, coyotebrush, mountain mahogany, and the like—are overrepresented in the composition of shrub species for the first few years after the fire. Over time, as the California lilacs grow back from seeds, shrub composition returns to what it was just before the fire.

Small trees that are commonly found in California riparian woodlands and chaparral habitats share the fire strategies of the shrubs. The heat of fire easily dries out the large, meaty seed that gives California buckeye its name. As a result, California buckeyes are obligate sprouters after fire, relying on their roots to send up new sprouts. When their branches have not been too severely charred by flames and heat, new

re-seeded manzanita by the entrance has flowers!

such an exciting sight this is. Their 1st year flowering post-fire sprouts can also appear in the buckeyes' crowns, sometimes within weeks of the fire. These stand out sharply to me, brilliant green against stark-white branches against deep-charcoal soil, when I first start visiting Cold Canyon in the early months after the fire.

I am stopped dead in my tracks by the beauty of a resprouting California bay laurel the first March following the fire. Growing on a steep rise just east of the trail, the base of a burned tree's trunk is exposed by erosion, and I can see an entire tiny forest nearly exploding from the bulge. The miniscule shoots, flame red at their bases gradually shading to lemony yellow at their tips, are each sprouting from a bud that had lain dormant until the fire. I am so impressed by just how many dormant buds are packed into the root crown, the storage area where roots meet trunk, much like a burl but not as distinctively enlarged. The roots themselves also contain these multitudes. I find other bay laurel sprouts coming out of the soil right next to the burned parent trees, evidence of the activity of the roots just below the surface. Bay laurel seeds are thin skinned and sensitive to heat, but moderately intense fires stimulate germination, so that they send up new seedlings after fire. High-intensity fires will kill bay laurel seeds, though, a recurring story in my exploration of California's fire history and what it means for our future.

Toyons, whose role in slowing fire is so important to burn mosaics, are vigorous resprouters. Their seeds are short lived and do not generally last long enough in the soil to form seed banks that can be activated after fire. As a result, toyons are entirely reliant on the sprouts that emerge from their root crown. I was curious about how long it would take for resprouting shrubs to flower and fruit again after the fire, and noticed the first summer after the fire that the toyons that had not burned in the fire flowered as usual and had abundant red berries the next fall, one year after the fire. However, none of the newly sprouting plants had any fruit that fall, and I only began to see new green berries in July two years after the fire, ripening to red that November. California bay laurels are quicker to flower, with new buds appearing on branches within the same year that those shoots appeared.

In mature chaparral, shrubs are the foundation and the architecture of their ecosystem—their roots the hidden mesh holding the soil together; their branches the living rooms for lizard, bug, and bird; their canopies the roofs protecting prey from prying eyes. Even in the early months after a wildfire, when everything is open—the roof ripped off the landscape—shrubs rush to reclaim their status as shelter and sustenance. Dusky-footed woodrats collect bay laurel leaves to line their nests, protecting them from fleas, mites, and ticks; the leaves are full of volatile oils that repel these parasites. Coyotebrush begins to provide cover again for wrentits, white-throated sparrows, and other small birds. Poison oak, particularly quick to rebound after fire, brings early stability to the postfire soil and plenty of nutrition in its white berries to woodrats and to birds such as California towhees.

I had been told about the hordes of American robins that descend on the canyon every winter to stuff themselves with toyon berries, but only finally witness the phenomenon myself in February 2020, four-and-a-half years after the fire. On that day, I walk a few hundred feet along the trail and enter a patch of toyons, and the air above me explodes. Unseen until I startle them from their feasting, a good twenty birds zip out of the branches, some to resettle in the same bunch of shrubs, others dashing just ahead of me on the trail to the next toyons down the canyon. This scene repeats itself again and again on the hike. My companions are so lively and so numerous that I am borne along on their energy.

The drama in the midst of which I have found myself comes to its final act when, toward the end of my visit, I notice a little body, tucked into the sticks and leaf litter off to the side of the trail. A shock of rust-red feathers on the breast announces that this is a robin and that tragedy has befallen one of the flock. I had seen a pile of scattered feathers earlier in the hike where it looked as though

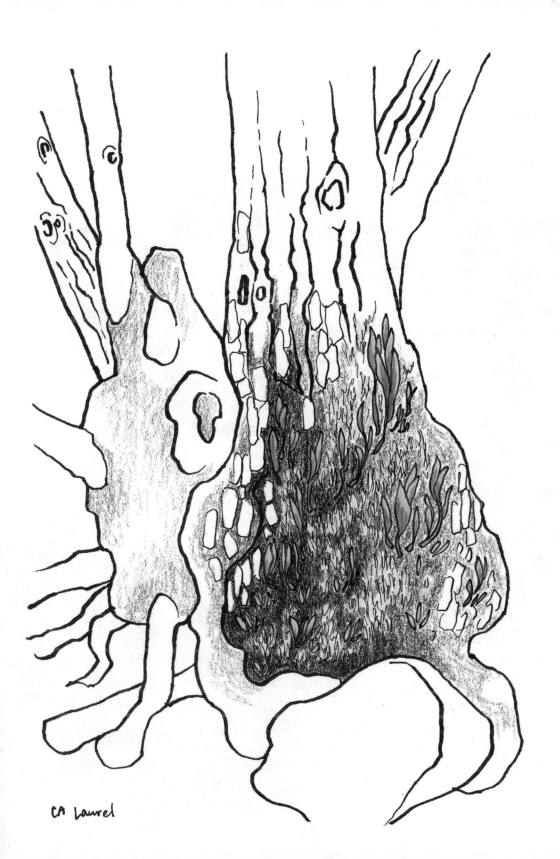

CA Laurel

tragedy befell this one –
I spotted it just down
the hill from the trail –
no signs of predation

several clearings full
of chaparral currant
Ribes malvaceum

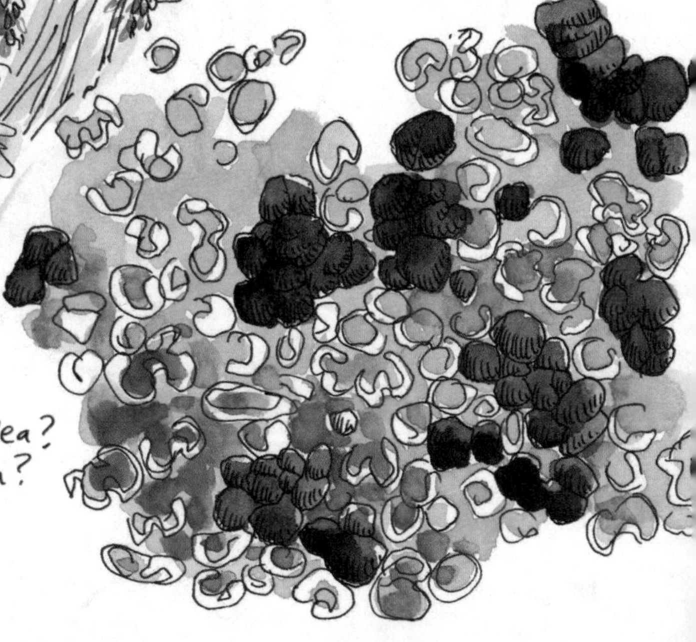

Lecidea?
Psora?

one bird had escaped a predator, but this one was not so lucky. I see no signs of attack—blood or parts missing—so its cause of death remains a mystery. Time passes. Lives begin and end. Shrubs in the chaparral sprout, grow, flower, and fruit, all the while serving as protection, food, structure, and shade. The species that benefit from their largesse may change as the shrubs mature, but the value of the gifts remains constant.

Close attention to Cold Canyon's hillsides, and growing knowledge about how life has adapted to these habitats and especially to fire have shown me that the role models I value most are chaparral shrubs. Theirs is the best recipe for life in difficult environments: hold on tight, grow deep roots, and always share with your neighbors. My favorite shrub is California mountain mahogany, and I reveled in my first glimpse of its new leaves in October 2016, just over a year after the fire—tough, thick little fan-shaped leaves, deep green. Mountain mahogany has the most beautiful seeds. They float away from their parent plant on feathery plumed tails, and when they land, the gently spiraling tails catch the wind and spin the seed down into the ground like a drill. After a fire, these seeds waiting in the earth grow again, as do sprouts from the burl of the original plant. The burned branches, though, do not go to waste. They are a home and a feast for the creatures that come to this burned land, drawn to the opportunities laid bare.

mountain mahogany
Cercocarpus betuloides
basal sprouting

Chapter Four

AN EXPLOSION OF COLOR
Wildflowers Seize the Day

Wildflowers respond exuberantly to fire, emerging to soak up the sunlight now that the tree and shrub cover is gone. They fill the landscape with color, wasting no chance to use all of the resources suddenly available to them in this time of open space and new beginnings.

The canyon, flung open by the fire, has not looked like this for nearly thirty years. Sunlight, shining through charred limbs and blackened snags, reaches the ground in places that had long been in full shade. It will be many years before the canopy reaches its prefire height, but each year, resprouting shrubs and trees grow higher. Now is the time.

This is a magnificent opportunity for some species. Many plants are unable to compete in mature ecosystems, growing only in scattered open glades here and there or disappearing altogether. These plants, mostly annual wildflowers, grow best in disturbed environments where their competition has been removed.

Taking full advantage of the burned landscape, the annuals grow abundantly for a few years and then decline, crowded out by perennials. But even then they are not truly gone. Their seeds will bide their time in the soil, waiting for the next fire. The life blooming, buzzing, and fluttering all around me at Cold Canyon keeps fresh in my mind just how natural fire is. Wildflowers are not merely the most colorful signs of recovery from a catastrophe. They avidly profit from the event and turn it to their advantage. Fire is an integral part of the ongoing life of the ecosystem.

It is February 2016, the winter after the fire, when I spy the first one. Walking down the trail, surrounded on both sides by new herby green growth in soil damp from recent rains, I see a flower: Henderson's shooting star. This early-season bloomer looks just as its name suggests, with delicate pink petals streaming behind the cone-shaped stamen "star" that seems to fall to earth. The shooting star is a perfect celebratory start to several eye-opening seasons of new discoveries and colorful flowers.

Fire-followers

On a gray day in May 2016, the first spring after the fire, I come to Cold Canyon midmorning and let myself in at the gate. The canyon is still closed to the public, and I am visiting with special permission from the university, which is allowing researchers to continue their work. I slowly inhale the unusually cool, damp air. The heat of summer will soon be upon us, well before the calendar registers the season's official start. Noting the colorful flowers at every turn, I stop to draw a chick lupine in full bloom, bright yellow with orange tips. Only once my pen is moving across the paper do I notice something new. I stop and look up from the lupine. Intertwined with the lupine and also spreading up the slope behind are distinctive fuzzy plants with long stalks growing from a low rosette of leaves. The stalks are lined with drooping bell-shaped flowers in pale yellow. The air feels still to me, but the bells nod in response to the gentlest currents.

Whispering bells! Here is a wonderful surprise. I have been reading about fire-following wildflowers to get an idea of what I might find on these explorations. I know this year will reveal treasures, but each one delights me nonetheless. This is at the top of the list. To be sure, it is less showy than the chick lupine I was drawing or some of the other vivid flowers nearby, but it is a quintessential fire-following annual, and it has not been seen at Cold Canyon since shortly after the last wildfire, nearly thirty years ago. This shy arrival has a lot to say about how

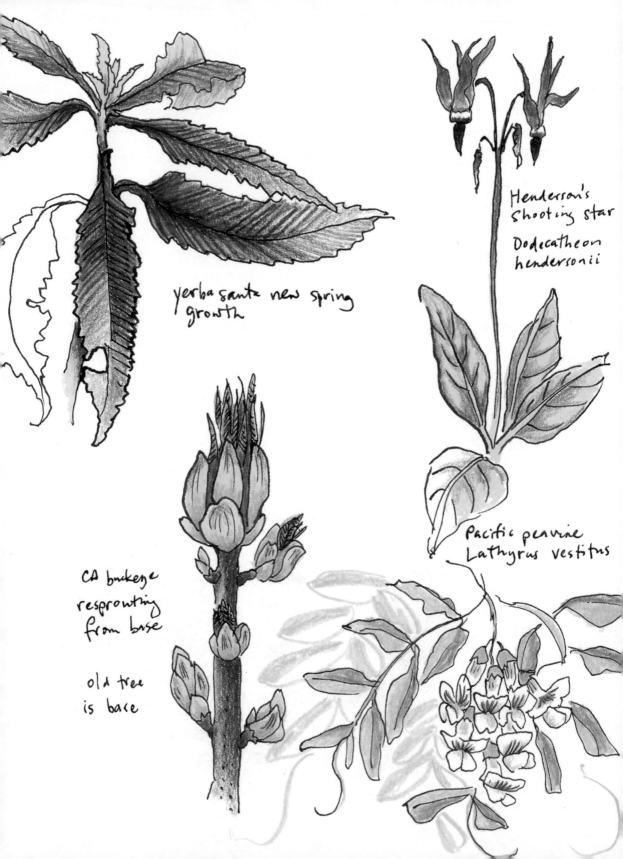

yerba santa new spring growth

Henderson's shooting star
Dodecatheon hendersonii

Pacific peavine
Lathyrus vestitus

CA buckeye resprouting from base

old tree is bare

some flowers evolve to depend on fire, taking advantage of the unique environmental conditions it creates.

As the Wragg Fire ravaged the landscape, its scorching heat blasted the ground. Chemicals released by burning vegetation penetrated the surface. In the soil lay dormant seeds, undisturbed for decades since their parents last grew here. They've been waiting since I was a teenager. The plants' hairy, sticky leaves and stems are like Velcro, ensuring that seeds stick to their parents and enter the soil right in that spot, protected from dispersal on the wind. It is lovely to think now, as I add fuzz to my whispering bells drawing, about what those hairs are for: ensuring that seeds remain in the soil where their parents successfully matured and flowered and then decayed to become part of that same soil. When fire returned to the canyon, the seeds were perfectly placed to receive the smoke's message.

Nitrogen dioxide in smoke tells a whispering bells seed that it is time to germinate. Wildfire means that the ground will be perfect for new plants to grow:

whispering bells
Emmenanthe
penduliflora

chick lupine
Lupinus
microcarpus

fertile, ashy soil, full of nutrients. The new whispering bells sprouts have emerged from their decades-long rest into open sunlight, in a place that until now was too deeply shaded by the shrubs and trees that came to dominate five to ten years after the last fire. With less competition for vital resources—sunlight, nutrients, water, and space—whispering bells will thrive here for a couple of years. By then, other plants will crowd in and over them, and the nitrogen dioxide in the system will have returned to prefire levels. Whispering bells seeds will stop germinating and fall again into their long slumber, waiting like Sleeping Beauty for their next enchanted awakening.

The landscape in which the whispering bells have appeared is a stark study in contrasts. The green of spring is all around me, with small shoots of shrubs appearing between the dead black limbs and freshly risen annuals and grasses low on the ground. The new growth does not obscure how dark the ground still is, marked by layers of ash from burned vegetation. Looking up the slopes to the ridges on either side of the canyon, I see lines of ghostly tree limbs and branches: the finest, thinnest dead twigs on each tree merge in the distance to form rivers of purple-gray.

I am struck by the thought that right where I stand, whispering bells grew nearly thirty years ago and, I hope, will grow here after the next fire. I was a girl when whispering bells grew here last and will be an old woman if the next fire waits another thirty years. These plants are a window through time, tying past, present, and future together in a continuum of long, patient waits and fleeting emergence.

Amid the beauty of their flowering, I think about that future. What will happen to whispering bells as the climate continues to warm and destabilize and we experience fires of greater frequency and intensity? If a fire is too intense, heat will penetrate the soil deep enough to kill waiting whispering bells seeds, which are unlikely to be buried more than four inches under the surface. If fire burns the habitat again too soon, whispering bells will not have time to mature, flower, and set seed. Without a full seed bank waiting beneath the surface, whispering bells will not be able to grow again after the next fire. Whispering bells have evolved to match their life cycle to the natural fire regime of their chaparral habitat home. Changing fire regimes undermine the strategies that whispering bells and other fire-adapted annuals have honed over their evolutionary histories. If more frequent or more intense fires destroy the number and diversity of seeds waiting in an ecosystem's seed bank, the health and resilience of that ecosystem will be compromised. I wonder whether I can count on these whispering bells appearing again after the next fire.

Fire-stimulated germination is widespread in the borage family, to which whispering bells belong. I have long loved the flowers in this family—fiddleneck, with its tight curls of tiny orange trumpets; phacelia, looking like soft, fuzzy, curled-up caterpillars; popcorn flowers in cheery sprays of white—all of them with their charismatic hairy stems and leaves. Most members of the borage family, though, are not as closely tied to fire as whispering bells. Many other borage plants germinate in response to wildfire, but also continue to grow from seed during the intervening years and do not disappear completely from their ecosystems.

whispering bells
Emmenanthe penduliflora

One member of the family, yerba santa, employs two responses to fire. As with whispering bells, smoke cues seeds waiting in the soil to germinate. Yerba santa also vigorously resprouts from its rhizomes after fire, much like some shrubs from their burls. Rhizomes are technically stems, but they grow horizontally just under the soil surface, sending out both shoots and roots as they spread. Protected from fire by the powerful insulation of the soil, rhizomes are primed to immediately send up sprouts afterward. Yerba santa combines the two strategies to rapidly repop-ulate a habitat after fire. It is a hardy perennial that remains abundant at Cold Canyon, even when the last wildfire is a distant memory.

fiddleneck
Amsinckia
menziesii

This tough survivor is also cunningly able to turn fire to its own advantage, just like chamise. When flames reach yerba santa, the waxy, resinous leaves burn furiously. A stand of yerba santa intensifies the fire, encouraging it to spread further and burn hot-ter, consuming the other trees and shrubs nearby. In the process, yerba santa burns up, but its rhizomes are ready to immediately grow again, spreading out-ward to claim more space in the habitat, now that slower-growing perennials have been removed. I watch yerba santa coming up green after the fire, in large patches along the sunniest banks of the creek. When I crease a leaf, its smell is sweetly medicinal. This first new growth is the rhizome in action, sending up new sprouts. It takes longer for seeds to germinate. It takes longer still for the new plants to produce flowers. None of the plants flowered in that first year—I have to wait two years to see the first pretty little pale-purple, trumpet-shaped flowers.

Fire-stimulated germination is not limited to the borage family. On my first hike through the canyon in December 2015, the long, thin leaves of wavy-leaved

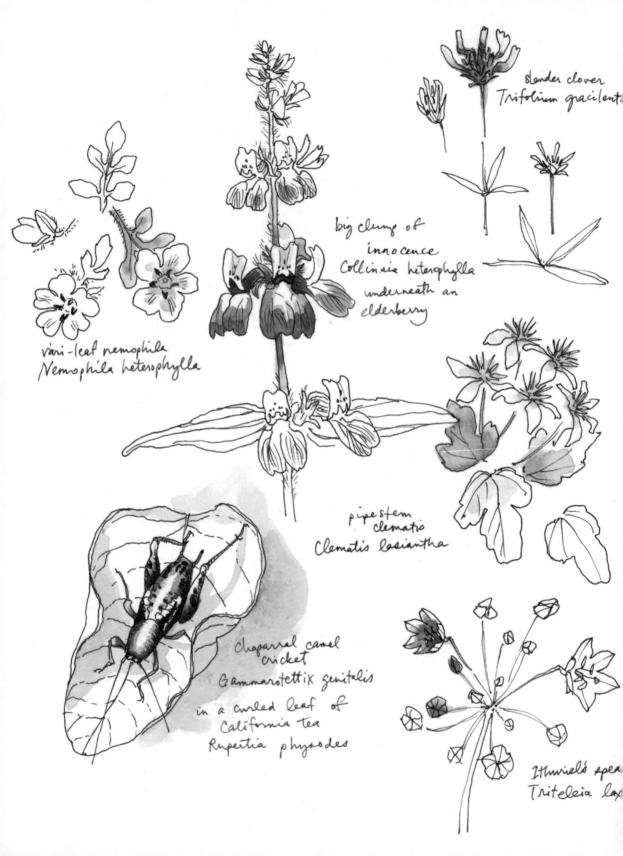

slender clover
Trifolium gracilent[um]

big clump of
innocence
Collinsia heterophylla
underneath an
elderberry

vari-leaf nemophila
Nemophila heterophylla

pipestem
clematis
Clematis lasiantha

Chaparral camel
cricket
Gammarotettix genitalis

in a curled leaf of
California tea
Rupertia physoodes

Ithuriel's spea[r]
Triteleia lax[a]

soap plant are strikingly green against the blackened earth. I watch the plants extend their tall flowering stalks, reaching my height of six feet. The delicate pale-pink flowers remain tightly curled during the day; it is only at night, when their moth pollinators are out, that the flowers open into spindly stars, their pollen-bearing anthers standing out like a spray of yellow sparks. I've seen them opening in the early evening, the thin veins of pink down the center of each petal glowing in the setting sun.

Wavy-leaved soap plant is always present at Cold Canyon, and throughout California chaparral habitats generally, but it particularly flourishes after fire. Soap plant first resprouts from bulbs. Later, new plants grow from seeds that germinated in response to fire. The dual reproductive strategy of bulbs and seeds gives soap plant flexibility in its response to changes in its environment. It quickly recovers from aboveground trauma by sprouting from its bulb. It preserves long-term variation by continuing to grow from seeds that have been produced sexually, with genetic material from two parent plants.

I feel a tiny jolt realizing that the soap plant seeds that are just now germinating and sending up new green sprouts will not produce flowers for a decade. It is strange to me that it takes so long for the plant grown from seed to be able to reproduce. For something as large and substantial as a tree, I expect a long time to reach maturity, but soap plants seem like more ephemeral beings that would mature rapidly. And it is interesting to know for sure that the soap plants that I see flowering in the first few years after the fire must have regrown from bulbs, not seeds, since they were able to flower so quickly.

Life underground

Walking in Cold Canyon in June 2016, almost a full year after the fire, I am baking in the midsummer heat. I pause to survey my surroundings in a full three-dimensional panorama. Above me, the sky is so vivid that it temporarily washes out my view of the hilltops when I lower my eyes slightly. Not even a wisp of cloud breaks the sky's smooth gradient from pale to brighter blue, though when I look up again, I see two vultures circling on thermals high above the ridgeline. I let my eyes wander down the slope, following the paths of the ghostly gray branches of burned and desiccated trees. Closer to the canyon bottom, things become greener: California manroot and chaparral false bindweed vines climbing, western redbud leafing out, California bay laurel and California buckeye growing rapidly, and plenty of annual herbs still green and flowering. Blue elderberry has exploded in puffs of creamy-white flowers.

I root myself in one spot and turn slowly around. To the east, Pleasants Ridge rises above undulating hills covered in the skeletons of chaparral shrubs and bare, blackened trees in blue oak savannahs. South, up the canyon, the hills recede into

EAST   SOUTH

the distance, the farthest still covered in green trees, untouched by the fire. To the west, the top of Blue Ridge is pale and parched, without much in the way of green now that the main flush of spring growth and blooming has ended and we have moved into the summer heat. I look north, back down the canyon toward the entrance and past it to the summer-yellow hills near the Monticello Dam, and finally I look down at my feet and the hard-packed trail surface.

Beneath my feet, unseen, there is much going on. Aboveground, the wildflowers are peaceful and serene, opening to the sun in the morning and closing as evening falls, but under the surface they are hard at work, literally reshaping the soil. The health of the postfire habitat rests on a knife's edge, and the work they do will make all the difference. When the Wragg Fire roared through, ash remained, blanketing the ground. By burning plants and plant litter on the ground, fire released their nutrients, including nitrogen, phosphorous, carbon, and sulfur. Most of these remain in the soil, making it richer for plants to regrow and new seeds to sprout. The catch is that all of these usable nutrients are in the ash or right at the soil surface, where they are easily washed away by rain or blown away in the wind. And nitrogen was vaporized by the fire, lost to the soil for the time being.

WEST   NORTH

Springing up shortly after fire, annuals and short-lived perennials such as poppies, lupines, phacelias, delphiniums, and penstemons bring immediate color into the altered landscape. Not just pretty faces, they, like the shrubs I have been so admiring, guard against erosion by holding soil in place in a web of interconnected subterranean scaffolding. Their roots also play a critical role in capturing soil nutrients so that they are not rinsed out of the system. By absorbing and using resources in the soil, the plants bind the nutrients into their living tissue. As the annuals die at the end of their growing season and are recycled back into the soil by invertebrates and microbes, the nutrients become available again for other plants. This process is an exquisite example of recycling and renewal launched by fire-followers after a wildfire. Without it, the habitats here would be indescribably poorer and fire more truly a destructive cataclysm.

It is impossible to resist the charms of lupines, one of the great joys of spring. Their spears of white, purple, and magenta flowers are extravagantly arresting, and I will always be awed by a field full of them. They are a magic carpet, stitched in intricate patterns, rolled out over the undulating hills. Cold Canyon has a bounty after the fire. Arroyo lupine and miniature lupine appear first, in March 2016. Arroyo lupine has big, fleshy leaves spread out in the characteristic lupine fan, and miniature lupine is appropriately tiny, with stalks that have only a few whorls of flowers rather than a long spear of many blooms like arroyo lupine. In May, there are two more: silver bush lupine, with its skinny, hairy leaves, and chick lupine, yellow instead of the usual purple of most lupines. By that time, arroyo lupine has gone to seed and sports large, hairy pea pods in abundance.

Lupines are overachievers when it comes to capturing nutrients. Most plants rely on bacteria in the soil to convert nitrogen in the air into more usable forms. Lupines have taken matters fully into their own hands and have brought the bacteria right into their own tissue, in nodules that form on their roots. Inside, the bacteria metabolize nitrogen into compounds the lupines use to make the amino acids and proteins they need to grow. In return, the lupines give the bacteria protection and energy. When lupines die, their tissues return all the metabolized nitrogen to the soil, where it becomes available to other plants.

As their fruits attest, lupines are members of the pea family—legumes. Almost all members of the family are nitrogen fixing. At Cold Canyon, I watch deerweed, a shrub with small yellow flowers, and western redbud, with its deep-pink flowers, reappear the first spring. Pacific peavine, California tea, and several native clovers also emerge that year. It is not a coincidence that many legumes return quickly after fire in chaparral and woodland habitats. They exploit their advantage in pulling nitrogen from the air to grow in conditions that are more difficult for plants without integral bacterial helpers. Legumes are the best-known family of nitrogen fixers, but a few other plant families have also invited bacterial associates into their roots. In chaparral and oak woodland habitats like Cold Canyon, these prodigious nitrogen fixers include California lilacs, mountain mahogany, and alders.

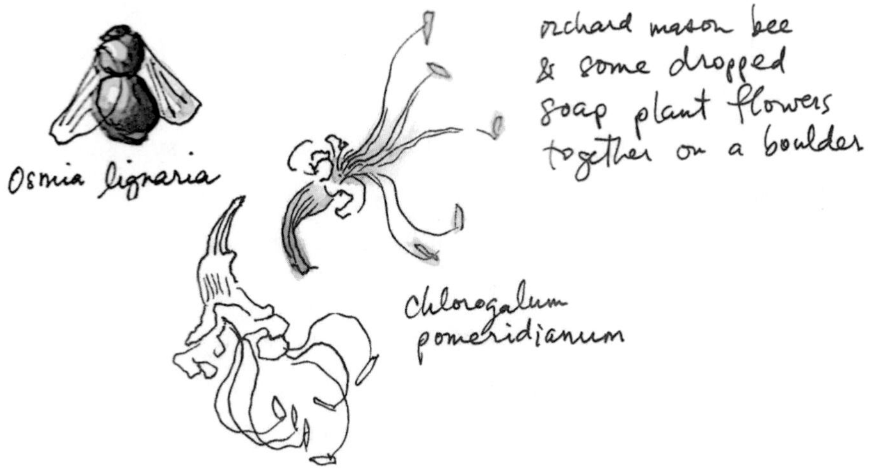

Osmia lignaria

orchard mason bee & some dropped soap plant flowers together on a boulder

Chlorogalum pomeridianum

On this hot June day, having taken stock of my surroundings, I know there are connections being strengthened below me in the soil, invisible to the human eye and so easy to forget. I have visited the canyon throughout the winter, spring, and early summer after the fire. I have walked through the unfolding drama of life responding in vibrant splashes of color and have seen annual plants experience a full reproductive cycle, like the lupines that sprouted, flowered, and set seed. It is in these aboveground cycles that I am reassured of the regeneration occurring in the soil, as legumes and bacteria find each other and establish the nurturing relationships that sustain them and the rest of their ecosystem.

The complexity of weeds

Familiar from sidewalks and roadsides everywhere in California, nonnative red-stem filaree is common along the trail at Cold Canyon, with its pretty pink flowers and distinctive beak-like seedpods. On my visits, I often catch myself dismissing the nonnative plants I see along the trail. Too often I reflexively shake my head, thinking, "What a shame the fire opened up all this space for weeds to exploit." The easy dichotomy is to view native plants as healthy for the ecosystem and introduced species as unhealthy. Once I start thinking deeply about the work done by early arrivals to the postfire landscape, though, it is easy to see that even the weeds make contributions.

Like their native pea family relatives, bur clover and hairy vetch are nitrogen fixers that help enrich the soil for future plant growth. Other lovers of disturbed ground sprout readily after fire too, such as filaree and dove's foot geranium, both common weeds. These nonnatives help hold the newly exposed soil in place and contribute nutrients to the soil when they die, the same as the native annuals. The same qualities that make all of our favorite native fire-following annuals

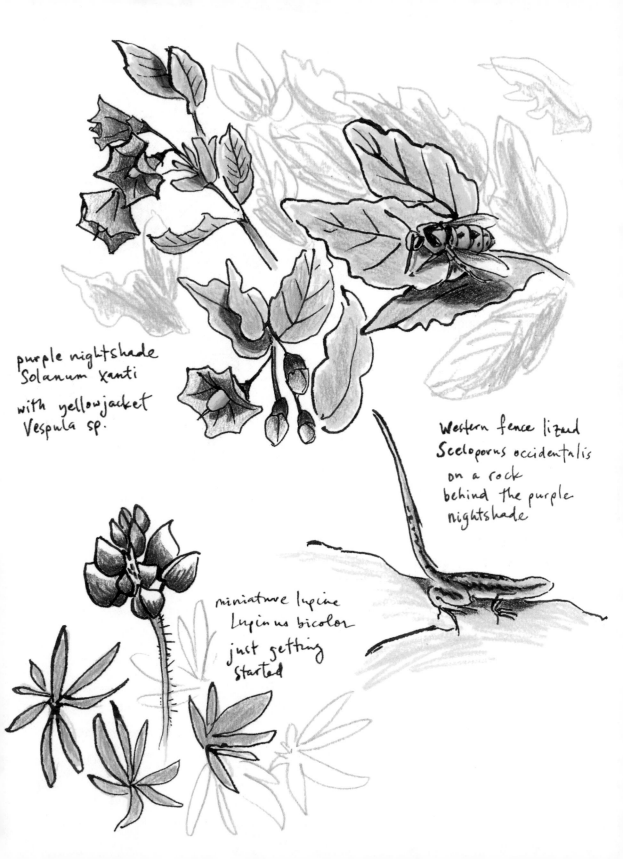

purple nightshade
Solanum xanti

with yellowjacket
Vespula sp.

Western fence lizard
Sceloporus occidentalis
on a rock
behind the purple
nightshade

miniature lupine
Lupinus bicolor
just getting
started

proliferate after a disturbance—the ability to grow in soil that has been depleted of nutrients such as nitrogen, eagerness to exploit abundant direct sunlight, tolerance for drought—are the qualities that enable introduced species to spread in local ecosystems.

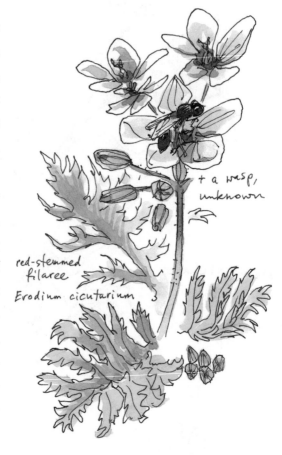

+ a wasp, unknown

red-stemmed filaree
Erodium cicutarium

Just as studying this canyon brings the story of a burned landscape to life, these investigations lead me to question my black-and-white judgment of introduced species. Concerns about the impacts of nonnative plant species on a habitat are undeniably real and important. Plants that thrive in habitats far from their original home are generally hardy and able to tolerate environments poor in water, shade, and nutrients. Once established, these plants often outcompete native species for these scarce resources, eventually ensuring that fewer native plants survive. Over time, the diversity of the ecosystem diminishes, as many different types of native plant are replaced by just one or a few nonnative species.

But this is not the whole story. There is space for a more nuanced view of the newest species in an ecosystem, the plants introduced from elsewhere that find a foothold here, just as plants from this California ecosystem have traveled the globe and become weeds in other places. A weed, after all, is simply a plant that is growing somewhere that humans would rather it not. Seep monkeyflower, for example, a western North America native found in Cold Canyon, has become a successful weed in New Zealand after being introduced as a garden ornamental. Fiddlenecks are California natives often considered weeds in their own native state, not to mention elsewhere in the world where they have been introduced. I look at the nonnative clover and red-stemmed filaree at the side of the trail, and am reminded of the hardiness that gives them a foothold in a disturbed land. Their presence here is complex: taking resources that before would have belonged to the native flora, but participating fully in the reestablishment of vegetation and succession of habitats after the fire.

I realize, as I walk these dusty trails admiring and sketching flowers, that the flowers are flourishing now, but are at the same time paving the way for their replacements and preparing their own demise. It is a potent image of beauty in the immediate moment and continuing the cycle into the waiting future. Walking the canyon's paths with the fire-following annuals, I step into the stream of passing time.

Each spring after the fire, the annual wildflower palette changes. Some flowers appear immediately after the fire and then disappear, following the pattern set by whispering bells, which is gone by the fourth postfire spring. Many, such as lupines and yerba santa, explode immediately and hang on, eventually taking a more modest place in the mature communities at Cold Canyon among the chaparral shrubs and in the oak woodlands, grasslands, and riparian corridor. Still others take a few years to appear in any great numbers, such as the clarkias—elegant clarkia, red ribbons, and four-spot—but then blanket the hillsides in color.

As I take stock of the changes I've witnessed in the canyon, I am filled with gratitude for my front-row seat to this unfolding spectacle. I feel a part of the

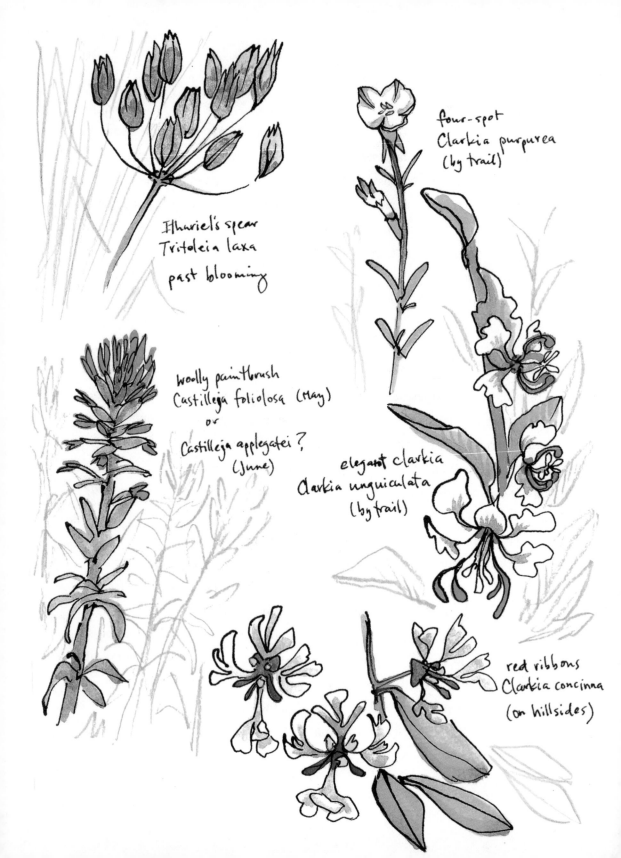

Ithuriel's spear
Tritoleia laxa

past blooming

four-spot
Clarkia purpurea
(by trail)

woolly paintbrush
Castilleja foliolosa (May)
or
Castilleja applegatei ?
(June)

elegant clarkia
Clarkia unguiculata
(by trail)

red ribbons
Clarkia concinna
(on hillsides)

narrative in a way that is impossible without witnessing each stage. Having watched each flower appear in its own season and seen the vigor of life reasserting itself in this stark, opened, breathing landscape, I find my own ideas of beauty expanding. A mature, leafy, shady canyon is a wonderful place, but I am so much the richer for the new perspectives offered by the fire. It is the act of looking closely and repeatedly at Cold Canyon's habitats that makes possible my shift in understanding, in a way that reading about fire never would. As I record each noteworthy find, pen in hand, drawing the ink lines into my sketchbook takes my observations out of the realm of the purely objective and gives them emotional weight. After nearly thirty years of growth and yearly deposits into the seed bank by flowering plants, this was a landscape prepared to burn. And this is how I come to fully understand the message in the tapestry of color in a newly burned landscape, after an appropriate interval between fires. This is natural. This is normal. This is a healthy ecosystem.

Chapter Five

FLOWER-FOLLOWERS
Pollinators

As flowers fill the canyon, more life follows. Animals rush to the scene, finding sustenance and shelter in the nectar, pollen, and greenery that quickly appear. Insects and birds recolonize the burned landscape and return the favor by pollinating the flowers.

Whispering bells, the magical flowers that grow at Cold Canyon only for a few years after a wildfire, are participants in an intriguing mystery. There is an elusive bee that collects pollen only from this particular flower. The bee is so rarely spotted that it has no common name, being known only by its scientific name, *Protodufourea wasbaueri*. It is a very small bee, less than a quarter-inch long, with a black head and thorax and a shiny reddish-brown abdomen. In the intervals between fires, which could be thirty to fifty years, the bee is never found. What a strange existence! *P. wasbaueri* nests in the ground like the other members of its family, the Halictidae, commonly referred to as sweat bees, though not all are drawn to sweat. I wonder whether *P. wasbaueri* somehow remains dormant underground all this time, waiting, just like its host flower, for the conditions to be right to burst into a frenzy of short-lived activity. So far, this bee has been found only in Southern California. I would dearly like to know whether it also pollinates whispering bells in Northern California, and if not, who does.

The open spaces cleared by wildfire are excellent opportunities for ground-nesting bees like *P. wasbaueri*. Mining bees, digger bees, membrane bees, and sweat bees find abundant food in the nectar and pollen of the new wildflowers and plenty of exposed soil in which to build nests, wide open to the sunshine. I wonder whether some of these bees might have survived the fire, insulated and safe in their underground homes. Certainly other bees will arrive after the fire, too, to take advantage of the new opportunities. Wood-nesting bees are less likely to survive the fire, but colonizers from nearby unburned habitats will find ample new resources in the burned landscape. The burned trunks and branches are inviting new sites for the construction of cityscapes by carpenter and mason bees.

As all these bees hurry to the plenitude of flowers and nesting spaces in the years following the fire, they themselves ensure the health and prosperity of the flowering plants. Their pollination helps the flowers thrive and build up their underground seed banks in preparation for not only the next year but also the next fire. I start each spring at Cold Canyon full of anticipation for the creatures I will find enjoying the new season's flowers. In these pollinators, I know I will see evidence of renewal and the beautiful reciprocity between plant and animal, each ensuring each other's health, survival, and reproduction.

Life cycles intertwined:
Butterflies, moths, and their local hosts

A large, dark shape flutters past, and before I catch myself, my brain registers: bird! Then the erratic nature of the fluttering sinks in, and I revise my impression: butterfly! Pipevine swallowtails are impressively large for butterflies, with wingspans up to five inches, and their deep-blue wings only add to the impression of something substantial passing by. I follow the blue-black shape as it dips and bobs across the trail and over to a gentle slope where there is a young oak tree, blackened, and lots of green, herby vegetation low to the ground. I see lavender-pink twining snake-lily, nodding in the sun, and California manroot tendrils reaching up. At the base of the oak are new, soft, yellow-green leaves of pipevine.

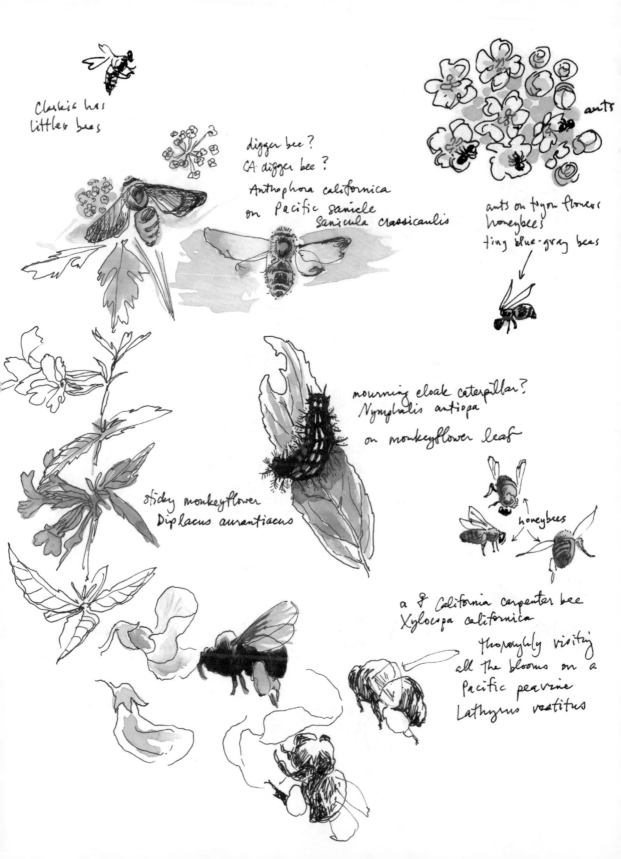

Clarkia has littler bees

digger bee?
CA digger bee?
Anthophora californica
on Pacific sanicle
    Sanicula crassicaulis

ants

ants on tyson flowers
honeybees
tiny blue-gray bees

mourning cloak caterpillar?
Nymphalis antiopa

on monkeyflower leaf

honeybees

sticky monkeyflower
Diplacus aurantiacus

a ♀ California carpenter bee
Xylocopa californica

thoroughly visiting
all the blooms on a
Pacific peavine
Lathyrus vestitus

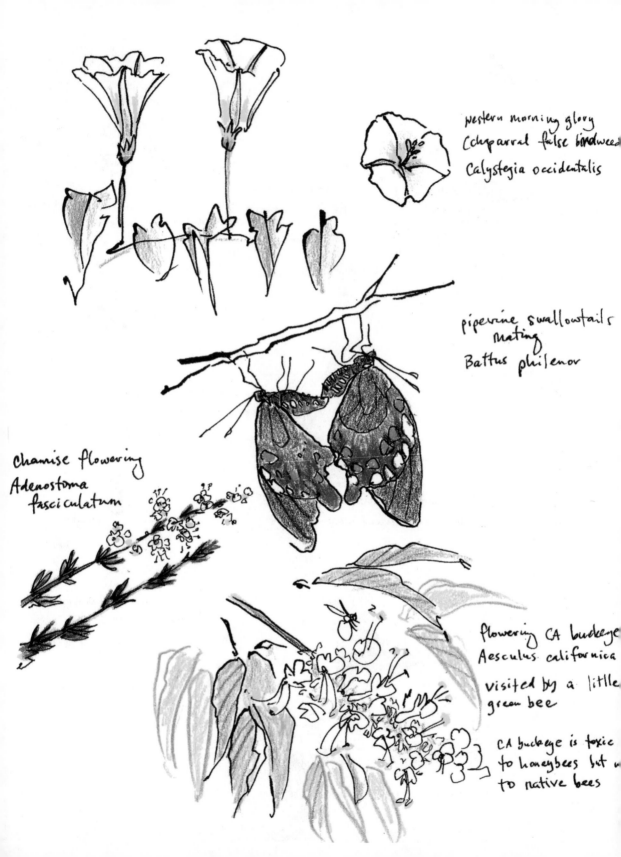

western morning glory
Chaparral false bindweed
Calystegia occidentalis

pipevine swallowtails
mating
Battus philenor

Chamise flowering
Adenostoma
fasciculatum

flowering CA buckeye
Aesculus californica

visited by a little
green bee

CA buckeye is toxic
to honeybees but n
to native bees

The butterfly I am watching lingers on several of the pipevine leaves, resting and moving, resting again and moving on.

California pipevine, like other vines, grows easily after wildfire, resprouting from underground rhizomes and capitalizing on abundant sunlight. As the only host plant for pipevine swallowtail caterpillars, pipevine draws the butterflies back to Cold Canyon within months of the fire. Butterflies are often able to fly away from fire, but they are short-lived creatures: adults live for only about a month. The adults that flew to safety ahead of the Wragg Fire are not the ones that return when pipevine starts to regrow. I know that the butterflies I see here after the fire have come from outside the burned habitat. As fires cover larger and larger areas in California, butterflies will find it much more difficult to escape at all. They require the patchiness of historical fire regimes, where fires burned smaller areas and left other spots unburned. A mosaic of untouched areas, like the ones I see in Cold Canyon after the fire, provides critical sheltering sources for butterflies who can return to the burned areas. We know how important mosaic patterns of burning are, for butterflies, for birds such as black-backed woodpeckers and spotted owls, and for so many other species too. Watching the patterns of wildfire change in the western US, I wonder what the new patterns of larger, hotter, more frequent fires hold in store for butterflies, birds, and everything else, as their mosaics disappear.

Like most butterflies, pipevine swallowtail caterpillars and adults have completely different diets. While the caterpillars depend on pipevine alone for food, the adults visit a number of flowers for nectar. I often inadvertently follow them as they travel up and down the canyon. They stop to feed at blue dicks and Ithuriel's spear, two purple flowers in the asparagus family growing alongside a large patch of pipevine near the entrance to Cold Canyon. Higher up the canyon, they bob along until they reach some of the large patches of yerba santa or visit the plentiful California buckeyes growing near the creek and climbing up the canyon slopes.

Pipevine swallowtail caterpillars are as attention grabbing as their parents: deep, velvety brown with electric-orange bumps. They seem to be everywhere this first spring, eating pipevine stems and leaves and also crawling across the trail.

I find a few pipevine plants, but not many, so how can there be so many caterpillars? At first I wonder whether the caterpillars will eat up all the pipevine, making it difficult for the plant to grow the following year. It turns out that this is unlikely. A caterpillar munching on a pipevine leaf stimulates the leaf to step up its production of toxic aristolochic acid. The caterpillar finds a little of this acid beneficial and sequesters it in its body as a defense against birds and other predators. Too much aristolochic acid, however, tastes terrible to the caterpillar, which will move on to new leaves. I have seen the partially nibbled leaves—nibbled, but not wholly devoured. The few plants I see must be only the tip of the iceberg. I am sure there is plenty of pipevine elsewhere in the canyon.

pipevine swallowtail caterpillar (Battus philenor) on pipevine

The intertwined life cycle of pipevine swallowtail and its California pipevine host is common among butterflies. Caterpillars are often dependent on a single plant or plant family for their food, so finding a butterfly is an important signal about its host plant. I do not expect to see so many butterflies in an area—unless they are in the middle of their migration—without also expecting to see the host plant somewhere nearby. Thinking of host plants, I have been wondering how California lilacs fared in the fire. These common chaparral shrubs were abundant at Cold Canyon before the fire, but lacking burls, both species found here must grow from seed after fire, so they are taking a while to show up again postburn. Each year, I keep my eyes open for evidence of them—hairy-leaf ceanothus and wedge-leaf ceanothus. Unsuspecting, I nearly stumble over an important clue. One January over three years after the fire, a kaleidoscope—this is truly the term for a butterfly swarm—of California tortoiseshells is gathered on a patch of damp trail.

Just as pipevine swallowtails lead me to California pipevine, when I see large numbers of California tortoiseshells at Cold Canyon, I suspect that California lilacs are probably rebounding. After all, tortoiseshell caterpillars feed only on California lilacs. And sure enough, shortly after finding the butterflies, I come across both ceanothus species thriving, hairy-leaf ceanothus throughout the canyon and wedge-leaf ceanothus higher up on the slopes. The next year, over four years after the fire, both species are full of flowers and industrious insects.

A crowd of tortoiseshells congregating on a patch of mud, slowly opening and closing their wings, is a vision. It upends our usual image of butterflies as ethereal creatures delicately sipping nectar from colorful flowers. In reality, some butterflies are far earthier. Consider the mourning cloak. Each spring after the fire, I see them flying past me at eye level, immediately recognizable by the outer strip of creamy white on their otherwise dark maroon-black wings. Far from the pretty image, mourning cloak adults shun flowers almost completely and prefer to feast on mud, sap, and dung.

Unlike pipevine swallowtails, California tortoiseshells are migratory and spend only part of their life cycle in the canyon. Adults spend their winter in Cold Canyon and other foothill canyons, storing fat in the fall and finding sheltered places in trees and rocks to lay eggs that will hatch, eat, and form pupae that remain dormant until the days warm and lengthen again. I observe them in large numbers from January to March this third spring after the fire; the females are likely laying eggs on California lilacs, though the ones I find are mostly congregating on mud puddles, gathering minerals and nutrients from the water and soil. These are probably all males, who will pass the minerals and nutrients to females in their sperm, improving the survival chances of their offspring.

Mourning cloaks and California tortoiseshells have similar life cycles, with a winter generation in the foothills and a summer generation in the mountains. The eggs they lay at Cold Canyon will hatch, and the caterpillars will feed voraciously, pupate, and emerge as adults in June. This summer brood is drawn to higher elevations and often further north, where adults will breed in summer and lay eggs on their high-elevation plant hosts. The adults born at Cold Canyon will then die, having fulfilled their life's work of traveling to the mountains and laying the eggs of the next generation. They will never return to their birthplace. Their eggs develop into caterpillars that spend the rest of the summer at high elevation, pupate, and in late September return to the foothills and places like Cold Canyon to prepare for the next winter. What is it like to be drawn to a place you have never seen, to birth a new generation that only longs to return to the home you will never see again?

Butterflies are not the only lepidoptera active in the daytime. When I hike around the Blue Ridge–Homestead loop one early March day four-and-a-half years after

our dry February has had a visible effect
on the creek — I've never seen it so
low & scummy this early in the year —
& it is completely dry down closer to the
highway

another patch of CA pipevine
Aristolochia californica

popcorn
flower

Plagiobothrys
nothofulvus

California tortoise shells
Nymphalis californica   mud puddling – MANY at the Cold Creek
crossing & MANY on the trail up the
other side

the fire, several flashes of orange catch my eye, and I watch a pair of moths come to rest on milkmaids, a common early spring wildflower at Cold Canyon. Their forewings are camouflaged in jagged brown stripes, but their hindwings are vivid orange on top. The bright color stands out sharply against the white flowers as the two moths pause in their flight. At first I assume they are butterflies, but they let me approach closely enough to see that they do not have the club shapes at the ends of their antennae that are the mark of a butterfly. They are moths, part of a group referred to as underwing moths for the bright colors and patterns only on their hindwings. But these are only visible when they are in flight. The striking hindwings are entirely covered when they rest with forewings closed on top.

Looking up the moth later that day, I discover that it has been collected regularly at night at Cold Canyon by John De Benedictis, a retired UC Davis entomologist. I had the great fortune to join him on a collecting trip he made in May 2016, the first spring after the Wragg Fire, and this underwing moth, Verrill's underwing, was one of the species he found that night. How, I wonder, can it be that this moth, collected at night with John, is also out and about in the day? It turns out that underwing moths keep surprising hours. They are nocturnal, but also fly for an hour or so right around noon. Is this to visit flowers only open during the day? For mating? I did see two moths flying and landing together.

The collecting trip that May after the fire with John was enlightening. Having up to that point explored the newly burned canyon for a few months observing and drawing anything that caught my eye, I jumped at the opportunity to see Cold Canyon through the lens of deep scholarly familiarity with this ecosystem. John has been collecting moths twice a month at dusk at Cold Canyon since the 1980s, shortly after the last major wildfire. He was watching closely to see how moths responded after the Wragg Fire, to compare with his observations after the earlier fire. He usually finds the largest number of species in May. On a good night, he can collect about a third of the roughly 275 species present at that time of year. The numbers collected the May I joined him would help indicate how the moths were faring after the fire.

extreme close up of buckbrush flowers + an engrossed wasp
Ceanothus cuneatus

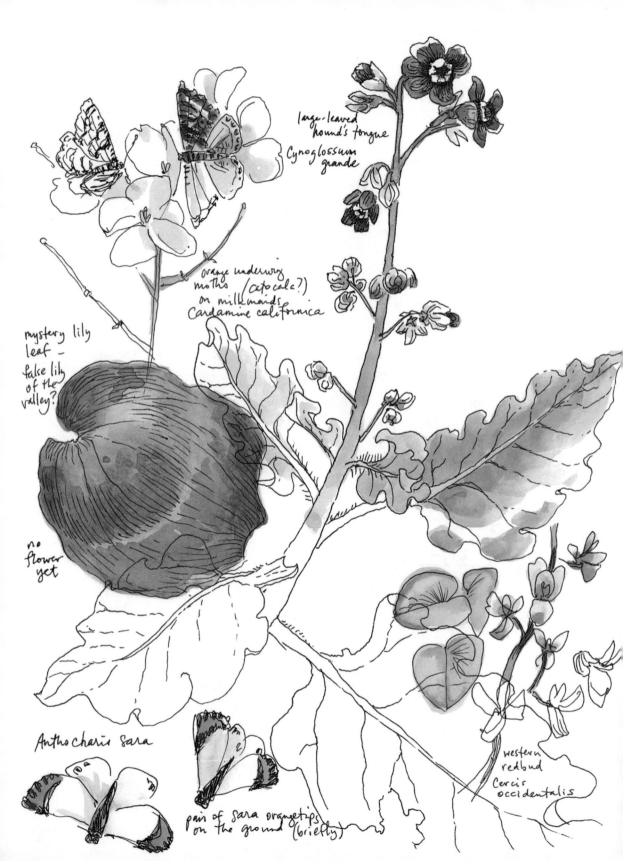

large-leaved
hound's tongue
Cynoglossum
grande

orange underwing
moths (catocala?)
on milkmaids
Cardamine californica

mystery lily
leaf –
false lily
of the
valley?

no
flower
yet

Anthocharis sara

pair of sara orangetips
on the ground (briefly)

western
redbud
Cercis
occidentalis

On our visit, I helped John suspend a sheet across the path just past the entrance to Cold Canyon. He hung a fluorescent light against the sheet, emitting unfiltered UV light, a mixture of UV and white light, to attract the insects using the canyon trail as a flyway as evening darkens to night. With the light quickly fading in the canyon, his bearded face under baseball cap and glasses stage-lit by the glow from the sheet, John told me about the other long-term collecting he does in his own backyard in Davis. I was immediately reminded of other entomologists I have known and worked with: I know his species well. Inveterate collectors, they have an insatiable curiosity about the world and all the many-legged things in it. Even those with research projects in far-flung places are always just as curious about all the wonder and unanswered questions in their own backyards.

John watched the sheet closely while we talked, narrating the early arrivals. In addition to the moths he was looking for, there were plenty of other flying insects drawn to the light. We saw longhorn beetles, which had flocked to the area in response to the chemical signals emitted by trees in distress, ready to lay eggs in the burned wood. There were many types of flies, some scarab beetles, and many more roaches than usual. John speculated that the roaches may be attracted to debris on the ground after the fire, thicker than usual in the spring.

And we saw many, many moths. Leaving the rest of the insects to their own devices, John collected the moths for later identification. The crickets were singing around us as he scooped the moths up in small vials when they landed on the sheet, keeping up a running commentary as he went. He took the collected moths home to identify—many require a microscope to see the features that reveal their species characteristics to John.

Many of the moths were tiny. Easy to overlook, these micro moths are intricate and beautiful when viewed up close. John told me how a couple of miniscule moths in the leafroller family have responded to Cold Canyon's fires. Leafrollers feed on plant tissue—stems, roots, buds, leaves, seeds—but have hosts specific

moth collecting at dusk

bulb has combination of
black light & white light
this sheet is set up across the trail (catching moths traveling along the
trail corridor)
when John sets up parallel to the trail,
he finds a very different set of species

John DeBenedictis

Geometridae
land flat

Noctuidae
recumbent

scarab

fly

longhorn
subcortical
see them on
fallen trees —
they detect trees in
distress

set up across the trail

to each species. After the last fire, John watched as one leafroller species, which eats the low-growing plants that appear first after fire, grew scarcer and scarcer as its host plants were shaded out by taller shrubs and trees. An oak-eating leafroller was hard to find after the fire, but slowly became more common as the oaks regrew. Were there any signs of a similar pattern after the Wragg Fire? John had observed that oak-eating leafroller numbers were down considerably after the fire, and so were the numbers of other oak-associated moths. It appeared that at least as of that first May after the fire, the leafrollers were bearing out John's predictions.

Both of these leafrollers are only about a half-inch long and do not look like much at first glance. But under a hand lens, their forewings are patterned in intricate designs of cream and rusty red. Their hindwings are silky white, and both pairs of wings are fringed with silvery hairs. If there is one thing that I learn over and over again studying nature, it is that looking closer will always be rewarded. Each minute examination—of a plant, a rock, a fungus, an animal—reveals worlds within worlds of discovery and beauty.

The evening grew late. Afterward, when John and I continued our conversation over email, he told me about some surprises from the evening, once he had finished identifying his finds. There were some moths that had not been collected in Cold Canyon before. One was a larger moth in the owlet moth family with intricately scribbled dark gray and cream markings. The other two were micro moths, one a striking beauty in the mompha moth family in stark white with red streaks and black dots, and the other streaky silver and black in the twirler moth family. Were they here now because of the fire? Or was this a coincidence and just another twist in the ongoing story of a regular sampling project? Overall that night, John collected considerably fewer than the ninety moth species that would have constituted a good night before the fire. He found forty-nine species this time, not surprising given how many plants, both in diversity of species as well as

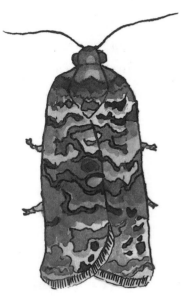

fruittree leafroller
Archips argyrospila
caterpillars eat fruit tree & oak leaves

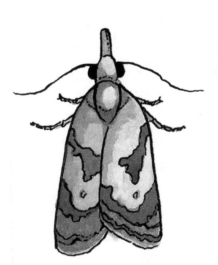

Sparganothis senecionana
a leafroller whose caterpillars eat
low-growing, herbaceous plants

sheer numbers, were missing from the habitat after the fire and how many moths depend on those plants.

On the evening we collected the moths, I headed home before the night grew too late, but John remained, observing as the early evening flyers gave way to moths active later, a solitary witness to the nightlife of the canyon. I walked carefully along the dark path back to the road and listened to the night-rustlings in the brush to either side of me. I had a flashlight but was trying not to use it, the better to observe all that was around me rather than being blind to everything but the narrow beam ahead. The insects that flitted past me as I left were just whispers in the darkness again, going about their own mothy business, unmolested by scientists or artists.

Fierce territorialists: Hummingbirds

Tiny and bright, another pollinator flies in California chaparral and woodland habitats. This one is not an insect, but its size sometimes obscures the distinction as it whirs past. At the height of summer when not much else is moving, I am sometimes briefly unsure whether it was a hummingbird or a grasshopper that just buzzed my head. With a wingspan of only five inches, Anna's hummingbird is about the size of the largest pipevine swallowtails. A year-round resident, Anna's is by far the most common hummingbird at Cold Canyon.

Interestingly, they are relatively recent interlopers in Northern California's chaparral and woodland habitats. Originally only found in Southern and Baja California, they are drawn north by our gardens. They are more comfortable around humans than other hummingbirds and are happy to make use of the new suburban bounty. They have expanded their range as far north as Vancouver, British Columbia, and now stay year-round throughout this range. Eucalyptus trees

Calypte anna
Anna's hummingbirds —
a couple of them are busy
along the streambank in
the sun — plenty of CA fuchsia
Epilobium canum

along with gardens and hummingbird feeders help them supplement their diets in the fall and winter when they run out of native sources of nectar.

In places like Cold Canyon, however, hummingbirds find year-round nectar. Spring gets all the attention for showy, colorful floral displays, but Cold Canyon's mild winters mean that its flowering season never fully ends. Four years after the fire, annual wildflowers are still going strong. Each spring, hummingbirds have a feast of appealing flowers to choose from. We think of hummingbirds as being particularly drawn to red, orange, and bright-pink flowers. And, although it is true that their eyes are more sensitive to these colors, recent research reveals that color is not the primary reason they visit specific flowers. Instead, they learn which flowers have the most nectar and remember where to return for these rich resources. This is why their diet at Cold Canyon includes orange flowers (monkey-flowers) and red flowers (penstemons, canyon delphinium, and warrior's plume), but also California pitcher sage (light purple) and several manzanitas (pale pink).

Colorful annuals and short-lived perennials—monkeyflowers, penstemons, delphiniums, and warrior's plume—provide the bulk of the hummingbird's spring diet. As the birds return to the canyon in the years after the fire, though, woodier subshrubs such as California pitcher sage and shrubs like manzanita are added to the menu.

Come August, most of the flowers have faded, and the streambed is dry. This is when California fuchsia shines, blooming from midsummer and into the fall and serving as the primary late-summer source of nectar for hummingbirds. In turn, the hummingbirds are important pollinators for this plant. I watch the birds zip from stand to stand of fuchsias, the deep red-orange, trumpet-shaped flowers standing out in diagonal sprays from the plants' silvery-green leaves. By waiting until later summer to flower, the fuchsia ensures that it will have its hummingbird pollinators all to itself without needing to compete with any of the spring bloom-ers. Once California fuchsia has finally stopped blooming, chaparral currant takes

hummingbird at the top of a
dead oak, looking quickly back &
forth between down & to the side,
likely in response to the calls of
other hummingbirds I could
hear nearby
Anna's hummingbird, Calypte anna

over. It can bloom as early as November, and its small, fuzzy, pinkish-red hanging bells are the next to attract hummingbirds.

I am amused by the contrast between hummingbirds' looks and their behavior. Though pocket-sized, jewel bright, and cute, Anna's hummingbirds fiercely defend their territory and avidly fight off competitors. They are fancy aerialists. The males use dramatic dive displays in courtship, and both sexes aggressively warn off intruders by diving and by zooming toward their target head-on. Sometimes this includes chasing away bumblebees, wasps, moths, and other kinds of birds.

Although it may often seem as though they are, hummingbirds are not always in motion. On a bright scattered-cloud November day, I spend a long time watching a male Anna's hummingbird perched high in an oak. He is quiet the entire time I watch him, but extremely attentive to the calls of other male humming-birds nearby. I hear them singing: a series of buzzing sounds followed by a whistle and a few short cheeps, then repeated. At about ten seconds, it is one of the longest songs sung by hummingbird species. I watch as he turns his head in four different directions over and over in sequence, listening to the chatter of his competitors. Only males sing. They also spend a lot of time declaring their space and monitoring the activity of other males, as I observed on this day. I cannot say, though, why the male I watched was silent for such a long time.

I started noticing Anna's hummingbirds in the summer of 2018, four years after the fire. Different species of hummingbirds respond differently to fire, and Anna's seems to wait a while to return to recently burned areas. It may take two years or more for them to fully recolonize a habitat. This aligns with what I observed, but I wonder about the reasons for the delay. Wildflowers are abundant in the first few years after a fire, so lack of food cannot be the reason it takes years for the birds to return.

It turns out that Anna's hummingbirds like heights, more so than many other hummingbirds. They survey and defend their territory from high perches and build their nests higher than other California hummingbirds. Up to twenty-five feet off the ground, Anna's nests are terribly soft-looking creations of lichen, spider web, moss, and other plant fibers. I would love to see one at Cold Canyon, but thanks to their camouflage and elevation, I have not spied any yet. Inside these tightly woven cups, females incubate two pinto bean–size eggs. Once the chicks hatch, their mother keeps them stuffed with insects and nectar until they fledge after about twenty days. They stay close to the nest for a few days and are then off on their own to forage for nectar and insects themselves.

Anna's
high in
an oak

Their preference for height may explain Anna's hummingbirds' response to wildfire. At Cold Canyon, they were likely waiting until their high perches became appealing again, once greenery had begun to regrow on the taller trees and shrubs, providing them with some cover where they perch and nest. Leafy cover is critical protection from the sharp eyes of their predators—scrub jays, crows, and smaller raptors such as kestrels and Cooper's hawks.

Not all local hummingbirds respond to fire in this way. Some of these sparkling fish of the sky, whose iridescent feathers shimmer like scales and who move sinuously from flower to flower as if through water, become even more abundant in areas that have just burned. Though I have not seen them in Cold Canyon myself, two other kinds of hummingbirds are occasionally found there. Rufous and black-chinned hummingbirds both pass through in the fall as they head south down the Coast Range to winter in Mexico and southern Texas.

Black-chinned hummingbirds nest much closer to the ground and find suitable spots immediately in the new low growth of shrubs after a fire. They may also be taking advantage of reduced competition in Anna's hummingbirds' absence. Rufous hummingbirds have been observed foraging in open burned areas with explosions of wildflowers along their migration routes, and they may rely on burned areas as important stopovers for sustenance on their journey.

These three hummingbirds are living evidence that fire's impact is not monolithic or uniform. Slowly watching as these many disparate pieces of the local ecosystem puzzle are revealed and fall into place is revelatory. Just as fire creates new openings in the ecosystem for annual wildflowers to thrive, as soon as the wildflower pieces of the puzzle are placed, they in turn create new opportunities—openings in the jigsaw—for hummingbirds and all the other lives that depend on nectar, pollen, and vegetation for their sustenance and growth.

Anna's
hummingbird
Calypte anna

bush monkey-flower
Diplacus aurantiacus

Chapter Six

THE RELATIVITY OF TIME

Oak and Pine in Life and Death

So much life returns in abundance after fire that it is tempting to immediately tally the living and the dead. But trees exist on a very different time scale, and their lives and deaths caution against hasty conclusions.

"Look at this burned bay laurel. Do you see the way those branches are all pointing the same direction?"

Dead tree branches just over my head etch lines into the electric-blue sky, and I am transfixed. From the thicker supporting branches to the finest twigs, they all swirl in the same direction, performing a ghostly dance choreographed by the Wragg Fire's fierce, hot wind. Even though the air around me is completely still, I can easily envision the wind whipping around these trees as the fire blazed and they were frozen in this shape.

It has been a year-and-a-half since the fire, and a participant in a field sketching class I am leading at Cold Canyon has just pointed out these shapes in the trees to me. Miriam Morrill is a biologist and a specialist in fire and communications at the Bureau of Land Management (BLM). She is also an artist, and I see that she has been making notes and drawings in her sketchbook that capture some of the signs of fire behavior still legible in the landscape. This is not a language that I know, and we are excited to compare notes.

She explains that she sees more trees and tree skeletons on Blue Ridge than she would expect had the fire advanced up that slope from the bottom of the canyon. She surmises that the fire instead came from the west, over the top of the ridge, and backed down into the canyon, burning less intensely moving downslope than it would have had it been charging upslope. I tell her that this is what I know to have been the case, based on Jeffrey Clary's description of the fire's progress. Miriam says that she also notices that the branches of the leafless trees where we are standing near the creek are all pointing in different directions, as if different eddies of wind were whirling around each one. From this, Miriam concludes that the fire became more intense at the bottom of the canyon before racing up the slope on the other side. As the Wragg Fire paused here, the intensity of the fire created its own weather.

Strong winds gusted and eddied among the folds and pockets of the hills. Where the fire did not fully burn the vegetation, its heat dried out the branches. Losing their moisture made them permanently inflexible, pointing in the direction of the last wind they would ever feel. This phenomenon is termed *foliage freeze*. Time stopped, arrested, and I am held there too, caught in this still, quiet day but also in the midst of the roaring frenzy of fire and wind of late July 2015.

This could be the image of violence preserved, jarring me out of time on a peaceful day. I might see this as the life force of these trees sucked right out of them by the wind, with their macabre skeletons still here to remind me. If fire is only a catastrophe from which this ecosystem must recover, the brutality of that image is appropriate. But if fire's place in the ecosystem is subtler, then those frozen branches might equally be seen as a reminder of the continuity that underlies the fire, tying the seemingly singular event to the history of the landscape as well as its life to come.

Disturbance has a past and a future and blends more easily into both than it would seem. And now, as I stand here in the present, the frozen branches are important clues to the behavior of the fire. Fire leaves signs behind on the land that are often fleeting—erased by wind and rain and footsteps—so it feels like a race to find and read them before they disappear. Patterns of ash and char, curled

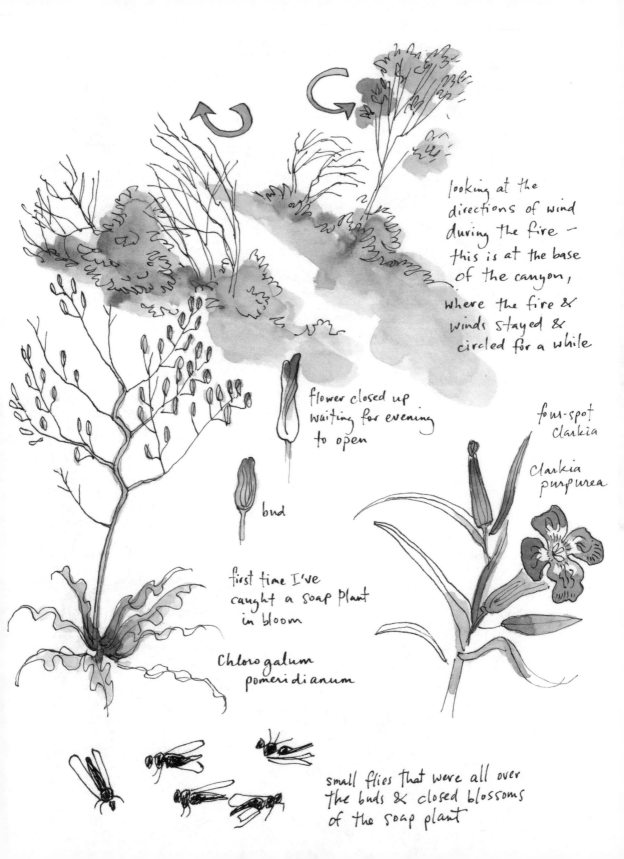

looking at the
directions of wind
during the fire —
this is at the base
of the canyon,
where the fire &
winds stayed &
circled for a while

flower closed up
waiting for evening
to open

bud

four-spot
Clarkia

Clarkia
purpurea

first time I've
caught a soap plant
in bloom

Chlorogalum
pomeridianum

small flies that were all over
the buds & closed blossoms
of the soap plant

the fallen blue oak
after high winds

ladybug pupa

mating
ladybugs
Coccinellidae

more examples of swirling winds
in the fire

oak →

CA bay
laurel

leaves, fallen tree trunks and grass stems—all are quickly obscured by the movement of animals, the fall of rain and rush of wind, and the growth of new vegetation. These twisted branches, though, remain. The fire's passage is frozen in the trees' bodies, and the trees' writhing limbs marking this path are emblazoned on my mind.

Oaks: Anchors in time

Growing up in California's Central Valley ensured that water worries indelibly marked my subconscious. I am a child of brown summers and green winters, of regular drought and water scarcity. I was a toddler during the 1976–77 drought and have vivid memories of my mother explaining to me why we couldn't flush the toilet every time we used it. Even as a child, I approached each winter with concern: Will there be enough rain this year? Will the rivers dry up? I find nothing more reassuring than rain and nothing more terrifying than endless cloudless summer skies.

As I got older, I began to understand the ways life here has adapted to make the most of the rain we do receive. I am reassured by hardy species that get by on little water and conserve their moisture in ingenious ways, such as the blue oaks standing tall in the woodlands and savannas that ring the Central Valley. These are important members of Cold Canyon habitats, the trees that Jeffrey was concerned about after the Wragg Fire. Blue oaks are of middling size for oaks, with the wildly crooking branches common among oaks that make their limbs look as though they are dancing ecstatically. Their leaves are compact, with only wavy margins, not the deep lobes of some of the other oak species. The waxiness of their leaves helps with moisture retention in their often-arid habitats.

Staunchly Californian, blue oaks are endemic here—found nowhere else in the world. They live at lower elevations in the Coast Ranges and the Sierra Nevada, as well as on the southern end of the Cascade and Klamath Mountains. A few grow in the Central Valley itself, but they mostly prefer to be up in the hills. Though I live in the flatlands of the valley, I am glad to be close to the hills and mountains, and it is to these foothill habitats that I turn for guidance in how to live in an often-parched land.

Of all of the deciduous oaks in California, blue oaks are the most able to withstand drought. Their taproot—their main central root—can grow deep into the ground to find the water table, to depths of eighty feet, though they can also focus their energy on growing shallower roots if water is available higher in the soil. They need soil that is relatively dry and well drained, and are found on soils that are poorer in nitrogen, phosphorous, organic matter, and other nutrients than the soils that support other California oaks. On these soils, they cultivate communities of other hardy species by holding the earth in place against erosion and using their taproots to bring water to the surface, incidentally making it available to other species as well. Before introduced annual species came to dominate California grasslands and savannas, blue oaks grew alongside bunchgrasses such as blue wildrye and purple needlegrass, similarly water-conserving species. The oaks and grasses mutually supported one another, sharing resources via fungal mycelial networks.

Now, introduced annuals such as redstem filaree, cheatgrass, and wild oat have largely replaced the bunchgrasses. The introduced species compete with young oaks for space, water, and light, just as they outcompeted the native bunchgrasses for these resources. As in the rest of their range, blue oaks in Cold Canyon shelter quite a few introduced annual species, but they are also home and sustenance to many other creatures. Nuttall's woodpeckers rely on them for foraging and nesting. Dusky-footed woodrats build at their feet and eat their acorns. Fallen branches are important gathering places for western fence lizards.

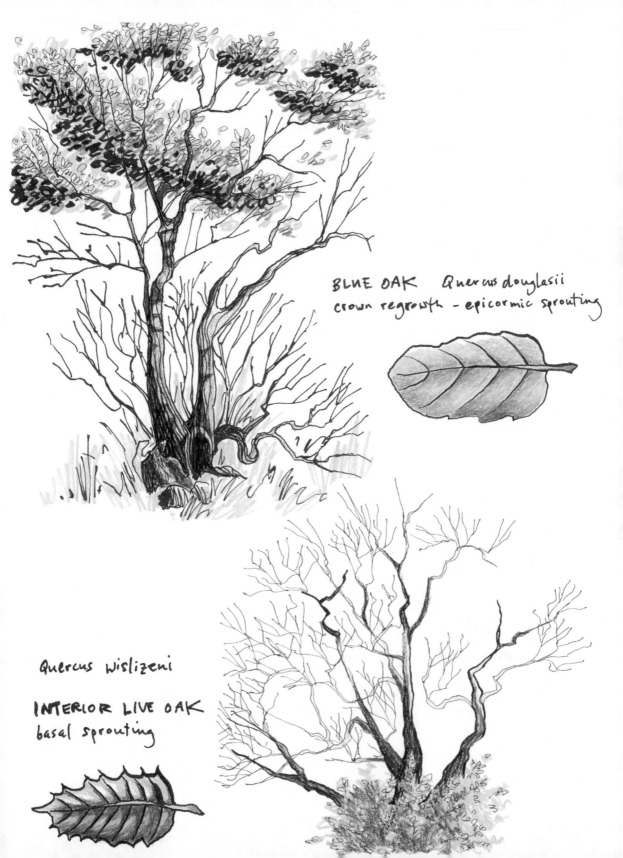

BLUE OAK   Quercus douglasii
crown regrowth - epicormic sprouting

Quercus wislizeni

INTERIOR LIVE OAK
basal sprouting

I watched an
oak titmouse
poking around at
the side of the trail

Baeolophus
inornatus

Oak titmice—birds the soft mousy brown of their namesakes—defend year-round territories in their canopies.

It is easy to see the wildlife that depends on the oaks, but equally important to understand the less visible forces at work. Blue oaks are critical to the quality of the soil around them, increasing its nutrient content. This is thanks to the fall of leaf litter, which increases the nitrogen in the soil. It is also because trees capture moisture from the air that otherwise would have evaporated. Instead, the water droplets adhere to the leaves, eventually aggregate into larger drops and then fall to the ground. The drops bring along important nutrients —potassium, phosphorous, and magnesium, for example—that were present in the air and are concentrated when the drops form.

There are three kinds of oaks growing in Cold Canyon, two of which are trees—blue oak and interior live oak—and scrub oak, which takes a shrubbier form. Interior live oaks tend to be found in the bottoms of the canyons, as they prefer the wetter areas in the riparian zones, and these are often too wet for blue oaks. Blue oaks generally grow on the hillsides. The distinctions are not absolute: there are certainly blue oaks growing in the canyons and live oaks on the hills, but the general pattern holds.

Over the five years of my visits, when I look closely at oaks, I try to deci-pher the puzzle of their health and survival. In a landscape of rapidly sprouting annual plants and fast-growing shrubs, trees are not as easy to assess. There are no immediate answers to how the oaks at Cold Canyon are faring. In the areas closest to the creek, some oaks did not burn at all and are doing fine—these are mostly interior live oaks. A little further from the creek, there are more interior live oaks, and some of these burned. Those that burned are sprouting, strong shoots growing up from their bases, from their root crowns. The brand-new leaves in their chartreuse skin are spiky and fresh. Further up the slopes, some of the blue oaks are sprouting. On the blue oaks I see, the sprouts are not at the bases of the trunks but higher on the tree, on the branches. These differences are characteristic of the two oak species: live oaks tend to regrow from their bases, blue oaks from their crowns.

The oaks that are able to survive fires will benefit from them, especially if the fires were low intensity. Fire removes accumulated litter beneath the trees, which helps reduce the numbers of insect pests that feed on acorns, such as filbert worms and filbert weevils, two of the most common in California. Fire also helps remove some of the oaks' competitors for resources, such as annual grasses, though it can also open opportunities for other competitors—thistles, filaree, and the like—to gain a foothold and claim the open turf for themselves.

The world underneath the blue oaks' canopy is much different now than it was before incursions of plowing, plants, and livestock. Fire can still be a healthy force, but that is no longer always the case, now that fires burn hotter and higher, and more often kill the crowns of trees, making it hard for the trees to survive and resprout. The bark of mature blue oaks is thinner than other similar oaks, which increases the trees' susceptibility to fire as they age. It is more difficult for acorns to grow under competition from introduced plants and in our rapidly drying environment, with droughts becoming more and more common.

All of this is to say that one year, three years, five years in, it is too early to tell how the oaks are doing at Cold Canyon. Trees challenge our impatient animal desire to know what is happening. Acorns take a very long time to make more acorns. Seedlings take a long time to become saplings, which take a long time to become mature trees. Time stopped for the branches frozen by the heat of the fire, but most of those trees are still alive and sprouting green at their bases. Trees live and die slowly, but it is difficult to remember this in the context of a disturbance like wildfire. The fire can feel like a catastrophe, and tallying the damage afterward feels so urgent. Trees move in their own time, and it is hard for me to comprehend when I am so quick, so mobile, so unrooted.

Oak gall wasps

Sometimes I go hunting for marvels, and sometimes they are sitting right in the middle of the trail, in shocking bright-pink glory. On a day when I arrive at Cold Canyon planning to focus on oak regrowth patterns, it is a strangely appropriate gift to find a crackly, dry blue oak leaf in front of me, covered in tiny galls. There are two different kinds of gall on the leaf, both elaborately structured and very pink. I pick up the leaf and sit down on a rock beside the trail to wonder at the details of these tiny homes, nurseries to the microscopic babies within.

The interaction that creates these intricate structures is an amazing tale of manipulation, and a relationship maybe even more strange than the complex interaction fostered by horntails, fungi, and the distressed trees in which they lay their eggs. Once again, it is wasps that are responsible. This time, very much unlike the large, somewhat alarming horntails, the wasps are no bigger than about a quarter of an inch. Some of the smallest gall wasps in the world are only one millimeter long, the size of a comma on this page.

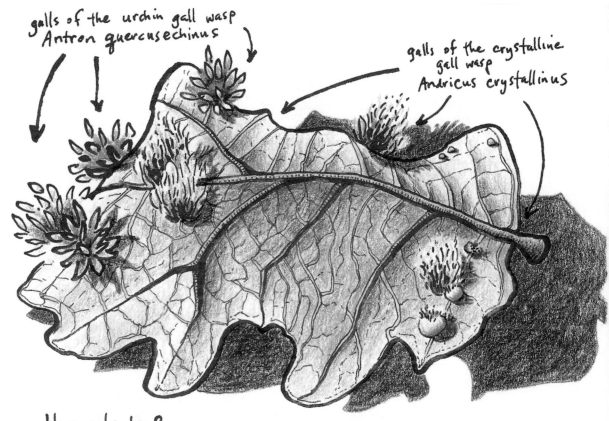

galls of the urchin gall wasp
Antron quercusechinus

galls of the crystalline
gall wasp
Andricus crystallinus

blue oak leaf
Quercus douglasii
fallen leaf spotted right in the middle
of the Homestead Trail

URCHIN GALL
Antron quercusechinus

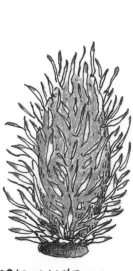

CRYSTALLINE GALL
Andricus crystallinus

Andricus sp.

galls on interior live oak
Quercus wislizeni

Female gall wasps lay their eggs in rapidly growing parts of trees, such as twigs or leaves like the one I am holding in my hand. Once the eggs hatch and the wasp larvae begin to eat the plant tissue, a chemical in their saliva, or perhaps the mechanical process of their feeding itself, stimulates the plant to redirect some of its own cells to produce a protective outer structure that surrounds the larvae. This is a defense response by the plant, sequestering the larvae so that they do not eat its other parts. But it has great benefits for the larvae as well. The gall is both shelter and, inside, more food for the ravenous larvae, which comfortably feed until they mature and chew their way out of the nursery as adults. It does not seem as though the wasps do any real harm to their host plants, though they do of course consume some resources that would otherwise be used to meet the plants' own needs.

What is most amazing, and apparent even on the leaf I've just found, is that each species of gall wasp stimulates a very specific and unique structure of gall. One of the kinds of gall on the leaf has spines sticking out in all direction. This is the home of a batch of urchin gall wasp larvae. The other kind is almost furry, and is made by crystalline gall wasps. The gall shapes are even expressed in the wasps' scientific names. The urchin gall wasp is *Cynips quercusechinus*—the species name means "oak hedgehog," emphasizing its spikes. The crystalline gall wasp is *Andricus crystallinus*, inspired by the delicacy and translucence of its fine "hairs." Two different species, with two characteristic gall shapes. And there are over a hundred different gall wasps known so far worldwide. How on earth do the chemicals in the saliva of the larvae dictate the *shape* of the gall that the plant cells will build?

Most gall wasps are specific to a single type of tree, usually an oak. It turns out that blue oaks have the largest known number of different gall wasp species, at forty-one and counting. They also appear to have the greatest diversity of shape and color of galls. I am looking at the galls just a little after one year since the fire. I try to guess which of the blue oaks around me dropped this leaf. I wonder whether it was a tree that burned, and this was a new leaf since the fire, or one that survived the fire intact. Perhaps the wasps whose offspring were reared in these galls came to Cold Canyon after the fire, or perhaps they survived the fire as larvae themselves.

The effects of fire on oak galls have not been extensively studied, but it appears that gall wasps need time after a fire to return. There must be oaks for them to return to, either newly grown oaks or ones that survived the fire. There must be sources near the burn for them to come from. And some wasp larvae surely survive the fires, sheltering in the oaks that do not burn and remain cool enough that their leaves are not all killed by the heat. Adult wasps are not likely to survive the fire themselves, but then, they generally live only about a week, so each wasp truly spends most of its life—about a year—as a larva.

How funny that wasps have twice been my windows into the endlessly intricate webs of interactions that compose these ecosystems. First the horntails, who rush to burned trees to lay their eggs and inject their symbiotic fungi. Now the gall wasps, who bend the oaks to their will but are dependent on their hosts for shelter and protection when the world around them burns. Without being present in these places—burning and burned—I would have remained ignorant of these beautiful mysteries. The wasps' relationships are just glimpses into vast silken webs of stories that humans have not yet even dreamed. Start traveling along just one exposed thread, and how many more nodes in the silk might we find? The ones we do see tantalize us with the many that are yet unknown.

Gray pines: Waves of loss and return

Gray pines, towering over the other trees at Cold Canyon, seem to me the embodiment of solidity and permanence after the fire. They have an underappreciated beauty, being arguably rather spindly and dull in comparison with some of the more majestic pine species. But I think their long, pale-green needles are pretty, especially in the bright summer sun. And while their needles are not densely packed enough to create a whole lot of shade, I find they create striking silhouettes against wintery overcast skies. In the early years after the canyon burned, I am anxious to count the survivors and the lost, to take inventory, even if anecdotal, of the fire's casualties. Studying the gray pines, I can see green needles on what look like two-thirds of them, so I assume they have survived fairly well. But on a winter hike with Jeffrey Clary and Sarah Oktay, the Reserve's current director, just over three years after the fire, I learn that the truth is likely more complicated.

Gray pines, also known as foothill pines, are often found in the blue oak woodlands and savannas that are interspersed with chaparral habitats in the California foothills. Like blue oaks and chaparral shrubs, they are hardy and thrive in

Daldinia sp.

Sitting
on a rock in the trail:
fallen wood from oak

Pinus sabiniana
Some of the grey pines have
new needles at the very crown
only & some were completely
killed

toyon at the creek
crossing has berries
(resprouting toyons
elsewhere
do not)

completely bare
of new needles

new needles over
entire tree

places with drier climates and less nutrient-rich soils. Unlike many other plants, they do not have root, trunk, or bark adaptations that allow them to survive fire. Gray pines are extremely pitchy, even for a pine. They are torches in a fire, thanks to the resin in their needles, cones, bark, and wood. Because they do not contain the burls or other root structures that allow many chaparral shrubs to regrow, a gray pine too damaged by fire will not grow back.

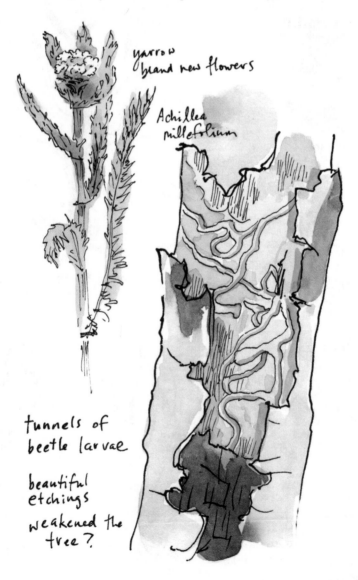

yarrow
brand new flowers

Achillea
millefolium

tunnels of
beetle larvae

beautiful
etchings
weakened the
tree?

Instead, gray pines must start all over again, growing from the seeds protected inside their enormous, spiny cones. I see cones, open and dry, with seeds long spilled, all over the canyon. Picking them up and turning them in my hands, I wonder whether their seeds are unfurling now, nestled underground where they landed after dispersing when the cone opened still high on its tree. The heat of fire stimulates germination by weakening or breaking the seed's coat and allowing it to begin development. Gray pine seeds are also able to germinate without fire, but there are other pine species, such as lodgepole and knobcone, that do require fire for germination, at least in some parts of their ranges.

This all sounds reasonably straightforward: gray pines mostly die in fires and eventually return to the landscape as new sprouts. It is the timing of their dying that is a surprise. Jeffrey points out that even though many of the trees at Cold Canyon still have green needles in their crowns, they may already have been killed by the fire, either because part or all of them burned or because the heat of the fire was too great and killed their tissues. Set inexorably onto the path to their fate, they are continuing to function while slowly winding down. In their diminishment, they are now home to organisms that they would have easily fought off while healthy. The fire drew pine sawyer beetles—a kind of longhorn beetle—and their larvae are now tunneling through the pines' wood. Bark beetles, such as pine engravers, will also have come, finding nourishment in the wood of the dying trees.

These wood-boring beetles and their relatives are usually healthy members of forest communities, consuming only trees that are already dead or dying and returning the trees' nutrients to the ecosystem. But in the increasingly stressed habitats of the western US, some species, such as the pine engravers, have become decidedly unhealthy. In the face of plentiful dead wood during years of drought and fire and excessive logging, the beetle populations explode. Voracious new generations feast on living trees too, making for even more fuel in wildfires and escalating the vicious cycle. While we are most familiar with large expanses of dead pines and firs in the Sierra, gray pines are not immune to these amplifying effects of climate and beetle. As I walk beneath a pine with silvery-green needles left on only a few of its higher branches, I see the fine line between health and disease, between beetles as beneficial recyclers and beetles as forest destroyers.

I am learning that dying is a completely different phenomenon for a tree than for all of us more ephemeral creatures. It is not a single event in time but a very long process. How smooth is the continuum of living and dying and how hard to say where some organisms are on that spectrum. There are no quick answers in assessing the results of upheavals like wildfire, at least for trees, as I watch the aftermath play out slowly over the years.

Gray pines are common in chaparral habitats, but they require plenty of time to recolonize between wildfires, after the fires have mostly killed off the existing

Blue Ridge

trees. On the one hand, if wildfires occur too frequently in chaparral, there will not be enough time for new gray pines to grow from seed. As the window for recolonizing closes, gray pines will slowly disappear from these habitats. On the other hand, if fire is completely absent from the chaparral ecosystem, gray pines will take over—enough gray pines will eventually colonize that the blue oaks cannot compete for space and sunlight. Fire—at least a healthy fire regime—keeps the balance in these blue oak and gray pine foothill habitats.

After my hike with Jeffrey and Sarah, before I head home to the valley flatlands, I stand next to a gray pine and put my hand on its bark. Time slows to a crawl as I deliberately calm my quick animal breaths. Time stops while I try to think in tree time. Here time is measured in roots creeping, tunneling, and connecting with fungal mycelia and other roots. Time passes in rings of wood expanding, thickening, drying, and cracking into bark. And time is the slow, slow pull of senescence, embarked on long before the tree's final end. Senescence is set to the tiny music of the jaws of beetle larvae scraping and gnawing their intricate way through the tree, just below the surface of the bark.

This is a kind of sorrow, deep and abiding. There is nothing that will stop the onward pull of time and the tightening of death's grip. The last green needles will brown. The wood will fully dry. The tree will continue to stand for a long time, entirely dead, waiting for the gust of wind or shift of soil that will send it crashing to the ground. But I am also, just as deeply, moved by the cycles in which the pines and I are enveloped. As though my awareness of the process allows me into the rolling pattern. Nothing is what it once was, nothing in the view ahead of me can stay this way forever, and we are all senescing even as we are full of life.

The gall wasps whose tiny homes I marvel at on blue oak leaves live only a week as adults. A blink of an eye. What would they make of my ponderously long and slow life, beyond the limits of comprehension? Just as I struggle to understand how a living tree can also already be dead.

Chapter Seven

CORNERSTONES

Lichens in Rapidly Changing Ecosystems

Often overlooked, lichens are ecosystem cornerstones, whose lives tie everything together: soil, rocks, trees, animals, and air. Lichens only slowly return to an area that has burned, and some take decades to reappear. Diversity in wildfire timing and severity is critical in maintaining the mosaics that preserve unburned areas where surviving lichens shelter.

I peer into a dense forest full of life. Long, thin branches, the palest yellow-green, sway a little, arching over gently curling mint-green leaves pressed close to the ground. A few cups of green with dark-brown centers are scattered among the leaves. Here and there are scattered flashes of gold, like clusters of flowers among the shrubs. I think of stepping into the scene and strolling beneath the shady trees. An oak titmouse scolds me from above.

These are not trees, or shrubs, or flowers. The leaves are not actually leaves. They are lobes, and these are not plants at all. And I could gather this forest up easily into my cupped hands. This tiny forest is an ecosystem of lichen growing on the trunk and branches of a blue oak, several species of lichen making an intricate world, one in which I would very much like to get lost. The lichens here are all commonly found on bark and wood: the long branches are strap lichen, the green curly lobes are rosette lichen, and the scarcer golden lobes are sunburst lichen.

I am laughing a little, thinking about the attention that I am paying these lichens. The bird is interesting too, but my focus right now is entirely on the lichens. I imagine my ninth-grade biology teacher nodding, glad that I have finally caught up with her. It has come to seem so important to be acquainted with these beings living slow and quiet lives, foundations of their ecosystems.

The blue oak is a small one. Its trunk is no more than fifteen inches around. I am looking at healthy green lichens on this side, but if I move around to the other side, the view changes. Here, the lichens are no longer green. Directly in front of me, the lobes and branches of the lichens are withered and brown, and below me, they are blackened and burned away. The oak burned on this side as the fire rushed past, and though the oak survived the fire with minimal damage, the lichens on this side will not survive.

In the years I have been watching postfire changes in oak and chaparral habitats, it has not appeared that lichens thrive after fire in the way that many plants and fungi do. Areas on rocks and wood where lichens have burned away or been withered by heat remain bare, certainly for as long as I have been watching them. I am eager to understand how lichens are affected by fire and whether they take as long to regrow as it seems. I wonder whether more frequent fires will mean that some lichen species will be unable to regrow at all and whether we will see a slow reduction in lichen diversity. Lichens lay the foundations for their ecosystems by changing the air, the rock, and the soil around them. They are themselves important sources of food and shelter for many other organisms. If lichens begin disappearing, the consequences will be deep and lasting for the intricately balanced network of earth, air, fungus, plant, and animal that depends on them.

An intimate association

Lichens, by their very existence, are a challenge to my animal-centric concept of self. What makes an organism an organism? In the popular imagination, it seems so obvious that an animal is a single unit, an entity by itself. Likewise, plants are usually (though not always) discernibly separate units. An animal is a thing, a plant is a thing—whole, complete, and easily recognizable.

QUAIL RIDGE
RESERVE

49° overcast
starting to clear
very windy
8:40 AM

oak titmouse
scolding me from
above

Baeolophus inornatus

A lichen, by contrast, is only itself when two different organisms come together. The body of the lichen is a fungus, but a fungus that has taken into its structure the cells of algae (a plant) or cyanobacteria. Like animals, fungi do not make their own food. By harboring the cells of other organisms that photosynthesize—cyanobacteria or algae—some fungi have cleverly gained the ability to have food made within their own bodies. And in so doing, they become lichens.

What are we to make of this relationship? It can be argued that the fungal partner in the relationship is actually a parasite, subsisting on the carbohydrates the cyanobacteria or algae produce by photosynthesis. Or perhaps the relationship is a true symbiosis, because the fungus provides protection and a comfortable environment for the algae or cyanobacteria. There are strains of algae that likely cannot exist anywhere outside a lichen partnership. Perhaps thanks to my childhood spent partially on my father's family farm, my favorite description of the relationship is of the fungus as a farmer, tending its crop of algae.

Lichens have existed for at least four hundred million years. Long enough to prove that this is a very successful relationship. And long enough for them to have had a significant impact on the makeup of their—and our—ecosystems. Lichens lay the foundation for life in their environment. With acids they secrete and the slow creep of their fungal threads down into the structure of the stone, they break down rock to create soil. They enrich the soil yet more by trapping water, dust, and silt. The

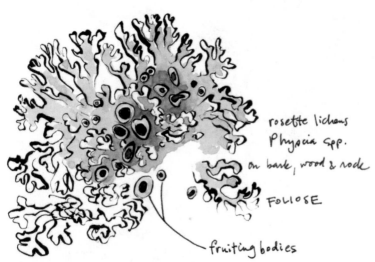

rosette lichens
Physcia spp.
on bark, wood & rock
FOLIOSE

fruiting bodies

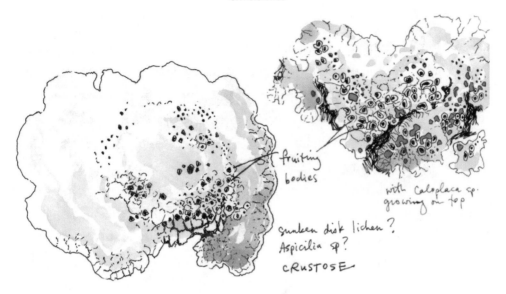

fruiting
bodies

with caloplaca sp.
growing on top

sunken disk lichen?
Aspicilia sp?
CRUSTOSE

lichens that contain cyanobacteria fix nitrogen in the soil and provide nutrients to plants and fungi. A wide range of animals—from insects to birds to deer—eat lichens. They are a key nest material for some insects, mammals, and birds, especially hummingbirds.

These hard-working, unsung farmers are also extraordinarily sensitive to the quality of the air around them. The changes that humans have made in recent centuries are registered in the bodies of lichens, and in their eventual disappearance from habitats in which they once flourished. Pollutants pumped into the atmosphere by the burning of fossil fuels can damage lichens. The toxins are readily absorbed into lichen tissues and, once inside, disrupt the photosynthesis carried out by algae or cyanobacteria. If pollutant levels are high for a sustained period, lichens will gradually disappear from the area. This is why in cities, very few species of lichen are able to grow. The yellow-orange firedot lichens I see forming crusts on sidewalks and other city concrete are some of the few that are able to tolerate high urban pollutant levels.

Lichens are an important barometer for ecosystem health, and their sensitivity to air pollutants is a warning to everyone. The same environments that are unhealthy for lichens are unhealthy for most other living creatures, including people. Sulfur dioxide interferes with our breathing and weakens our hearts and lungs, making them more susceptible to diseases. Our sensitivity to air pollutants is only the first of the things we share with these beings, seemingly so alien. This almost certainly extends to wildfire smoke, too. Little research has been done yet into how the intensifying and lengthening periods of smoke in the western US affect lichens. But because wildfire smoke contains some of the same chemicals as anthropogenic pollution—including sulfur dioxide—lichens are likely suffering in the wake of recent megafires.

Are we truly that different from lichens? The more we learn about the importance of the ecosystem of bacteria living in our guts, the clearer it becomes that we rely on these cells, which are not our own, to get the nutrition we need from the food we eat. So are we single organisms? Or are we also a collective, like lichen, tending our own farms of bacteria deep within our bodies?

In the field

The lichen-covered oak I am examining stands on a high hill at Quail Ridge Reserve. Like Cold Canyon, Quail Ridge is a part of the UC Natural Reserve System. It is not far from Cold Canyon, just a mile or so northwest as the crow flies, or a short drive on Highway 128. Quail Ridge sits on a peninsula in Lake Berryessa, not too far from the dam. Dramatic ridges and canyons throughout the Reserve provide topographical and geological diversity that has fostered rich and varied vegetation. There are five different species of oak in its woodlands, well-preserved grasslands full of native perennial bunchgrasses, and three different types of chaparral—chamise, California lilac, and scrub oak. It is mid-spring 2021. Nearly the entire Reserve burned in the LNU Lightning Complex Fire last

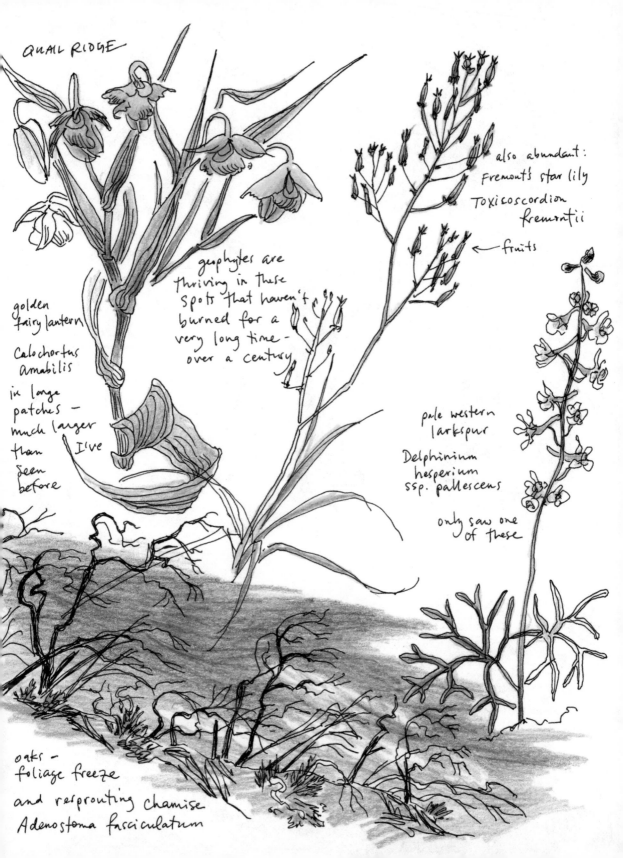

QUAIL RIDGE

also abundant:
Fremont's star lily
Toxicoscordion
fremontii
← fruits

golden
fairy lantern
Calochortus
amabilis
in large
patches —
much larger
than   I've
seen
before

geophytes are
thriving in these
spots that haven't
burned for a
very long time —
over a century

pale western
larkspur
Delphinium
hesperium
ssp. pallescens

only saw one
of these

oaks —
foliage freeze
and resprouting chamise
Adenostoma fasciculatum

Jes & Jesse up a slope
scouting a spore trap location

checking sites
mapped on
a phone

& pounding
stakes into
the
ground

surrounded by
charred branches
& whispering
bells

Emmenanthe
penduliflora

spore traps
look like this

stark views of the burn's
mosaic of severities:
areas with nothing but bare dirt,
areas with blackened chaparral branches,
& areas with still-standing trees
& shrubs

August, and I am getting my bearings on a Saturday morning before I join two ecologists for part of their day in the field setting up a new experiment.

I meet Jesse Miller and Jessica (Jes) Coyle at the Quail Ridge Field Station office, where they are gathering gear and testing walkie-talkies. The terrain is steep throughout the Reserve, and the roads are mostly narrow trails. We will be driving to their test sites in a 4x4 Gator. I met Jesse in my quest to understand how lichen populations fare after fire. Having read his research findings demonstrating interesting and varied responses to fire in different kinds of lichen, I was delighted that his website featured groups of students posing in lichen "wigs" at the end of a field day, alongside pictures of his research projects. I promptly reached out for a phone conversation, and he offered to let me tag along while he and Jes finalized their study sites. I'm looking forward to a fun and enlightening day in the field.

We are starting out high on a ridge, where the wind comes in still-cold gusts that will slowly warm on this late April day. The view makes evident the ruggedness of the land all around. Ridges, folds, valleys, and peaks—flat land is rare here. My impressions before meeting Jesse in person are proved correct. He is easygoing but also full of excitement about lichens and ecology. Tall and gangly, he towers over Jes as they look over their map of field sites and decide on a route for the first half of their day. He introduces me to Jes. Her enthusiasm for ecology matches Jesse's, as she tells me about her interests in using lichens to understand broad questions about biodiversity and how species are geographically distributed. Their friendly banter as they load up the back of the 4x4 sets the lively tone for the day.

Jesse has already been to Quail Ridge to scout out the locations where they will be setting up their experiments. They are installing lichen spore collectors. On this trip, they will be making final decisions for each location and hammering rebar into the ground to support the spore collection boxes. As we bounce along the trail, we point out wildflowers to one another—fields of golden fairy lantern in larger patches than any of us have seen before, large swaths of Fremont's star-lily, fields of whispering bells, twining snake-lily, white foothill delphinium, Fernald's iris. In between exclamations about flowers or patches of oaks still hanging with lichen garlands, I get to eavesdrop on their conversations about how they are setting up the experiment and how to ideally situate their collection sites.

Little is known about how lichens repopulate an area that has burned. Research so far has shown that lichens return slowly after fire. In a recently published paper, Jesse looked at burned sites in Cold Canyon and Quail Ridge, comparing sites that had burned at different times, from over one hundred years ago to just three years before the study. Cold Canyon burned in 1988 and again in 2015. The paper noted that Quail Ridge has sites that burned in 1953, 1988, 1996, and 2005. The study was completed before Quail Ridge burned nearly completely in 2020. Jesse and his coauthors found little evidence that lichens have any particular advantage after wildfire, the way that some fungi, animals, and plants do.

fruiting bodies are
tiny outgrowths on
the lichen
branches

beard lichen
Usnea sp.

FRUTICOSE

Instead, lichens regrow in burned areas according to their general colonization abilities: lichens that are always the first to colonize new or disturbed areas are the first to appear after fire, and species that are slower to colonize can take thirty, fifty, or one hundred years to appear again.

The lichens that Jesse and Jes are studying are primarily those that grow on bark and wood, but lichens can grow on just about any surface, as long as it holds still long enough for lichens to find and colonize it in their unhurried way. Substrates can be cement, metal, and plastic, but are most often rock, wood, bark, and soil.

When we look closely, the myriad forms of lichens begin to reveal themselves, each a different component of our metaphorical forest in miniature. There are three basic types of lichen, based on their overall shape. Foliose lichens look like leaves, with layers of flat lobes only lightly attached to their substrate. Fruticose lichens are longer, more like bushes or branches. Sometimes they are upright and cup shaped or shrubby, and sometimes hanging and hair-like. Fruticose lichens are often attached to a surface at a single point, whereas foliose lichens are attached at multiple points along their extent. The final type of lichen, crustose, is flat and grabs its substrate tightly. If you try to remove a crustose lichen from whatever it is attached to, you will bring some of that surface along too.

In Jesse's recently published study, he documented the lichens that return first after fire: the smaller foliose lichens, ones that form small, leafy rosettes on trunks and branches, and are hardy enough to grow on burned wood. These start appearing as early as three years after a fire. The next lichens to reappear, after a decade or so, are larger foliose lichens. After a couple of decades, fruticose lichens return to the landscape. The lichens that take the longest of all are the cyanolichens, the lichens that contain cyanobacteria instead of algae and may be foliose, fruticose, or crustose in form. The study sites have shown that they do not appear until sometime between thirty and sixty-five years after a fire. It might seem that large things such as trees are slow to regrow after fire and that small things such as lichens must come back quickly—size can be confounding; the short lives of tiny gall wasps are more familiar than the very long lives of lichens. But the lengthy return times that Jesse found for some lichens upend this facile assumption. They also make a strong argument for the preservation of stands of old-growth chaparral. The shrubs present in stands of chaparral that are allowed to reach the century mark are critical havens for other species, such as the slow-returning lichens in Jesse's study.

So how do lichens recolonize after fire? Unsurprisingly for such wonderfully complicated creatures, their reproductive mechanisms are also complex. Most lichens have two means of reproducing, and it is unclear which method is more important in responding to fire disturbance. The fungal parts of lichens are able to reproduce sexually by making fruiting bodies (similar to a mushroom in function but not shape). The fruiting body contains spores that disperse and combine with spores from other members of that species to create new individuals with genes from each parent. However, these new individuals are just fungi, with no algae or cyanobacteria to begin with. The new fungi must find algae in the environment to take into their bodies to complete the formation of new lichens.

Lichen fungi can also bring their symbiotic partner along with them in dispersal, by forming tiny outgrowths that are made of both fungus and algae or cyanobacteria. The outgrowth granules break off of the lichen and are spread by wind, water, or animals. Where they land, the granules attach to the substrate and grow new lichens without needing to find new algae or cyanobacteria. This flexibility in reproduction helps lichens colonize areas devoid of life, such as empty rock faces.

Lichens have no means of surviving fire outright, and are killed when their substrates burn or when they are burned off nonflammable substrates such as rock or soil. Pioneers are required to recolonize a habitat: new lichens from

early afternoon light
looking toward the
furthest north end
of Blue Ridge

button lichen
Buellia sp.

sunkendisk
lichen
Aspicilia sp.

goldspeck lichen
Candelariella sp.

firedot lichen
Caloplaca sp.

dust lichen
Lepraria sp.

a sampling of lichens on a boulder
on the trail to Blue Ridge

a map of the side of the
boulder looks like this

unburned areas must make their way into the burned area after the fire. Lichen spores and vegetative granules are brought to the burned landscape by wind or animals, but this means that there must be living lichens near enough to the burned area for the spores or vegetative granules to reach it.

Once spores and vegetative granules manage to reach the burned area, they need to find places to land, attach, and grow. The bark- and wood-dwelling lichen species—epiphytes—have to be able to find shrubs and trees on which to make their home in a newly burned area. Some lichens can grow on burned wood, but not all can, and if the fire was intense enough, even burned wood can be scarce.

Jesse and Jes are trying to find out which of these two requirements—suitable substrates or sources of new spores from outside the burned area—is the greater obstacle to lichen regrowth after wildfire. The rebar posts they are setting out today will soon be outfitted with spore traps that will collect spores and vegetative granules in fine mesh nets. The collected materials will be analyzed genetically to identify which lichen species are successfully dispersing spores into the air at all of these sites.

Jesse and Jes have an easy camaraderie, and their enthusiasm for ecological fieldwork is infectious. Both are teachers first and foremost: Jesse is a lecturer at Stanford University, and Jes is an assistant professor at St. Mary's College. Jesse worked full-time for several years in the field doing surveys of rare plants, but, as he tells me, he likes people and collaboration, so he returned to graduate school in order to be able to combine fieldwork with teaching.

Their love for field ecology keeps them returning to the field, to conduct their own research and to create research opportunities for their students. It is relatively easy to set up the spore traps now, when most of the chaparral shrubbery is gone or just charred skeletons. But as soon as the new green growth of chamise and manzanita and toyon fills in again, checking the spore traps will become much more arduous. Even before then, the poison oak will have taken full advantage of the open spaces to come in thick and lush. We already have to dodge it in some places. A high poison oak tolerance will be a requirement for student researchers, Jes jokes.

I love being out here with ecologists. As a biologist and artist, I treasure these times in the field, fully engaged in an ecosystem. Being present in the landscape and drawing what I see in front of me make my drawings more lively and real. This is why Jesse and Jes are here too, because they know how important it is to offer students this immersive experience. And how important it is for their own well-being to refresh and reconnect with the world that they are studying.

As we drive, the researchers explain to me that each experimental area is a group of three sites: one surrounded by severely burned land, one nearby just at the edge of the burned area, and another one, also nearby, in an area that burned at low severity. The low-severity sites experienced only ground fires, which means that many of the trees escaped relatively unscathed, and their lichen populations along with them. Jesse and Jes ensure that each low-severity burn site contains a source of lichens—trees or shrubs that still have all of the lichen species that were present before the fire. They agree that this means fruticose species such as beard lichens must be present. These are the long, fine lichens that hang like delicate, pale-green hair from tree limbs. Beard lichens take longer to reestablish after they are removed from an area, so if we see them at a site, it is reasonable to conclude that the lichen community there is fairly mature.

It is not difficult to find groups of sites that meet these criteria. Driving between sites, we marvel at the patterns of more and less severely burned land. It is so easy to see the map of a wildfire, the perimeter of the fire outlined and filled in, and imagine a scorched wasteland throughout that entire shape. In reality, this is almost never the case. Especially in ecosystems that have experienced fire occasionally and at varied intervals, the pattern of burning forms a precious mosaic. This is what we see at Quail Ridge today. In the 2020 fire, some hillsides were thoroughly burned, so that not even charred stumps are left of the chaparral shrubs that had densely crowded them before the fire. Other hillsides look untouched, having burned lightly beneath the oaks, leaving the trees unscarred and the ground to fill in quickly with new green spring growth. Many sites are between these two ends of the spectrum, with standing blackened shrub branches and still-bare earth just starting to turn green again.

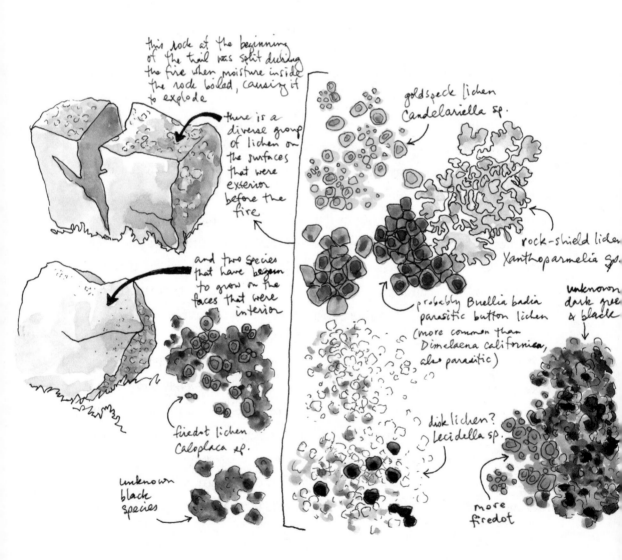

this rock at the beginning of the trail was split during the fire when moisture inside the rock boiled, causing it to explode

there is a diverse group of lichen on the surfaces that were exterior before the fire

and two species that have begun to grow on the faces that were interior

firedot lichen
Caloplaca sp.

unknown black species

goldspeck lichen
Candelariella sp.

rock-shield lichen
Xanthoparmelia sp.

probably Buellia badia parasitic button lichen (more common than Dimelaena californica, also parasitic)

unknown dark green & black

disk lichen?
Lecidella sp.

more firedot

At Quail Ridge, I see, over and over again, refuges holding living trees and lichens, and understand their importance as sources of spores for lichens to recolonize more deeply burned areas. It drives home the critical importance of the burn mosaic. If Quail Ridge had burned uniformly at high severity, there would be nowhere for lichens to hide and persist. There would be no sources of living lichens near enough to reach the hearts of the severely burned areas for a very, very long time.

Lichen diversity

My favorite time to look for lichens at Cold Canyon is winter, when the bare landscape exposes surfaces usually hidden by the leaves of shrubs and trees. All along my hikes, I keep my eyes open for the lumps, bumps, frills, tendrils, and rings of lichens clad in orange, yellow, buff, brown, black, green, and all the colors in between.

I have been keeping close watch on lichens on a rock near the entrance to the Reserve. Truly a touchstone for my experiences here, the boulder came to my notice on my first visit after the fire. It was here that I learned how rocks are fractured by steam in a fire, breaking apart to expose new surfaces. I have watched the new rock faces since then for clues about some of the slowest and quietest changes in an ecosystem, as the rock slowly weathers and as the first traces of colonization by new life appear. The original exterior of the rock was covered by more than six different lichen species—these survived the fire, despite heat high enough to fracture their substrate. On an early January visit four-and-a-half years after the fire, I can see that a couple of the survivors have begun to grow on the new faces. These are crustose lichens, growing flat and close to the rock, so enlaced with its surface that I would not be able to remove them without bringing along some rock too.

whiskered jelly lichen
Leptochidium albociliatum
on a mossy rock

Here are the things I think about. Are the two lichens that have begun to grow on the newly created face faster colonizers? Does the south-facing orientation of the new rock faces perhaps favor the first two colonizers? How long will it take for all the species on the old faces to colonize the new face? There is so much to discover, and I wonder what else this old sandstone friend will teach me.

Rock surfaces attract foliose lichens too. Some of these are the same species that like to grow on trees, and others are partial to rocks alone. Later in my walk, after I cross Cold Creek, now swiftly flowing, and head up the hill, I encounter several foliose lichens. The fire burned here, too, but like the crustose lichens I've been following, these seem large and well established enough to have been here before the fire. The morning mist has left them damp, so they are all moist and green, which tells me that they must be photosynthesizing. With no roots to draw water from the ground, the lichens lie dormant during the hot, dry summer, when there is next to no moisture in the air. In that state, they are neither growing nor photosynthesizing.

Speckled greenshield lichen is an interesting specimen, reminiscent of lettuce leaves draped on a fallen log. Growing with other mosses and lichens, it forms a lush, self-contained world, one that I know is teeming with microscopic beasts—tardigrades, rotifers, nematodes, springtails, and mites. Whiskered jelly lichen, nestled in moss on a boulder, looks like wavy black miniature elephant ears. Intriguing white whiskers sprout on the bottom edge of each ear, and inside the top inner parts of the ears are little red balls filled with spores.

Lichens are a treasure hunt, yielding a trove of magical new finds in color, shape, and texture as the reward for paying close attention to my surroundings. The eureka of finding a species new to me is complemented by the pleasure of finding new spots harboring some of my particular favorites, such as disk lichens. I love them for their tile-like pattern of concentric rings and the way the black fruiting bodies stand out against the white lichen body and define these rings. The ones I am examining are large, covering a good fraction of their boulder substrate. I think they were probably fire survivors. Lichens on rocks have an advantage over those growing on trees. While they certainly can burn, their substrate does not. I have seen plenty of evidence of this in my observations of numerous rock lichens along the trail, even shortly after the fire.

Dog lichen, green and leafy-looking, is growing *on* moss on a rock. This association may be harmful for the moss, as chemicals secreted by the lichen can kill the moss, with the by-products of the moss's decay increasing lichen metabolism. I see interactions upon interactions, all laying the basis for the growth and development of the other organisms here. Layered, in a way, like my visits to Cold Canyon, each one resting on the previous as the months pass after the fire. I see my understanding of this ecosystem growing and changing as the layers accumulate.

At first I feel relief, watching green leaves appear so quickly, in shrubs resprouting and vines extending in sunlight and fresh structures to climb. Then satisfaction, in the discovery of so many lives—flower and fungus, wasp and lizard, bird and beetle—enriched by the newly burned landscape. Only later awe and sorrow, for the slowly dying pines, and a new appreciation for lives lived at such a vastly different pace than my own. Like the pines, lichens remind me that the impacts of fire are felt far longer in the landscape than seems immediately obvious, some lichens returning only long after the ash is gone and the charred wood is hidden beneath lush new growth. So too the fundamental processes of the ecosystem, at whose base is the work of the lichens, methodically and timelessly creating soil from stone and wood.

Perspective shifts

Lichens offer a cautionary story about wildfire, and about the dangers in generalizing the effects of fire on a habitat. Chaparral is known to burn easily, and fire ecologists have hypothesized that fire intervals of as little as thirty years are healthy. However, Jesse's research shows that some chaparral lichens require several decades and perhaps as long as a century to return. Thirty years may be too short for full recovery of all the lichens. And I realize with a start that this probably means that not all of the lichens at Cold Canyon had returned before the Wragg Fire, not quite thirty years after the previous fire. Lichens' lives are inextricably entwined with the shrubs that host them. When large swaths of chaparral burn, as is happening more and more frequently in California, the slower of the bark- and wood-loving lichens will have a harder time returning, until they eventually disappear from areas where they were once common.

another mossy rock glowing in the sun

pile of feathers probably from an unsuccessful attack on a robin

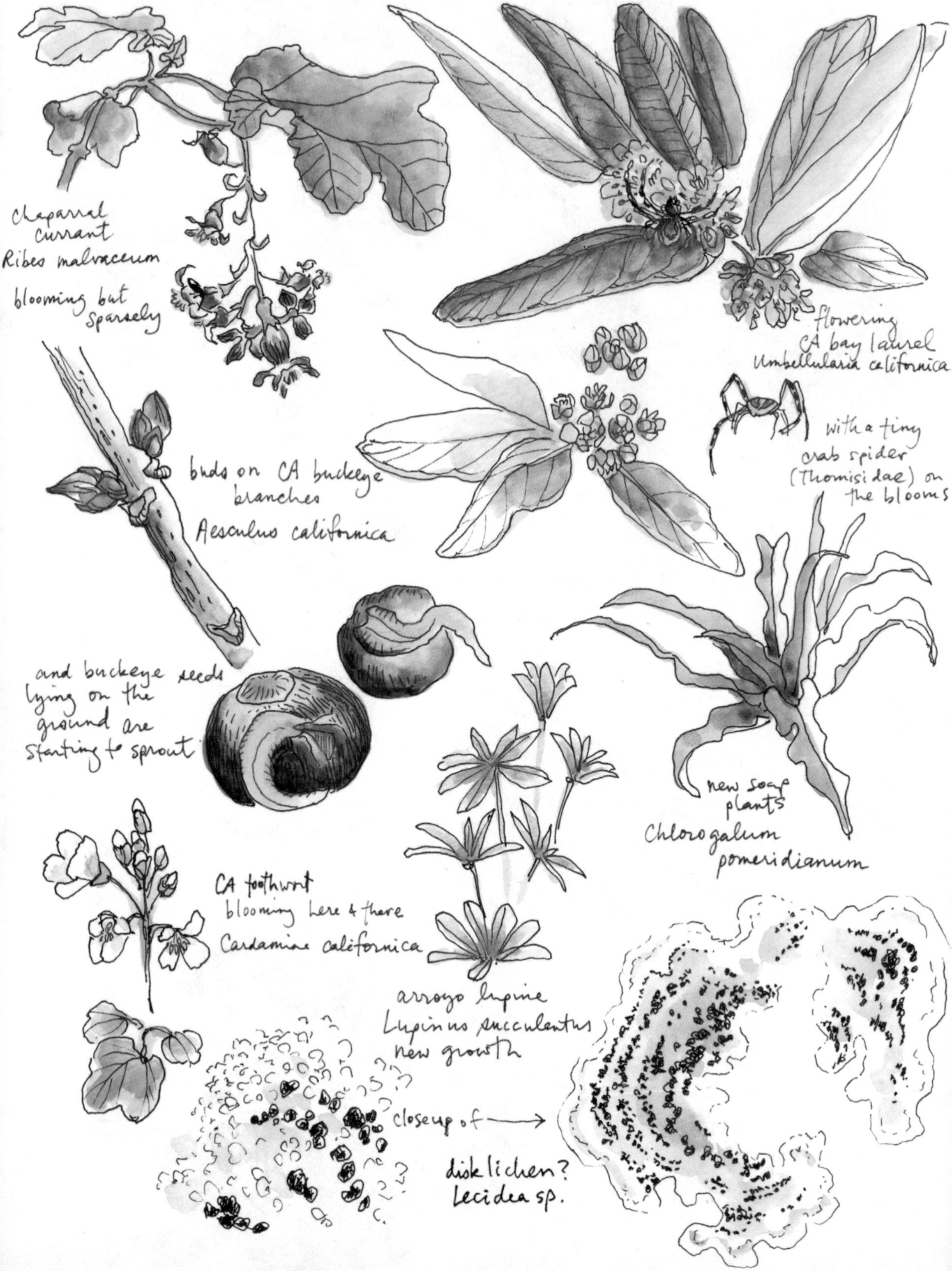

chaparral
currant
Ribes malvaceum

blooming but
sparsely

flowering
CA bay laurel
Umbellularia californica

with a tiny
crab spider
(Thomisidae) on
the blooms

buds on CA buckeye
branches
Aesculus californica

and buckeye seeds
lying on the
ground are
starting to sprout

new soap
plants
Chlorogalum
pomeridianum

CA toothwort
blooming here & there
Cardamine californica

arroyo lupine
Lupinus succulentus
new growth

closeup of →

disk lichen?
Lecidea sp.

There is hope, though. In his recent study, Jesse found that while many species of lichen were absent from large patches of burned chaparral, oaks in and near the burned areas were more resistant to the fire and survived with their lichen communities mostly intact. Jesse found that almost all of the lichen species missing from the burned chaparral were still represented on the oaks. It is the mosaic pattern of burning that we saw on the hillsides at Quail Ridge that ensures lichens survive after fire, recolonizing burned areas from unburned areas, or from the trees that survived within the burned areas. But—and this is the challenge—recolonization will only work if we can avoid large, homogeneous megafires.

There are many reasons to care about lichens—their contributions to the soil, to the air, to the diets of plants and animals—but let it also be for the window they give us into the creativity of life, to the questions they raise about how an organism is constructed. I think about the relationship between these clever fungal farmers and the crops they tend within themselves, wanting not to make the lichen more human in the comparison but to make myself that much more lichenous. Peering carefully at the unassuming organisms coating rocks and sprouting like hair from trees takes me deep into the mysteries of life and its endless fantastical forms.

Lichens will always remind me of how vital it is to step back and question my assumptions—about what is interesting, what is beautiful, what has value. They ask me to notice the smaller details in the landscape and understand that some of the most important ecosystem processes are not immediately obvious. It is through this careful attention that we are learning what lichens can tell us about the danger to biodiversity if fires are too frequent or severe in chaparral. Lichens point us to all we stand to lose—as markers of all the places in the world that are becoming less healthy, less inhabitable, and as reminders of what we are doing to ourselves as well as the world around us.

Chapter Eight

BLAZING A TRAIL
Mammals of All Kinds

The long human history at Cold Canyon has shaped the contours of its ecology, and the relationship has been reciprocal. This canyon has become an unparalleled place of learning for scientists and the public. And it has given us eyes into the world we cannot see and the life that continues when we are not there.

I often played a game, looking out the window on car trips with my family. Where have people walked on the landscape? If every human footprint left a mark, is the entire world covered? Is there anywhere our feet haven't touched? I searched the hillsides we passed, seeing the gray shadow of human tread covering everything, wondering whether there might be a bright glimmer anywhere that no human had ever touched. Maybe there, on that distant mountain? Not at the very top, I would tell myself, but somewhere along the side, somewhere inaccessible, somewhere overlooked. Could there be anywhere I had passed by, even if I only saw it from afar?

My thoughts then were consumed with the idea of wilderness and a yearning for places unaffected by humans. People were something distinct, a group I wished I could pluck out of the world and tuck away into a box, and in so doing save the natural world. But slowly I started to think about those mythical places with no human footprints. How much would that matter, really? Humans have changed everything around us, all around the world, air, land, water. In my mind, I watched the dark gray footprints evening out to a light gray film over the planet.

All organisms change their environment. The differences are in the scale of their impacts. Humans alter natural processes the world round, but we are not something set apart from nature, except in our own minds. As we change the world, it changes us. Hiking at Cold Canyon, I might wish to be an impartial observer, but my breath removes oxygen from the air around me and adds carbon dioxide. My feet press into the soil or the sand or the rock, compressing them and changing the tiny biome of life right there, of lichen or moss or grass or fungus or bacteria. My presence changes the behavior of animals nearby: the frog fallen silent in the creek nearby, the fox waiting quietly in the shrub up the hill, the bird scolding me loudly from the tree branch above. I try to remain conscious of the changes my presence makes in the habitat all around me and also to understand that those surroundings are changing me too. Changing my body, as I breathe the air and touch the leaves, rocks, and soil around me, and changing my mind as I learn and grow in my understanding of what is here, what is evolving, and how it all interacts.

As the canyon grows and changes after the fire, humans are observers of the process, sure, but we are also movers and changers ourselves, shaping the future of the wild with every step on the trail, pet we bring with us, and artifact we leave behind. Humans have been here, in this canyon, for a very long time, though who we are and how we use the land have changed dramatically. The canyon has been home and livelihood. It has been a place of rich resources and hard work. And it has become a place of respite, research, and recreation. Over its long history, it has been shaped by fire—fire started by lightning long before humans arrived, perhaps fire used intentionally by early human inhabitants to tend the oak woodlands, then fire long excluded once it became a danger to human property. Now, with Cold Canyon accessible to the public, fire's presence here has opened the door to a new understanding and appreciation of its role in the ecosystem. Knowing the canyon is impossible without knowing the intertwined pasts of landscape, fire, and people.

With each visit over the months and years after the fire, I am learning the

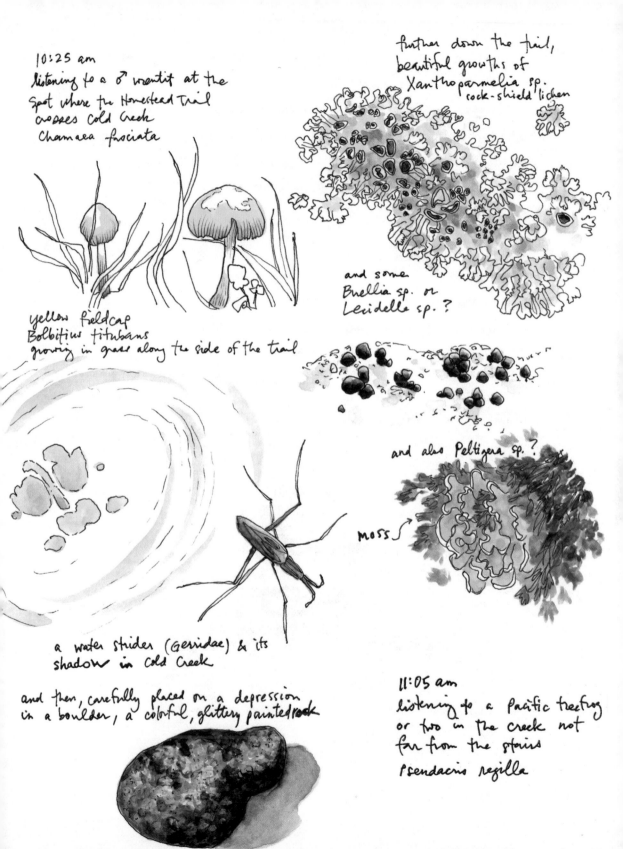

10:25 am
listening to a ♂ wrentit at the
spot where the Homestead Trail
crosses Cold Creek
  Chamaea fasciata

yellow fieldcap
Bolbitius titubans
growing in grass along the side of the trail

further down the trail,
beautiful growths of
Xanthoparmelia sp.
  rock-shield lichen

and some
Buellia sp. or
Lecidella sp. ?

and also Peltigera sp. ?

moss

a water strider (Gerridae) & its
shadow in Cold Creek

and then, carefully placed on a depression
in a boulder, a colorful, glittery painted rock

11:05 am
listening to a Pacific treefrog
or two in the creek not
far from the stairs
  Pseudacris regilla

planes and edges of this specific place. Only through repeated direct experience can I grasp the fullness of the habitat here, how it looks, feels, smells, and sounds. And those visceral discoveries bring sympathy and understanding. They stitch me into my surroundings and let me change with them over time.

Echoes of time and history

One morning in January, three-and-a-half years after the fire, I catch a twinkle out of the corner of my eye. Looking closer, I find a brilliantly painted rock, fist-size, tucked into a ledge on a boulder. It is painted in bright shades of hot pink and turquoise and dusted with gold glitter. I think about the person who painted it so carefully and wonder how long it will stay there. Will it go home in the pocket of another hiker, a happy treasure and reminder of their visit? I hope it does—as beautiful as painted rocks may be, their acrylic paints introduce more plastic into wild places.

a cairn at the intersection of the trail & creek

These are the bits and pieces I keep watch for along the trails. They are evidence that Cold Canyon is well used and well loved. Evidence that while each person's presence here changes the ecosystem, the land is changing them too, their emotional connection made tangible in their offerings. People flocked back to Cold Canyon as soon as it reopened after the fire, eager to hike again in a favorite natural area and, I'm sure, to see for themselves what the burn looked like.

On that January visit, I find another interesting trace. At the place where Homestead Trail crosses Cold Creek, someone has built a cairn of carefully selected flat pinkish rocks. As I paint them in soft hues in my sketchbook, I imagine the person who hunted for the stones, carried them to this spot, piled them, then stood back to admire their work. Both the painted stone and the cairn, these temporary constructions, are clues to how beloved the Reserve is, as it has been for an inestimably long time.

Throughout the area in the Coast Ranges where Cold Canyon lies, mortars carved into the bedrock have been found, made by the Southwestern Wintun, who lived in the Sacramento Valley and around Cold Canyon for thousands of years before Europeans arrived. They are the southernmost of the larger Wintun group of tribes, whose ancestral lands extend north to near Mount Shasta. The mortars were once used for grinding acorns and other seeds into flour, and they bear witness to the long human history here, an indication of regular use of the area for untold generations. The Wintun cultivated this land with well-honed techniques, tending to the growth of plants important for food, shelter, medicine, clothing, and tools. Their land stewardship almost certainly included deliberate burning, which was widespread before European arrival. Fire was integral to promoting biodiversity and ensuring that plants grew in ways best suited to Native American dietary and cultural needs.

Humans have long been part of the ecology here, though colonization unbalanced the scales. Catastrophe for the Southwestern Wintun arrived in the form of Spanish settlement of the area in the early 1800s. Epidemics of smallpox and malaria were devastating, killing an estimated 75 percent of the Indigenous population of the Sacramento Valley. Under Mexican control of California, Wintun were forcibly relocated to Mission Solano, in what is present-day Sonoma County. The introduction of grazing livestock then also destroyed the plant ecologies that provided food and shelter to California's native inhabitants, exacerbating the deliberate genocide unleashed upon them. Wintun people today live throughout the Sacramento Valley, some as part of federally recognized nations, such as the Yocha Dehe Wintun Nation in the Capay Valley or the Paskenta Band of Nomlaki Indians in Tehama County. Many others are not included in these designated groups, but that should not obscure the fact that they are still here, tending land and community.

After forced removal of the Southwestern Wintun, Spanish and Mexican ranchers grazed their stock in Cold Canyon and the areas around it. Ranching continued in the newly created state of California, and the land began to be claimed as homesteads under the Homestead Act of 1862, a time still marked by the canyon's Homestead Trail, so named for the farm that stood at a spot right next to the creek. On this trail, I can step backward through time to the mid-1900s when John Vlahos and his family grazed cattle and goats on the hills above, having received the land in a 1938 grant. Some of the buildings' foundations remain, low rock walls in the bank above the stream, in a spot deeply shaded by bigleaf maple. It is a cool and peaceful spot and feels, in my imagination, like an inviting place to live and work. After the 2020 fire, more foundations were exposed further south of Vlahos's homestead, remnants of other settlement in the area.

Vlahos grazed cattle and goats on the hills above his home and stored the cheese he made in two underground cellars. I had always thought that the nearby creek and the deep shade of the homestead site kept the cellars cold. In a wide-ranging conversation about Cold Canyon past, current, and future, Reserve director Sarah Oktay explained that there is much more to it than that. The cellars took advantage of the lowest point in the nearby landscape, which forms a frost pocket. As air cools at night, it sinks and collects in hollows like this. This remains the coolest spot, freezing first, as the name implies, and also retaining morning fog. To further increase the cooling effect, Vlahos ran pipes from the spring down a vertical wall in the cellars. He picked this site so that the natural environment could do the work of food preservation, without need for costly ice or refrigeration.

Beyond their human applications, the cooling effects of this spot are of great ecological value. The water and lower temperature provide protection against fire, lessening its severity and allowing it to pass through without burning as much foliage. I have witnessed just how quickly the trees and shrubs here regrow after fire, with ample access to water and protection from the incessant heat of summer.

California towhee takes in the scenee looking downhill to the stream bottom from one of the homestead foundations

Cold Canyon's ranching legacy is marked by more than just foundations. The signs can be read in roads and footpaths and tracks of livestock. To this day, I can see terraces on the hillside northwest of the Homestead site. These mark the well-worn paths trod by countless goats and cows over the years of Vlahos's residence. There are other persistent ecological impacts here, too, in the form of introduced thistles and grasses. These plants continue to thrive in habitats disturbed by many years of grazing, and many more of them grow here than in the rest of the Reserve. High-severity fire can help eradicate nonnative grasses, but these were still evident after Cold Canyon burned in 1988 and again after the Wragg Fire. Their continued presence here may be an indication that the fire was of lower severity on this slope, or that the impacts of grazing are just that tenacious.

It has been a long time since any person has called the canyon home. Vlahos pastured his livestock here for thirty years and then sold half of his holdings to another private landowner, who sold the land to the University of California in 1979. Five years later, Vlahos's family sold the remaining parcel to the university. The land was allowed to gradually return to a more wild state, the roads disappearing into tangles of shrubs and the grazed hillsides slowly sprouting native chaparral plants alongside the introduced grasses fostered by grazing. I have often wondered what happened to the roads that Vlahos used to reach his home. Paul Havemann, Reserve steward for Cold Canyon, tells me that the old roads were never really removed from Cold Canyon and that they are strikingly evident after a fire. He has taken great pleasure in striking out cross-country after the Wragg Fire and mapping some of these roads. These have, as he puts it, been some of his "most exhilarating wanderings" at Cold Canyon.

Paul's words are thrilling. Here is another important part of the Reserve's history revealed by fire. The flames opened passage through areas that before were impenetrably dense with shrubs. Finding these roads deepened Paul's own

watched a ruby
crowned kinglet
in a laurel

Regulus calendula

looking up out of the
canyon to the east

bobcat
scat ?

gray fox
scat ?

experience of the landscape as he walked the old ways that were driven regularly by some of the canyon's long-departed residents. Just as I am taking advantage of the fire's revelations to see the canyon's ecology as a living and breathing entity through time, even Paul, who already knows the land here so well, finds new treasures when fire strips away the familiar enshrouding scenery.

The ripples of human presence

No humans live in the canyon anymore, but never has the landscape been so full of people. The Reserve sees around sixty-five thousand visitors a year, a number that has unavoidable and far-reaching impacts on the animals we observe, but also on everything we never see. No matter how lightly and responsibly we step, our actions shape the ecology of Cold Canyon.

Walking on the trail, I hear a small rustle in the thick tangle of toyon branches just to my left. I stop walking. The noise stops. I am holding my breath, and whatever has been alarmed by my presence is doing so too. I am determined to outwait it. Sure enough, after a few slow beats of my heart, the rustling starts again. Peering into the dark shade of the shrub, I spot a movement and then another. Eventually I am still long enough that the gimlet eye of a wrentit appears, the bird hopping from one low branch to another. The times that I catch sight of the source of noises, it is almost always a bird—a towhee or sparrow or maybe a wrentit—or very occasionally a lizard. Sonoma chipmunks I spot occasionally, usually above me in a tree, but sometimes low in a shrub. Crunching in the underbrush, calls filtering down the hillside—these are the signs of animals that are shy of humans, but not that shy.

There are many more things that are hiding while I am in the canyon, but I never catch sight of them. Save the bold chipmunks, it is mammals that are the most elusive, and I have small hope of seeing them in person. Instead I content myself with the evidence of their passage. Happily for me, some of this evidence is relatively abundant and hard to miss. On this visit, I step over several deposits of wild canine scat (not to be confused with the domestic canine scat I find all the time even though dogs are not allowed in the Reserve). A gray fox or a coyote left it in the middle of the trail as a marker of its territory. I am unable to say which it was, because their scats are very similar in shape and contents. Gray fox and coyote are close enough in size to have considerable overlap in scat size, and eat similar omnivorous diets of berries, insects, and small animals.

I can't tell which animal the scats belong to, but others can. Scats are dense with information for other foxes or coyotes passing by. Who was here? How long ago? Were they male or female? Were they healthy? There is information for me, too, in the still-bright skins of toyon berries studding the scat. It is a potent image of a complex system. Fox and coyote change their diets seasonally in response to food availability: insects and other invertebrates in the spring and summer, berries in the fall, small animals in the winter. The fall berries I see today are sustaining the fox or coyote, abundant and requiring no energy spent on a hunt. The wild canine's droppings in turn will enrich the soil with nutrients from which new toyons will grow.

I also spy scats that look more feline, with sinuous curves and abundant fur. Perhaps a bobcat left them, as they are also roamers of Cold Canyon. They seem small to be left by mountain lions, though these also are found in the canyon. But I cannot be certain that the scats are feline, since a coyote's scat can look the same once the coyote has switched to its winter diet and is eating more small mammals. These leavings prove that when we visitors scatter back to our homes at dusk, these predators scout the dark trails in solitude and silence. So much more is happening here than I will ever see in front of me. It was one great shift in thinking to understand that some plants continue to live during and after fire,

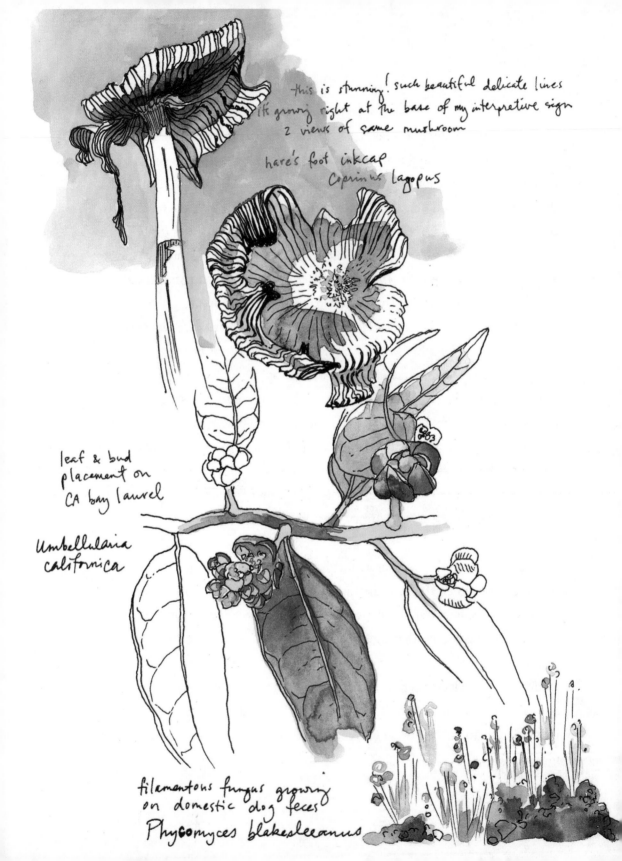

this is stunning! such beautiful delicate lines
it's growing right at the base of my interpretive sign
2 views of same mushroom

hare's foot inkcap
Coprinus lagopus

leaf & bud
placement on
CA bay laurel

Umbellularia
californica

filamentous fungus growing
on domestic dog feces
Phycomyces blakesleeanus

despite all the evidence of my senses that they had been killed. It is another to think about how active the world here is at night in my absence, something that I can know intellectually but that truly comes to life every time I spot the signs. And it is impressive how immediately these creatures are present after fire—scat and footprints appearing quickly on the trails still marked by ash.

But it remains the case that my presence, along with that of all the other human visitors to Cold Canyon and the domestic canines they often bring with them, ensures that the shyer mammals are not near the trails when people are. They are hiding in the parts of Cold Canyon far from the trails and are also spending time in nearby areas emptier of people, such as the state- and federally owned lands adjacent to this public reserve.

I wonder often, especially as I walk past a pile of dog scat decorated with the fine hairs of a filamentous fungus or watch a dog bound past me on the trail, far ahead of its owner, what effects these uninvited canine visitors have on the birds, other animals, and entire ecology of the Reserve. Too much dog waste can add excessive nitrogen to the soil and introduce parasites. Paul Havemann tells me that although dogs do affect the health of the canyon, he considers the scofflaws' dog walking worth the impact on the habitat because public access is at the heart of Cold Canyon's purpose. By exploring the rich ecosystems of Cold Canyon, visitors can come to know them personally and intimately, especially since other UC Natural Reserves nearby are protected from public impact. There are few other public hiking trails in the area, and people must be able to experience these oak, chaparral, and riparian habitats for themselves before they can fully understand their beauty and importance.

What is here when we are not

Every evening, we human visitors go home, taking with us our heavy footfalls, our loud voices, our strange smells, and our dogs. From dusk until well past the light of dawn, Cold Canyon belongs only to the nonhuman mammals and all the rest of the animals, plants, and fungi that call it home or travel through.

Even though human history marks this land in every way, Cold Canyon is a place where humans have chosen to step back in an attempt to rebalance the scales and prioritize the canyon's wild residents. As a UC Natural Reserve, the landscape remains open to researchers and the public while still shielding its inhabitants from greater impacts—overnight camping, horseback riding, bicycling, and motor vehicles. The protection of Cold Canyon's wild character opens a window into animal activities that we might otherwise never get to see.

Cold Canyon is host to many projects probing the secrets of its ecosystems, and to this end, Paul Havemann has installed a couple of trail cameras to assist. The cameras offer a window into the activities of usually unseen animals. Although the presence of the cameras themselves might have some small impact on animal behavior, it is safe to assume that what we see on the screen is a glimpse into the daily lives of animals with at least the immediate influence of humans removed.

One trail camera is installed near a pool in the creek where there is water year-round. I watch the footage, transfixed by animals coming to drink. In the day: a pair of scrub jays scooping up mouthfuls and lifting their heads to swallow; a chipmunk nervously approaching in quick starts and stops to quickly drink and dart away; a striped skunk at dusk reaching down from a rock to sip. A pair of foxes in the night, drinking for a long time—I imagine their gentle lapping. I find it deeply satisfying and even reassuring to see animals drink. Perhaps it is my perpetual fear of drought or just some common animal sympathy with seeing such a basic need met.

The look in the eyes of a coyote captured a couple of times over the span of a day makes the biggest impression on me. The coyote is poking about in the area just in front of the camera, sniffing the rocks nearby and the ground just in front of the camera. It gets so close that I can see right into its big, yellow, expressive eyes as it looks around warily while investigating the smells. So close that I can see a couple of hitchhiking ticks on and behind its left ear.

Mule deer wander by—fawn, adult, and antlered adult at various times. A dusky-footed woodrat makes a graceful leap straight over the pool and onto a boulder. A family of quail spend a while foraging in front of the camera, a few members at a time always keeping watch from the highest boulder. A bobcat prepares to leap, crouching low, ears flat, looking warily upward. At one point the scene bursts with towhees, both California and spotted, as they bathe, drink, and squabble, fluffing and preening.

All of this footage comes from just after the 2020 fire. I am amazed at how soon after the fire I see animals wandering through the frame. A coyote the morning after the fire and then the same one again or a different one late that afternoon. Skunk, rabbit, acorn woodpecker, fox, and bobcat, all within the next week. The area around the camera did not burn, and I picture them traveling along the riparian corridor, which was more protected from the flames. I study the images with a lump in my throat. I am more moved by this glimpse of animals navigating a burning terrain than I expect. There is no desperation or fear in their movements or postures. The fire is some distance away, but there is smoke in the air, and it is impossible that they are unaware of what is going on. In these images, Cold Canyon reveals itself as a place filled with refuges, even if the overall scene is one of destruction. Although I know that all but the most severe fires do have these pockets of safety, it is a very different thing to see that in action.

I tuck all these images into my heart and bring them with me on future visits to Cold Canyon, better able to guess at what is happening outside my range of

gray fox
Urocyon
cinereoargenteus

night time visits to
drink at the pool
Stebbins trail cam

striped skunk
Mephitis mephitis

dusky-footed woodrat
Neotoma fuscipes
taking several great bounds
up to & across
the pool

view. And better able to imagine the shapes of lives not at all like my own. A small step toward acknowledging and fighting my anthropocentric limitations, just as I have tried to do with lizards and newts and lichens.

An image from shortly after the 2015 fire tells another poignant story. One of the more striking images I saw after the fire was a trail-camera picture of the suspected last dusky-footed woodrat remaining in the canyon. In 2020, the scientists who had installed the camera published a paper about their postfire work. As part of a larger study about ticks, tick-borne pathogens, and tick mammalian hosts—especially woodrats—they had installed four cameras near the openings of known woodrat dens to see whether any had been able to burrow deeply enough to escape the fire. Only one of the dens still had parts of its midden, twigs and branches that had not all burned up. It was at this den that the cameras caught woodrat activity in the four months after the fire. There were pictures of it entering and leaving its den and once, carrying an acorn. This is a striking peek into the existence of a very fortunate but also probably very lonely survivor.

The consequences of removing woodrats from the habitat ripple far beyond this solitary holdout. Woodrat houses—built of sticks and lined with grasses and bark shreds—also provide shelter for a surprising number of other species, including other small mammals, reptiles, amphibians, and insects. The sophisticated construction of their houses further enriches the ecosystem by speeding decomposition of plant material and increasing soil moisture. And of course, woodrats are an important food for coyotes, bobcats, owls, and other predators. Although the woodrats are gone in Cold Canyon the first years after the fire, it turns out that another rodent, a kind of deer mouse, becomes very common right after fire, filling the gap in prey that would otherwise have been left by the woodrats.

Three different species in the genus commonly referred to as deer mice go through a sequential cycle of populations in chaparral habitats after fire. One species, the western deer mouse, appears first, right after fire. They are hardy invaders of disturbed areas, and do not climb, so they are not troubled by the scarce trunks and limbs of trees and shrubs. After a couple of years, western deer mice decrease while the numbers of brush mice grow. Brush mice, who need more cover, love scrub oak, California lilac, and mountain mahogany, and return to the habitat when those have grown large enough to shelter them. Finally, once the chaparral shrubs are reaching their mature sizes, after approximately ten years, a third species, California mice, become abundant.

For western deer mice, which habitat is the most preferred, the "best"? Certainly not the mature chaparral. These three very closely related mouse species each find a different postfire habitat stage to be the most suitable. And that is why all of the stages are equally important. Only by moving through all of them do all of the different organisms that evolved in these ecosystems have their chance to emerge, grow, and reproduce. It is a challenging concept for people who are so accustomed to thinking of the passage of time as a forward progression toward an end goal. And even understanding the concept with respect to mice, it is difficult to extend this observation to other mammals. I see in the field cameras how soon deer, bobcat, fox, and rabbit travel the burned area—this is still home, altered and certainly more challenging for some species, but not gone.

Being in a landscape and seeing the way that it changes, changes a person. This is very much my own experience at Cold Canyon, in my actual visits to the Reserve but also in these tiny windows into the hidden life of the ecosystem. I came to the project expecting to learn about fire and the habitats here, but have been surprised by just how transformative the experience has been. I am every day more aware of the radically different ways different organisms react to fire, and what fire means for their lives and their deaths. I will always be profoundly glad that there is so much happening in the world right around us, above us, and under us that we will never know. This is perhaps the greatest beauty in

sonoma chipmunk
Neotamias
sonomae

drawings from Stebbins
trail cam NRS 01
backdrop of boulders

bobcat
Lynx rufus

steller's jay
Cyanocitta
stelleri

coyote
Canis latrans

the world—that we cannot know everything, and that every new discovery only reveals more mysteries.

Shaping our view of fire

I have been traveling the paths through Cold Canyon all my life, participating on different levels as I have grown and matured. I hiked when I was young, eager to climb boulders, splash in the creek, and reach high places with inspiring views.

trail & slope stabilization work continues on the trail up to Blue Ridge

ripe CA buckeye fruit

Aesculus californica

tree is bare

signs of a mammal along the trail

gray fox?

As a teenager I was moved by a desire to get closer to nature, hoping to spot the species that made my heart beat fast, the hawks and falcons and vultures. As an adult, I am seeking the more finely grained knowledge rewarded by close study, conducting my own long-term citizen science project in fire ecology observation. I am working to better understand everything that lives there and to have a more personal, long-term sense of how it all fits together. Cold Canyon has also offered me a portal to the scientists whose research illuminates the effects of fire on these habitats and the dangers we are all facing from climate change and altered fire regimes. I am sometimes surprised to look back at all that this 638-acre space has meant to me. Over the years, Cold Canyon has been a comfortable, familiar outdoors escape and at the same time a source of endless new discoveries, rewarding patience and a willingness to look at familiar sights with open eyes and curiosity.

Although there is always a trade-off, given all our impacts on the landscape, both direct and indirect, I feel very personally the value of the gift of public access. If Cold Canyon were not open to the public, I would not have had any of these experiences. Most important, I never would have embarked on my artistic journey here after the Wragg Fire. And thanks to the fire, there is a new urgency to the public experience at Cold Canyon. Most people in California have not walked through a recently burned wild area, and there are generally very few opportunities to do so. Cold Canyon offered a rare experience for the public to explore an area less than a year postfire, and an even rarer opportunity for research into how people perceive this experience. Three UC Davis researchers conducted a year-long study between May 2016, ten months after the fire, and April 2017. They probed Cold Canyon visitors' knowledge of fire-related topics and their impressions of the fire's impact on the Reserve.

The study demonstrated that public understanding of this wildfire was thoughtful and nuanced. People expressed admiration for the resilience of nature and even the beauty of a burned landscape, though they also felt strongly the devastation and desolation all around them. The survey was administered both before and after visitors' hikes, and responses were often more positive after the hike, indicating that experiencing the regrowing habitat directly is important to understanding and appreciating fire adaptations and responses. This having been my experience exactly, I am excited to see it reflected in so many other visitors' responses.

Also probed in the survey were visitors' assessments of their knowledge about fire ecology. Quite a few people surveyed were at least passingly familiar with general concepts of fire as an important part of the ecosystem, and even the necessity of prescribed burns. Very few, however, were confident in their knowledge about specific fire regimes in California, or about how fire works in chaparral and oak woodland habitats specifically. All of our knowledge has limits—there is so much that is hidden and only occasionally glimpsed, like the old ruts of ranchers' vehicles, or the secret passages of cats and coyotes. But familiarity tends to breed affection, and when we are attentive and curious, our growing knowledge ties us to the cycles of life in this place.

This is the power of experiencing nature directly. This is what is gained in trade for those human footprints covering the wild in my childhood imagination. When we visit a place that is undergoing the upheaval of rapid and conspicuous ecosystem change after fire, we grow to understand the patterns of nature and the specific rhythms of our own home habitats. Especially if we are at the same time able to recognize all the parts of the system that are not immediately obvious to our own eyes, such as the animals that hide in our presence. That's what these years at Cold Canyon gave me, and what the Reserve offers every visitor whose heart broke when it burned.

oak

toyon

CA bay laurel

white pitcher sage
Lepechinia calycina

hairy-leaved ceanothus
Ceanothus oliganthus

① fox or coyote enjoying the toyon as much as the robins

② bobcat? coyote?

③ much smaller in comparison to others than it looks here
probably American robin since they are so active right here

Chapter Nine

THE FIRE CYCLE IN THE ANTHROPOCENE

Cold Canyon Burns Again

In a summer of catastrophic fires, Cold Canyon does not escape. A second burn five years after the Wragg Fire is a dramatic departure from a healthy fire interval in chaparral and oak woodland habitats. Cold Canyon illustrates the consequences of climate change, drought, and increased urbanization in the western US.

August 16, 2020, feels like a relief. I've been slogging through the dog days of this summer. I can well understand the dread of the ancient Greeks who gave us such an evocative name. This is the time that runs from mid-July to mid-August when Sirius, the Dog Star, rises and sets with the sun. Living in a Northern Hemisphere Mediterranean climate as we do in California, the Greeks and Romans thought that Sirius was giving off heat along with the sun. The double-barreled inferno beating down on earth incited all manner of ill effects: madness, drought, fevers, bad luck, wounds failing to heal, thunderstorms.

The thunderstorms that start in the early morning of the sixteenth certainly bear out the Greeks' fears. Thanks to the arrival in California of a large tropical storm's tail end, there are enormous, unusual thunderstorms throughout the northern and central parts of the state. These storms are full of electricity. Over the next three days, there will be more than twelve thousand lightning strikes recorded in Northern California, an unprecedented number in such a short span of time.

But all of that comes later. My first reaction on the sixteenth is happiness to see clouds in the sky, moister air, and a few raindrops here and there. The week before was a scorcher, reaching a temperature of 110°F the day before the storm. With our state slipping further and further into drought, even my usual fears about lightning and dry hillsides are completely overridden by my primal thirst for rain. The danger of the thunderstorms only begins to dawn on me gradually as more and more fires ignite and spread. It is becoming clear that this is not going to be a usual fire season. And the usual fire seasons are bad enough. California has experienced massive and devastating fires over the past decade, with significant loss of life. But never before so many and all at once.

When the skies are heavy and brown and the light that falls through my skylight is orange, it feels like apocalypse. I wonder how many people are in harm's way. The 2018 Camp Fire in Butte County was a lesson in what may be coming: when the town of Paradise was incinerated, eighty-five people died in that disaster, far more than in any other California wildfire. Casualties in the 2020 fires will not be as high, though there are a total of twenty-five fatalities in all the fires combined.

I live in a town surrounded by miles of agricultural fields and far from the dry hillsides, so I do not spend fire season worrying about my home or preparing to evacuate. Each year, though, the communities that are threatened by fires are in increasingly developed areas. These are joining the neighborhoods and scattered houses built in the "interface" between settled land and wildland, which are always at risk. People who do not live in the urban–wild interface can no longer remain blissfully unaffected by fires. Now, too, the smoke from these conflagrations affects us all. In the 2020 fires, communities far from the burning are nonetheless under the pall of smoke, often converging from several fires at once. An inescapable reminder of the rapidly changing environment that might be out of sight but is hard and harder to keep out of mind. We spend entire weeks in August and September reluctant to be outside in the severely unhealthy air, obsessively checking the air quality ratings throughout the day for better windows in which to exercise or run errands.

Over the tense days that follow August 16, many more fires are discovered, where lightning struck in more remote areas. It has taken a while for the fires to grow large enough for detection. I begin to wonder what this will mean for Cold Canyon. Since 2015, there have been fires every summer in the eastern Coast Ranges near Cold Canyon, and having observed and drawn the canyon's response to fire over the past five years, I knew that it was extremely unlikely that Cold Canyon would make it another thirty years without a fire—believed to be the minimum healthy interval between fires in chaparral. The Hennessey and Spanish Fires are discovered on August 17, both west of Cold Canyon but close enough that I start frequently checking the fire perimeter maps put out by CAL FIRE, the Forest Service, and the Bureau of Land Management.

On the morning of August 18, a new fire starts just near the entrance to Cold Canyon. By evening, this fire, the Markley Fire, has grown to twenty-five hundred acres. By the next day, the Hennessey, Spanish, and Markley Fires, together with six more fires in the vicinity, are beginning to merge. They are being called the LNU Lightning Complex, named for their local CAL FIRE unit.

So many modern wildfires are caused by humans—automobiles, campfires, power lines—that it is a little surprising to have this great outbreak of fires come from lightning, a natural source. The responsibility for the apocalyptic outcome, though, is arguably still on human hands. Climate change, drought, poor land management practices—all contribute to the catastrophic extent and intensity of the fires. Not to mention that the storm that brought the lightning was also part of a trend toward larger and more electricity-filled storms as the planet warms.

I am learning that it is important not to get too attached to tidy stories, though. Most of the fires in the LNU Lightning Complex are caused by lightning. But not all of them. At the time, I heard that there was an arson-caused fire at the

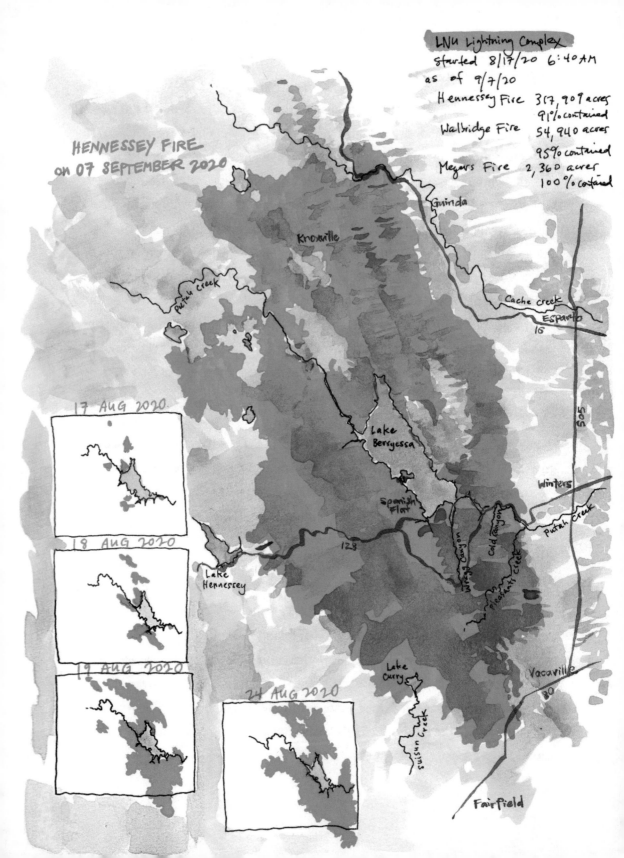

HENNESSEY FIRE
on 07 SEPTEMBER 2020

LNU Lightning Complex
started 8/17/20 6:40AM
as of 9/7/20
Hennessey Fire 317,909 acres
91% contained
Walbridge Fire 54,940 acres
95% contained
Meyers Fire 2,360 acres
100% contained

Guinda

Knoxville

Putah Creek

Cache Creek

Esparto
16

505

Lake Berryessa

Winters

Spanish Flat

Putah Creek

128

Wragg Canyon

Cold Canyon

Pleasants Creek

Lake Hennessey

17 AUG 2020

18 AUG 2020

19 AUG 2020

24 AUG 2020

Lake Curry

Vacaville

80

Suisun Creek

Fairfield

entrance to Cold Canyon, but misunderstood its scope. I thought it was a small fire that only burned right near the highway and then was put out. I thought that the Markley Fire, which burned all of Cold Canyon and merged with the rest of the LNU fires, was caused by lightning. It turns out, though, that the Markley Fire is alleged arson. And not just garden-variety arson, but arson to destroy evidence of a murder. In the midst of all these fires caused by extraordinary acts of nature—though their scale was exponentially greater due to climate change—this one was entirely human. The fire compounded the crime of the murderer-arsonist, because there were additional deaths when two people living in the fire's path were unable to escape in time. It took eight months for the investigation to conclude, for the full set of charges to be brought, and for the story to reach the news.

On the day I discover that Cold Canyon has burned again, I am surprised by my conflicting emotions. At this point, I've spent the past five years absorbed in a burned natural area and know to my core that the fire is not a destroyer but an important stage in a healthy ecosystem. The difference this time is that until now, all my insights have been into a landscape that had a nearly thirty-year interval between fires. After five years, the stakes feel much higher. What will happen when Cold Canyon's habitats have so little time to grow and change after the last fire? Will we start to see organisms and habitats fail to return or regrow? And I wonder about the whispering bells, which only germinate at Cold Canyon after fire. Has enough time passed for their seeds to be ready again?

Starting again, again

In the weeks after the fire, as I look forward to being able to walk in Cold Canyon once more, I catch myself repeatedly thinking impossible things. Wondering about the manzanita I watched bloom last spring for the first time since the

Wragg Fire, and how it is doing. Thinking about the full stands of California lilac that took five years to reach the height of my waist, and about the California tortoiseshell caterpillars that are dependent on them. Oh! And what about the three-leaf sumac that took several years to reach a size necessary to flower, and whose flowers I was finally admiring just last spring?

With a start, I remind myself: these are gone. In their place, charred limbs, or stumps, or bare earth. It is so strange to think that there can be essentially *nothing* there, when I was just looking at tall, sturdy shrubs and trees. Old friends that I visit and catch up with monthly. It feels as though the rug has been pulled out from under me.

And then I catch myself again. They're not gone, of course. The manzanita, the California lilac, the three-leaf sumac—they're all there, just not in the form I recognize. I've just demonstrated to myself how hard it is to internalize the new perspectives I've gained while studying fire ecology at Cold Canyon. I may know intellectually that fire is a usual, natural stage in a continuing cycle of life, but at one level I am also still in thrall to the metaphors of destruction and loss. I truly can't wait to get back to the trails, so that I can walk there conscious of the life thrumming underground.

My first visit to Cold Canyon is in September, a little less than three weeks after the fire started. The northern end of the LNU Lightning Complex is still burning and will not be fully contained until early October. In this area, though, the fire is out, and the roads have reopened.

I park alongside the highway and step out of the car into silence. It is a strange muting of everything. I feel as though my ears are covered with wool, as though the usual sounds of the place must be there and I am just unable to hear them. No cars pass on the highway the entire time I am there. The colors are dampened too, all browns, hinting only faintly at other colors in the spectrum: brown tending to rust, brown tending to ochre, brown tending to olive.

blue oak leaves curling in toward
the advancing fire
these are no longer an
indicator of fire direction
since the tree has
fallen

Blue Ridge

the beautiful tall oak
growing just past the
entrance at the highway
survived the Wragg Fire
but not this one

it anchored every
trailhead landscape
I painted (one every
six months after
Wragg) — the view is
very different now

it is quiet & still here
but I did spot one turkey vulture
above the ridge

I notice immediately that a landmark is gone. The fire has felled the great blue oak that marked the entrance to the trail just past the highway. Its survival and solidity after the Wragg Fire, as it greeted me in this very spot on my first visit to the burned landscape in 2015 and every visit until this one, made it an emblem of my questions and thoughts about the fire. I passed it each time I entered the canyon, and I drew it at least twice a year when I painted the view of the canyon from the highway to mark the passage of seasons and growth after the fire. I already miss it terribly. Is the tree still alive underground? Will I see new sprouts in the seasons to come? I hope so, very much, but cannot help but mourn the loss of the venerable tree, which I will not see in that form again. I will not be around after the hundred years it will take to reach that size, if it regrows at all.

9:00 AM   sunny & cloudless
~ 70° on arrival
45 days since fire
no rainfall since fire

coyotebrush
Baccharis pilularis

The next time I come to Cold Canyon, it is October. I am here on a day that the Reserve steward, Paul Havemann, is supervising a work crew. Cold Canyon is closed to the public, and even staff, volunteers, and researchers are never on-site alone, to ensure safety in a time when slopes are unstable and dead trees might fall. I come when trail work is being done. Paul and his volunteers are out every week rebuilding on the trails, clearing them, stabilizing them, and installing new signs to ensure that the Reserve is safe when it reopens to the public in the winter.

In stark contrast to my September visit, the air is alive with birds this October morning. A couple of Northern flickers dart across the highway, back and forth, as I get out of the car and prepare to hike. As soon as I head up the canyon, I see Nuttall's and acorn woodpeckers dashing back and forth too. It is not long before I hear wrentits calling from the remaining brush. The sounds indicate they are hiding in patches of desiccated but not burned shrubbery and also in pockets of trees and shrubs near the creek bed that were spared as the fire rushed through. I am seeing again a mosaic pattern of burning, just as I saw after the Wragg Fire and will see again at Quail Ridge. There are many patches of surviving vegetation. These islands are hubs of activity. A ruby-crowned kinglet buzzes across the trail just barely above my head. I see a couple of dark-eyed juncos foraging in what brush is left.

My greatest surprise comes when I am crossing the dry creek bed and an Anna's hummingbird flies past, on his way to a small patch of California fuchsia flowers. Still alluringly orange, they look like they are drying out for the season, though the hummingbird seems to be finding nectar in them still. It is fall and most of the vegetation has burned away, so I had not at all expected to see hummingbirds back in the canyon yet. The fuchsias and the jewel-bright bird are a nudge to remember that fires rarely burn everything and that the streambed is an important site of fire resistance, given the moisture just underground.

When I cross paths with Paul as he heads down the trail and I head up, he tells me about some of the perennial pools in the creek. One week after the fire, he was surprised to see that these pools were full to overflowing, fuller than they would ever ordinarily be in late August. It is proof, he says, of just how much of a sponge these hillsides are. Even after a long, dry summer, there is a lot of water in the ground. Most summers, that water is taken up by all the plants growing on the hills, long before it reaches the creek below. With most of the plants gone, the water made it to the bottom of the canyon and welled up in the pools. It is a thrilling demonstration of everything that is going on beneath us while we hike here, in stark contrast to the easy assumption that everything important is in the open air and visible to our eyes and other senses.

Water moving deep beneath the surface of the parched, ashy hills, barren of anything but occasional charred shrub limbs—driving home that day, I can't stop thinking about the full pools. The invisible flows of water through the system are a reminder that just as life continues after a fire, water continues too. Redirected but not destroyed. Five years into this project, the unseen environmental shifts that take place in response to disturbances such as fire continue to surprise me.

Traveling Cold Canyon these past five years, I did not truly believe that fire would also return so soon. Logically, I knew it must be coming, with so many fires in this area each summer, but I couldn't shake the dissonance between what I knew and what I actually expected to happen. We begin again in ash and dust, blackened branches and heat-withered leaves, but neither the canyon nor I are the same as we were five years ago. I now know the rhythms of renewal, and seek to understand the details of the pattern I could not yet see when I began to make a study of this place in earnest. The canyon has burned again after a much shorter interval, and the implications are both fascinating and concerning.

As I set out, walking the same path as ever from canyon floor to peak, I see, hear, feel, and breathe the postfire landscape. I am here to see what signs of the fire's passage I can read now that I am equipped with new knowledge and tools, especially one given to me by Miriam Morrill—a copy of *Guide to Wildland Fire Origin and Cause Determination*, the bible for fire investigators, published by the National Wildfire Coordinating Group. It is a thorough inventory of the indicators of fire behavior: how fires start, how they spread. I am not trying to draw any sweeping conclusions about the fire but using the guide to visualize what happened during the fire, in a place so familiar to me. It is another opportunity to begin to understand everything that happens here to which I am not a direct witness, just like the animals on the trail camera, the beetle larvae tunneling, or the newts tucked away safe underground.

ghostly marks of ash on the hillside: where a tree burned, toppled, then continued burning until completely combusted, leaving just a shadow of white ash

a few last hardy CA fuchsias in the dry creek bed AND one Anna's hummingbird visiting them

big red dragonfly - flame skimmer
smaller one - vivid dancer
cabbage white?

bigger - CA darner
orange sulphur?
cloudless sulphur?

white ash

the blue oak
from near the entrance
to the trail at the highway

new leaves from
base of redbud
Cercis occidentalis

the iron ranger
(painted by
Kirk Ehmsen)
survived its
second fire!!

what is resprouting?
- toyon
- yerba santa
- redbud
- coyotebrush
- bay laurel
- poison oak
- scrub oak (berberidifolia)
- spice bush

with few people
in the
Reserve,
mammal activity
is up - trail
cams have shown
regular mountain lion
use

Armed with the handbook, I walk carefully along the trail. The hard-packed dirt is unchanged by the fire, but there are piles of soft ash and dirt on either side. I see evidence everywhere of the heat and intensity of the fire: patches of white ash show where trees and shrubs burned completely, truly leaving nothing aboveground but ash. In some places, the combustion continued underground, and there are gaping holes where the tree continued to burn down its trunk and into its roots.

Where a burning tree fell and continued to burn, there are exact maps of the shape of that tree marked in white ash on the ground. I cannot help but watch, in my mind, the tree aflame, dark shadow of trunk and limbs haloed by dancing fire, falling to the ground in a great crash of sparks. The flames gradually burning themselves out, the tree reduced to molecules in the ash, the tracery of lines marking its final resting place.

Looking carefully at the burn marks on still-standing trees and shrubs, I make guesses about the direction in which the fire was passing and how fast. If a fire is advancing, moving quickly, especially uphill, and is not moving against the wind, the fire will wrap around and burn higher on the lee side of the tree trunk as it passes. In these places, there will be a steep angle to the char pattern on the trunk, higher on the side in the direction the fire was moving. Fire moving against the wind, or backing downhill, will make a more even char mark, level around the circumference of the trunk.

Fire behavior is also recorded in the ways leaves curl in the heat of nearby flames. In low-intensity fire, leaves that are near the fire but do not burn will curl toward the flames. The heat dries out the cells on the exposed side, which causes the leaf surface to shrink and curl inward. I look for foliage freeze, too, coming full circle to my original conversation with Miriam four-and-a-half years ago. I see interesting patterns of branches, stems, and needles frozen in different directions. This probably indicates swirling winds at the bottom of the canyon during

the 2020 fire, just as in 2015. Since there was plenty of frozen foliage left from 2015 just prior to the 2020 fire, I am sure I am seeing one maelstrom superimposed on another, a perfect image of the doubling of impacts of a fire coming so rapidly on the heels of the last.

Returning to another thing I first learned after the Wragg Fire, I come across patch after patch of rocks with interesting scars. Just as I discovered in 2015 that boulders can split apart as the moisture in them boils in a fire, I am now seeing the effects of rock spalling. The fire heats up the outermost layer of rock while deeper layers remain cooler, and the difference between these temperatures weakens the rock, causing the outer layer to flake off. Fire is a force remaking the landscape, hastening the decomposition of these flakes by knocking them to the ground where they wait for lichen, plants, bacteria, wind, and rain to return them to the soil.

I didn't know to look for any of these signs when I started visiting Cold Canyon after the Wragg Fire, when I was walking with eyes completely open to everything around me. No expectations and no agendas. Now, after five years of immersion in the landscape and five years of watching it change after fire, I have so many questions and so much more context for my observations. This is a chance to see some of the immediate effects of fire that I did not get to observe last time. And it is an entirely new view into what this short interval between fires will mean for the habitat.

Fire cycles

Coming to Cold Canyon regularly since it burned in 2015, I have been tracing the lines of an age-old cycle. Disturbances punctuate the life of all ecosystems. In California and throughout the western US, fire has been a key driver of change.

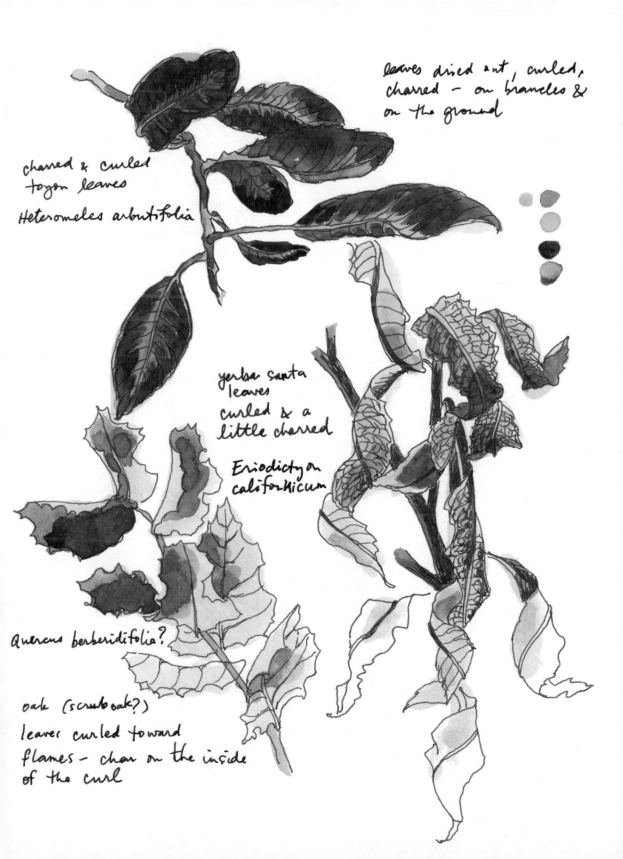

leaves dried out, curled,
charred — on branches &
on the ground

charred & curled
toyon leaves
Heteromeles arbutifolia

yerba santa
leaves
curled & a
little charred

Eriodictyon
californicum

Quercus berberidifolia?

oak (scrub oak?)
leaves curled toward
flames — char on the inside
of the curl

The ecosystems here evolved along with regular fire and have come to need it for their biodiversity, health, and resilience. In five years, I witnessed several of the stages along the path from fire to mature habitats. I saw the first flush of animals drawn to the burn, such as the wasps and beetles that make use of dead and dying trees and shrubs, and the birds and lizards that in turn eat the insects. I watched as the first plants reappeared aboveground, both those that grew from seeds as well as those that never died and simply resprouted from their underground organs—roots, rhizomes, bulbs, and burls.

After a couple of years of annuals and small perennials rushing to take advantage of the light and space opened up by the fire, larger perennials such as chaparral currant, pitcher sage, and yerba santa became more prevalent, having had time to grow large enough to flower and take their place in the habitat. With them came larger numbers of the animals, such as Anna's hummingbirds, wrentits, and California quail that rely on more cover than was available right after the fire.

Finally, in the year or so just before the latest fire, the shrubs were starting to return to dominance, growing large enough to start shading out smaller plants, and creating even more shelter for birds, mammals, amphibians, and reptiles. These stages of replacement are referred to as ecological succession. A group of species becomes dominant in the landscape and is then supplanted by a different grouping, each group following the next like waves, like the three species of deer mice and their population shifts after fire. Ecological succession is often thought of as a linear progression from a kind of blank slate to a full, ideal community of species. What my immersion in this process has taught me, though, is that the cycle of succession is not a targeted path with a final goal at the end. The so-called climax community of tall, mature trees and shrubs may feel like completion and the perfect end to the story, but every step along the way is the climax for a group of organisms. Even the still-burning land calls its siren song to some species.

I now know so many plants, animals, and fungi whose favorite habitats challenge conventional expectations of progress. The horntails who lay eggs in charred wood to give their offspring the best environment in which to mature. The fire-loving fungi who emerge to reproduce and disperse in the wake of a burn. The whispering bells germinating after a long wait deep in the soil. The woodpeckers who feast on larvae of beetles and horntails in dead or dying wood. The western deer mice whose populations explode in recently burned chaparral. This is their time. This is their desired end stage, not dense, shady mature chaparral or oak woodland.

Ecological succession in California habitats is the turning of a great wheel that starts with fire and ends with fire. When Cold Canyon burned in 2015, it had been nearly thirty years since the last fire. Only five years passed before the next. The cycle I was traveling was interrupted. The wheel bumped off onto the shoulder. Will it end up back on the same road, starting over again, or has it bounced onto another road entirely? That new road will not have the same stages leading to the same mature chaparral and oak woodland.

The tipping point

Fire has raced through these canyons and hills three times in recorded fire history—approximately the last hundred years—1988, 2015, and 2020, and up to five times in the hills just to the east of Cold Canyon. These numbers are very important. How many times a place has burned has lasting consequences for what grows there, as Jesse Miller discovered in his study showing that lichens reliant on old-growth chaparral didn't return until the seventh decade after a fire. And it is already clear that this third burn for Cold Canyon is a tipping point.

I am sitting in the cool green shade of the redwood grove along Putah Creek

patches of
peeling bark
- bubbling from
heat?

scrub
oak

char →

angle of
char

⟹ fire direction

white
ash

toyon
has the
same
pattern
as
the
scrub
oak

char

exposed
surfaces

flakes →

rock spalling:
flakes exfoliated from
rock surface when
heat caused a
breakdown in the
tensile strength of
rock's surface

on the UC Davis campus. It is morning on the last day of May, nine months after the 2020 fire, and the temperature will reach 104°F this afternoon. The coastal redwoods are incongruous and ill-suited to the climate in this hot, dry Central Valley town, but a most welcome meeting place this morning. I am talking to Ashley Grupenhoff, who is currently a doctoral student here, the day before she heads off for a week of field work in the Sierra Nevada.

Jesse introduced me to Ashley. Both have worked with Hugh Safford, a professor at UC Davis, regional ecologist for the Forest Service, and a leading voice in fire ecology. In her early work as a field scientist, Ashley studied bird ecology and population dynamics in places as disparate as Virginia, California, and American Samoa. While working on bird monitoring projects, she was evacuated from her Southern California home in a 2017 fire. That experience inspired her interest in fire ecology and all the thorny but fascinating questions about how to balance human life with the needs of millions of nonhuman lives.

Ashley's doctoral project is focused on monitoring prescribed burns in the Sierra, but this winter she also conducted a study at Cold Canyon, Quail Ridge, and Audubon Bobcat Ranch, a third local reserve about two miles northeast of Cold Canyon. All her sites are along the eastern side of the Coast Ranges, and were picked to sample a variety of times burned in the past century: from no burns at all to five fires in that time frame. What she is finding has profound implications for Cold Canyon and so many of the chaparral and oak woodland habitats in California.

After one or two fires, plants at the sites responded in much the same way as I observed at Cold Canyon after the Wragg Fire in 2015. All of the shrubs returned, both those that are able to sprout from their bases, such as chamise, toyon, coyotebrush, some California lilac, and some manzanita, and those that must grow again from seeds, such as other species of California lilac and manzanita. But after three or four fires within the last twenty years, Ashley does not see the obligate-seeding shrubs. They are disappearing from these systems, unable to grow from seed to the maturity needed to produce new seeds before the next fire comes. At least two decades are required after a fire for them to replenish their soil seed bank, certainly more than the meager five years that elapsed between the Wragg and LNU fires at Cold Canyon.

It is not only the obligate-seeding shrubs that are disappearing. Geophytes—perennial plants that grow from bulbs, tubers, or rhizomes—are also rarer at the sites that have burned three or more times. These are plants such as soap plant, lilies, irises, and brodiaeas, important components of the spring and summer color in these habitats. Both Ashley and Jesse told me about the differences they have seen between Cold Canyon and the spots in Quail Ridge that first burned in 2021. At Cold Canyon, the geophytes are failing to return this time, at least in the quantities we saw after 2015. Annuals, the other wildflowers that bloom so profusely after fire, are continuing to show up, although maybe not as many as before. At Quail Ridge, where this was the only wildfire in at least the last century, the geophytes are thriving: golden fairy lantern is growing in extensive patches, something not often seen here. Fremont's star-lily, twining snake-lily, Ithuriel's spear, blue dicks, Fernald's iris—all are popping up throughout the burned zones. Jesse and Ashley hypothesize that you can tell that an area has burned more frequently by its lack of geophytes and its conversion to mostly annuals.

Other aspects of succession are changing too. Deerweed is a vigorous opportunist after fire, a subshrub in the pea family that grows well in disturbed areas, helps enrich the soil by fixing nitrogen, and is eventually replaced when the slower-growing shrubs shade it out. However, Ashley has seen deerweed persisting much longer in places that are on their third or more burn in a century, as the shrubs that would have replaced it are failing to return. Deerweed is abundant at Cold Canyon, but Ashley has not seen any sign of germinating shrub seedlings such as Cold Canyon's two California lilacs, hairy-leaf and wedge-leaf ceanothus.

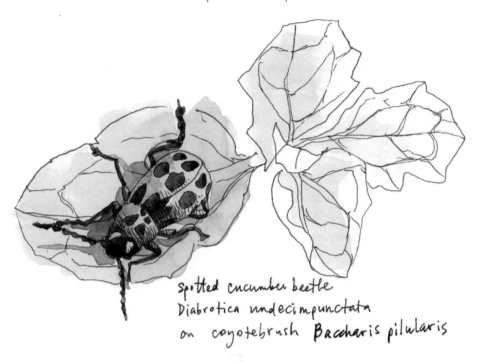

spotted cucumber beetle
Diabrotica undecimpunctata
on coyotebrush Baccharis pilularis

And although I have seen whispering bells at Cold Canyon this year, Ashley says they are far less abundant than they were after the Wragg Fire, and nowhere near as numerous as they are at the Quail Ridge sites that have burned only once in the last hundred years.

Cold Canyon has reached a precipice, it appears, and perhaps is already careening over it. All the benefits of fire, everything that has been a revelation to me in my wanderings through the habitats month after month over five-and a-half years, remain important in this landscape. But they accrue only at the intervals for which that habitat evolved. The chaparral habitats at Cold Canyon are healthiest when fire returns every thirty years or more, so that seed banks have time to replenish. Even the shrubs that can resprout from burls need time—at least six years—to rebuild their reserves of carbohydrates and nutrients so that future sprouting buds have enough resources to sustain them. Fires that occur too soon reduce dramatically the ability of resprouting shrubs to recover fully.

This is the threat of too-frequent fire, and the threat of climate change as a whole—that the environment is changing faster than organisms can adapt. It is impossible to separate the effects of ongoing drought, rising temperatures, urban development, human-caused ignitions, and increasing wildfires in California. They are a tangle of cause and effect, but are undeniably accelerating. As I pictured when I was little, our human footprints are everywhere on the map, both as a result of our actual presence and of the far-reaching consequences of our actions. Cold Canyon is a compelling example, where the consequences of years of heat and drought are now interacting with the aftermath of two fires, all challenging the organisms that live here to adapt or disappear.

Although my experiences have given me a very personal understanding of the natural place of fire in an ecosystem, scientists fear that once a place has burned too frequently, the habitat will be irrevocably changed and biodiversity reduced. As the shrubs at Cold Canyon begin to struggle now that the area has burned again so soon, we have almost certainly reached the point where some of the chaparral areas will begin to be replaced by grassland. Is this a problem? Aren't grasslands also important habitats? While it is true that native perennial grasslands harbor a great diversity of species, what will replace the chaparral at Cold Canyon is closer to a monoculture of introduced grass species. These nonnative grasses are annuals, in contrast to the perennial native bunchgrasses that once made up California's grasslands. The introduced grasses outcompete many other species, creating a landscape much lower in diversity and supporting far fewer species. Without shrubs, the habitat is less able to retain water in the soil, less able to stabilize soil on slopes, less able to capture and retain nutrients in the soil, and much more flammable than it was before. All of these changes perpetuate the cycle of frequent burning.

Introduced species are a paradox. It is important to understand the full picture of their role in the ecology of the place in which they are growing. They do

wrentit
Chamaea fasciata
in an oak

flesh fly
Sarcophagidae

foliage freeze —
much more difficult to
interpret
patterns
with frozen
vegetation
remaining
from 2015

woodpeckers were
extremely active — flashing across the
canyon from tree to tree or snag

magnified 10x:
rock shield lichen
Xanthoparmelia sp.

some charring
some staining
lots of heat-
killed spots

char on
burned
edges

looking west
patches of black, white
& tan

sometimes have positive effects on the habitat—for example, the nitrogen-fixing contributions that species such as bur clover or hairy vetch can make in disturbed habitats. But these effects do not alter the fact that introduced species can have extreme consequences for their adopted habitats. Introduced grasses accelerate the loss of chaparral shrubs and other species; they ensure their own propagation by changing the fire regime to favor them in the future and by greatly reducing the biodiversity of their surroundings. This is just one example of how a healthy fire cycle can be tipped out of balance into a spiral. Instead of the habitat circling all the way around to a mature state and burning again, fires occur sooner and sooner, and the habitat gradually loses the species that are unable to regrow or return in that time. The spiral accelerates and the habitat changes, eventually beyond recognition.

Every habitat has its own healthy fire interval and type of burning. Chaparral needs thirty to ninety years between fires for its full complement of species to regrow and return, maintaining a robust diversity. Chaparral shrubs and other plants also need the fires to be hot. The heat stimulates germination of native seeds and ensures that the seeds of nonnative grasses are killed. The introduced grasses did not evolve with this kind of fire regime, and their seeds cannot tolerate the heat. Hot, periodic fires help immensely with keeping nonnative grasses from taking over. Here lies the tension: hot fires are important for reducing nonnative grass seed banks. But nonnative grasses encourage frequent, low-intensity fires. As the grasses come to dominate, fire intervals are too short, and obligate-seeding shrubs do not have time to replenish their seed banks. And the fires are not hot enough to harm the nonnative grasses, which recover quickly and encourage the next burn soon after.

By contrast, oak woodlands can burn more frequently, as long as the fires are less intense, allowing the trees to survive, but burning off some of their pests and competitors. The differences between chaparral and oak woodlands have important consequences for their responses to controlled burning. Oak wood-lands can do well with controlled burns, which are usually conducted at low intensity. Chaparral generally does not, because its healthy fire interval is so long and because controlled burns are not hot enough to benefit chaparral species. Historically, Native Americans burned some chaparral precisely to convert it to grassland, to cultivate the native bunchgrasses that have so many important uses as food and as materials for tools, buildings, and other implements of daily life.

Ashley explained to me that the Wragg Fire burned very hot in Cold Canyon, but the LNU fire did not. In one way, this may be helpful, if one fire was more to the advantage of the chaparral and one was better for the oak woodlands. In another way, though, this is probably more bad news for the chaparral, with fire hot enough to remove the shrubs but not hot enough to kill off the seed bank of the introduced grasses.

The phenomenon of more-frequent fires converting chaparral to nonnative grasslands can be observed up and down the state, and has been best studied in Southern California. Chaparral is disappearing to rapid suburban development, and where it has not yet disappeared, the shrubs are all the same age, the result of fire burning over a large area and shrubs regrowing at the same time. This is a problem too. Chaparral fosters the most diversity when many different ages of plants are present. Just as Jesse has learned with lichens, wildfire is most bene-ficial when there are nearby reservoirs of species to repopulate the burned area. When fires burn uniformly over too large an area, rather than in a mosaic pattern, there are no islands of unburned habitat where species can shelter. All of this reduces the diversity of the habitat that eventually regrows. Old-growth chaparral is important for many species, and these species will eventually be lost if chap-arral burns so frequently that all the shrubs and trees are young, even if the areas have not been entirely converted to nonnative grasslands.

Ashley emphasizes that it is important not to view the repeatedly burned

several cairns in
the dry creek bed

plenty of human
presence even though
the reserve is closed

snail shell in the bare
dirt on a ledge along
the trail, lots of
exposed termite
burrows here too

new sprouts of
soap plant with
pretty fresh pink
tips
Chlorogalum
pomeridianum

this one is mostly
eaten - a bunch
seem to have been
browsed by deer (?)

landscapes as barren. On one field visit recently to Bobcat Ranch, to a site that had burned five times in the last century, Ashley was excited to see three beautiful yellow-orange birds making use of the habitat: Bullock's oriole, western tanager, and black-headed grosbeak. There was an intact oak woodland approximately two miles away, demonstrating the importance of the survival of unburned areas within a larger fire zone. While worrying about the effects of climate change and changing fire regimes, it is easy to forget that life will always return to the burned areas. But it will increasingly be an impoverished ecosystem, comprising just a few species instead of the multitudes that were once there. And the habitats will be the same for miles and miles, without the frequent shifts that lead to overall ecosystem diversity.

canyon
live-forever
Dudleya cymosa
on a boulder next to
the dry creekbed
these did not burn - I still see
dried stalks from last years flowers

Pacific sanicle
Sanicula crassicaulis
starting to glow up
all over the place

I find myself in an interesting limbo, watching Cold Canyon after two fires. In every direction, I see that this place is not barren. I see that some shrubs are doing fine, resprouting vigorously. I see whispering bells, and I see humming-birds. I see so many woodpeckers. I see bees and lupines and swallowtails. I have come far in understanding the complexity of fire ecology and all the different ways organisms respond. I am not the same person I was when I started, after taking in all these changes and letting them flow through me and out of my pen onto the page. I think of time differently, and what constitutes a life. And especially what fire means and how it fits into the cycles of an ecosystem.

So I know, both intellectually and throughout my being, that the second fire is not a tragedy. Life continues on, change is constant, and this truly is a beautiful thing. But I also know the importance of all the things we cannot see, such as the California lilac seeds that may fail to germinate because their seed bank is depleted. Or the California tortoiseshells that will not return to the canyon to lay the eggs of the next generations because California lilacs—their only host plants—are missing. I know that even though there is plenty of life thriving in the canyon after this fire, it may be less diverse than before.

We need diversity because it is only in diversity that we will find resilience. Diversity means that when one species or group of species or pocket of habitat or entire habitat struggles, there are others nearby that might possess qualities that allow them to survive or thrive. As some wane, others wax, and vice versa. But if we have vast swaths of land that are just introduced grassland, or just young chaparral, or just Douglas fir all the same age and size, what will happen when the conditions change and the rains cease or the temperatures rise? Everything will be affected at once, and there will be no reservoirs of survival on which to draw. And when the fires come—which is inevitable—everything will be consumed in the conflagration.

Chapter Ten

BRING FIRE WITH YOU

A New Old Paradigm

Fire can be a destroyer, or it can be a revitalizing force. Fire is itself one of the solutions to the problem of disastrously accelerating fire intervals. There are many examples of people and communities who already embrace a healthy relationship with fire, and it is vital to work with them in common cause, strengthening our ties to our neighbors and our local ecosystems.

The spiral can be broken. For nearly two hundred years, Europeans in the western US have been a powerful homogenizing force, through agriculture, urban and suburban development, introduced species—and a fire management policy with a single-minded focus on keeping fire out of ecosystems as completely as possible. We are coming to realize that this overriding fear is a self-fulfilling prophecy: preventing fire from occurring at healthy intervals ensures that when fires do burn, they are fearsome and disastrous. Increasingly, however, land managers are showing that letting wildfires burn can have enormous positive impacts. Even though Smokey Bear has been telling us for nearly eighty years to put out every fire, managers are slowly beginning to acknowledge a deeper human history with fire and to experiment with relaxing their strict fire exclusion policy.

Lynn Schofield's spotted owl research in Yosemite made her aware of the possibilities: since the 1970s, Yosemite has let wildfires burn so long as they are not threatening structures. The park has also used prescribed burning to maintain fire regimes more like those before the current fire exclusion period. These intentionally set fires, planned carefully, help maintain the health of the forest by recycling nutrients back into the soil, controlling numbers of pests and pathogens, reducing introduced species, promoting native species growth, and reducing fuel loads. By using prescribed burns and allowing wildfires to follow their natural course, Yosemite has achieved remarkable results, including reducing the severity of the 2013 Rim Fire where it burned inside the park. It is now the only area in the Sierra Nevada that has returned to a historical fire regime.

Lynn tells me enthusiastically about the dramatic satellite imagery of the Rim Fire burn. On it, I can see the stark boundary between the land within Yosemite and the land outside. Outside the park is a mixture of private land and the Stanislaus National Forest, none of which has been managed to embrace fire in the way that Yosemite has. Looking at a map showing burn severity, I can see that outside the park, the patches of each level of severity—high, medium, and low— are much larger. Immediately inside the park boundaries, the patches are broken up into tiny mosaics. The fire did not move across Yosemite as a monolithic force. Instead, it burned some spots very little and some much more extensively, and these severities alternate frequently over small areas. The patchiness creates many more refuges for fleeing species. It also forms islands where immobile species of plants, fungi, and lichens survive and send seeds and spores back to the more severely burned spots to recolonize after the fire. The burn mosaic forms more edges between more severely burned areas and those that are less severely burned or not burned at all. These edges are critical too, for species such as black-backed woodpeckers that prefer to move easily and quickly between burned and unburned habitats.

Fire is a peerlessly adept creator of biodiversity. But it can only do this when its own patterns are diverse: when it burns with variability in its heat, in its speed, in the heights to which its flames climb, in the area it covers, in the thoroughness with which it consumes vegetation. Calling this variety in burning style and scale *pyrodiversity* is helpful for breaking the ubiquitous image of fire as a single terrible force, only destructive, only frightening. The question is whether California and the western US can embrace pyrodiversity and step back to let fire do its life-giving work in the natural world. Without this, we are slowly losing the deep webs of species interactions in western ecosystems and will eventually lose the species themselves. I worry that I am watching this happen at Cold Canyon. And I fear that we have already stepped off the cliff and are falling past the point where the choice is ours to make.

Good fire

Fire has always been a companion of humanity. Throughout history, people have held many different relationships with fire, from embracing it as a partner to avoiding it at all costs, and everything in between. Since Europeans arrived in the western US, we have chosen the path of eradication. But no matter how much we might wish it, we will never be able to extinguish fire or manage it away. There will never be enough air tankers, brush breakers, or hotshot firefighters to keep fire away for good. We will always live with fire, and it is up to us to choose a better relationship.

Contrary to dominant forest management practices, there are many people in California who embrace a relationship with fire, foremost among them the Native Americans who have never forgotten their long-standing partnership with fire. Taking away the tribes' ability to periodically burn the lands on which they lived was a critical component of European settlers' program of genocide and cultural control. Fire was integral to Native Americans' cultivation of plants necessary for food, shelter, clothing, medicine, and tools. Settlers stole their fire and deprived them of access to all these basic needs. Since then, Native Americans have continued to burn when and where they can, an important act of resistance. Although their ability to burn has been extremely limited and even criminalized,

1120
prepping the
drip torches

2 parts diesel
1 part gasoline

1125
test burn

1150
getting started

"bring fire with you"

recent changing attitudes in state and federal government have created belated opportunities for a few tribes to direct larger-scale burns on their land and on adjacent government lands.

This cultural burning *is* controlled burning. But it is also so much more. As they have done for thousands of years, Native Americans burn to renew the landscape, to encourage biodiversity and the healthy growth of the plants they value. Just as important, they burn to renew their community ties, their heritage, their obligations to their ancestors, and their spiritual traditions. These cultural, historical, spiritual, and ecological dimensions of their engagement with fire are inseparable.

In 2019, Miriam Morrill, the artist and BLM specialist I first met at a workshop at Cold Canyon, organized a group of nature journalers to observe a few days of cultural and prescribed burning in the Klamath Mountains near the confluence of the Salmon and Klamath Rivers as part of a training program organized by the Karuk Tribe, the Mid-Klamath Watershed Council, the Nature Conservancy, and the BLM. It was a transformative experience to watch fire behavior up close and to learn from so many people for whom fire is a regular part of their personal, cultural, and professional lives. Given the long history of the government's willful ignorance of tribal fire practices at best, and racist criminalization at worst, it was most exciting to see the relationships that have been forged in the Klamath between the Karuk and their nonprofit and government partners. It is a sea change, with the government finally listening to what Native Americans have known all along. There are a growing number of other tribal burning programs throughout the state, in what is a promising trend toward cultural renewal and greater autonomy for tribes, and better relationships with fire for us all.

I have also had the great pleasure of participating in two cultural burning events at the Cache Creek Conservancy near where I live. Just sixteen miles as the crow flies from Cold Canyon, the Conservancy is home to a Tending and

Gathering Garden run in collaboration with local Native American communities. The garden is cultivated using traditional Indigenous methods, including pruning, coppicing, irrigating, and especially burning. Their newly established burning program brings together a broad cross-section of the local community, from university students to restorationists to families. The focus is on teaching the importance of fire in Indigenous culture and the methods Native societies use to tend the plants and habitats around them. It is an eye-opening vision of what community-level relationships with fire have been in the past and can be again: adults and children all involved in preparing the plants and tending the fires as they burn.

Native American burning practices are the inspiration for the more enlightened fire management policies that are now slowly being implemented by federal and state agencies in California, though that inspiration is not always recognized, and acknowledgment is rarely given to the original practitioners of these methods. Reading a published paper that described the Rim Fire's behavior in Yosemite, I was pleasantly surprised to see credit given to Native American land management work as the direct predecessor of the modern fire practices in Yosemite— allowing wildfires to burn and conducting prescribed burning—whose impacts on the behavior of the Rim Fire were so consequential to the spotted owls in the studies Lynn Schofield described to me.

Changes in government practices are part of a larger shift in public attitudes toward fire. The study of hikers at Cold Canyon conducted by UC Davis researchers uncovered a promisingly nuanced understanding of the value of fire in the ecosystem. Ashley Grupenhoff, the fire ecology graduate student, told me heartening news about the private landowners who lost homes in recent fires and now see prescribed burning as a way to help prevent future loss. In addition to her academic work studying the science of fire ecology, Ashley has taken an active role in fire itself. Not content with being a passive observer of fire's effects, she

along the north fire line

embers
fluttering

shooting flares
to light at
a distance

KLAMATH TREX

CACHE CREEK CONSERVANCY
tending flames in the deergrass

truly a community event – all are here:
tribal members, professionals, community members, children, students

became certified in wildland firefighting, obtaining the "red card" that proves her qualifications in fighting fire and conducting prescribed burns. For the past three years, she has managed a statewide fire monitoring program with CAL FIRE to better understand the effectiveness of prescribed burning and provide empirical data to help future planning efforts.

Something that often strikes Ashley when she is working a prescribed burn is the incredible level of knowledge possessed by the fire management officers (FMOs), the hotshots, and all of the other crew. They know the forest through and through and are intimately acquainted with how fire behaves. Theirs is a knowledge gained not through academic study but through daily experience over a lifetime of being in these habitats and working with fire. Their personal connection and firsthand observation are keys to the tectonic shift that is needed in society. Ashley's own example is important. Her direct knowledge of the entire process of burning and recovery informs her ecological studies of fire effects, helping her ask experimental questions based on real-world understanding of fire behavior and providing greater insights into the interpretation of her results.

Everyone I talk to about cultural and prescribed burning emphasizes the importance of showing people what fire looks like when it is allowed to burn at a healthy pace. Mark Stromberg, whose experience with newts at Hastings was so surprising, conducted a couple of prescribed burns there, years ago. Mark first experienced wildfire as a kid, growing up in Albuquerque, New Mexico, on the edge of a desert grassland where he spent all his free time looking under bunches of grass, catching grasshoppers and lizards, chasing snakes, and finding birds. He was devastated when the grassland burned, but then he watched, fascinated, as everything grew back, green and lush, after the monsoon rains. He saw native bunchgrasses growing back thicker and taller, mice and lizards back and active, birds returning. This experience with healthy fire led him to a doctorate in ecology from the University of Wisconsin–Madison, and a lifetime of commitment to grasslands research and conservation.

Mark speaks passionately of the educational value in showing photos to the public of firefighters lighting and tending fires, and in being able to point out the relaxed posture of the firefighters as they stand near the flames, dressed in protective gear but clearly at ease and in control. Even now, nearly fifteen years since the last time he participated in a prescribed burn at Hastings, I can see in Mark's demeanor how excited he was to bring fire to the land he loved so much and to be able to share this experience afterward through photos and conversation. Prior to working at Hastings, he managed the oak and grassland habitats at Audubon's Research Ranch in southeast Arizona, where they conducted many burns to study their effects on grassland. Wildfires were generally left to burn in that area, and Mark's whole family grew comfortable with fire in their lives.

Mark's wife was driving home one afternoon through the reserve while a fire crept along the ridgetop in her path. She calmly waited a few minutes and then drove through the fire front into the blackened, smoking grassland and the rest of the way home. This is an evocative image of cautiousness and comfort thanks to long familiarity with fire.

From personal experience, I know the power of standing close to a fire in the wild. At Cache Creek, I watch the small lines of flame creeping through deergrass, and fire racing upward and sparking as cattails burn like torches. In the Klamath, I watch flames meander at the feet of the trees in the forest, roar as they shoot up a tree, and smolder into embers deep inside a tree trunk.

For so many years, I watched intently as habitats grew and changed after fire. Watching controlled and cultural fires feels like finally reading the first chapter of my story, the behavior of fire itself. It is also like reading the first chapter of the story as it should be—humanity and fire working together in partnership. Being so close to fire is as exciting as I expected. It is also strangely calming to watch the crew treat the fire with grave seriousness and safety but also work with it as a valuable colleague. I see how clearly one can learn to read fire's behavior, to know how it will react when it encounters this fuel or that, to anticipate its next moves. It makes me think of an internship I had long ago with an arachnologist, learning to catch and study spiders. Watching them closely, I quickly developed an easy knowledge and comfort anticipating their behaviors, which meant that I could work with them unconcerned, even those I once found intimidating, such as black widows.

It is this ease that I see in the fire crews and the other participants in the burns—a healthy respect for a potentially dangerous force, but also a confident collaboration based on lengthy experience and attention. The feeling was encapsulated for me when I heard an FMO in the Klamath call out, giving the crew instructions to extend the active fire line using their drip torches, "Bring fire with

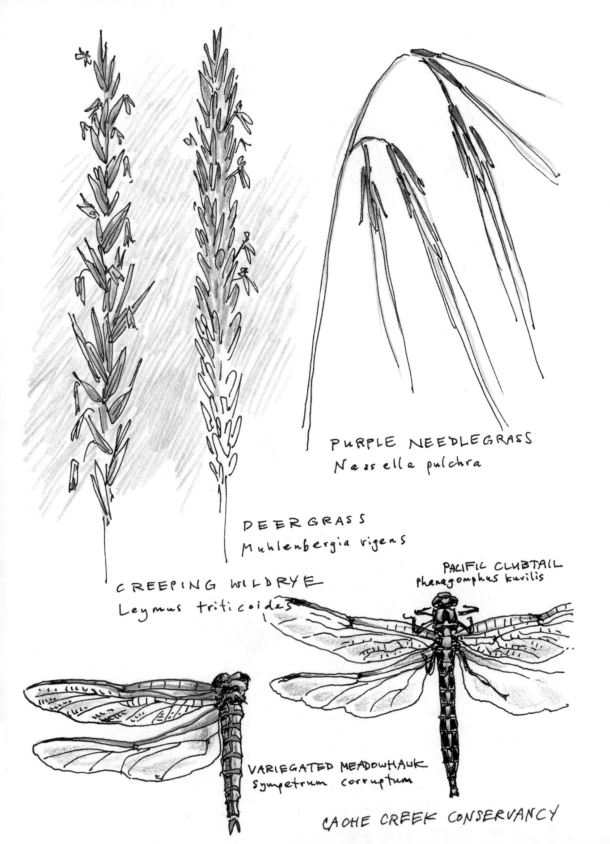

PURPLE NEEDLEGRASS
Nassella pulchra

DEERGRASS
Muhlenbergia rigens

CREEPING WILDRYE
Leymus triticoides

PACIFIC CLUBTAIL
Phanagomphus kurilis

VARIEGATED MEADOWHAWK
Sympetrum corruptum

CACHE CREEK CONSERVANCY

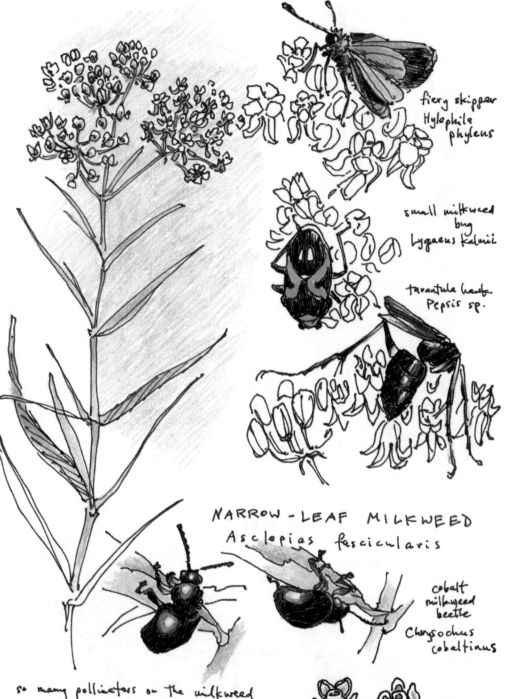

fiery skipper
Hylephila
phyleus

small milkweed
bug
Lygaeus kalmii

tarantula hawk
Pepsis sp.

NARROW - LEAF MILKWEED
Asclepias fascicularis

cobalt
milkweed
beetle
Chrysochus
cobaltinus

so many pollinators on the milkweed
(honeybees were also abundant on the
milkweeds, though not drawn here)

milkweed has been appearing from seed
abundantly since the January burn

like dogbane, milkweed fibers make very strong cordage

CACHE CREEK CONSERVANCY

you!" It is a companionable scene and one that stands in stark contrast to towering flames that stretch for miles and leave behind massive burn scars where all vegetation is gone.

We get there together

When I started this project, it was a solitary endeavor. I usually visited Cold Canyon on my own, exploring, drawing, and taking notes and pictures. This was the joy of the process, slowly getting to know the altered canyon and its changes and seasons over the years. On those hikes, I thought a lot about what was happening outside my perception—the animals hidden in shrubbery, the seeds and roots of plants underground, the diverse fauna living in the soil. I began to understand the relationships between organisms that are sometimes visible—pipevine swallowtail caterpillars feasting on California pipevine leaves, for example—and often invisible, such as mycorrhizal fungi, growing in or on plant roots and connecting plants to the soil and to each other.

And then gradually my own network began to expand, to mirror the connections all around me in the environment. Just as studying one organism after fire led me to another and then another via unseen threads of connection—as from tree to fungus to beetle to woodpecker—so too the human connections I made, following a serendipitous, illuminating path. My view of the rich and varied tapestry of fire ecology and ecosystem health has been filled with so much more color and detail thanks to everyone who has been generous with their time and thoughts. I chose Cold Canyon because it was open to the public, but also because I knew that there might be the chance to connect with researchers and land managers. That hope was resoundingly fulfilled.

What I had not anticipated when I started visiting and drawing Cold Canyon were the other connections that would flourish, too. My lucky meeting with Miriam Morrill first led me further afield, to the Klamath training program for prescribed burning and the hard-won and productive relationship cultivated there between the Karuk Tribe, conservation nonprofits, and government agencies.

SPLIT GILL FUNGUS
Schizophyllum commune

growing on the burned red bud stumps, looking quite dried out in the summer heat

WESTERN RED BUD
Cercis occidentalis

CACHE CREEK CONSERVANCY

And then those connections brought me back to the Cache Creek Conservancy Tending and Gathering Garden in my own backyard, where a strong community has been forged between Native Americans, the Conservancy, faculty and students at UC Davis, and the broader public.

We all have roots sunk deep, and the fungal mycelia that intertwine and connect our roots are our love for the lands on which we live and the ecosystems we immerse ourselves in, our commitment to the continuing health and biodiversity of these lands, and our understanding of the need for good fire, for the healthy flames that nurture a cycle of disturbance and renewal. The story I am telling has stitched these connections into its fabric in ways that I did not dream of when I stood outside the locked gate at Cold Canyon in September 2015, just after the Wragg Fire. These relationships, this fellowship, mark the way forward. This is how we will break the escalating spiral of fires that burn giant swaths of land at high severity and make it difficult for even fire-adapted species to recover. This is how we return to cycles of fire appropriate to their habitats. Our frequent summer and fall infernos are forcing us to become more familiar than ever before with fire and its aftermath, and as Californians we must decide what we want the future to look like. We can exacerbate the harm of wildfire by remaining stuck in a spiral of reaction only, fighting megafires with all of our limited resources. Or we can tend it as a restorative force, one that brings new opportunities to the inhabitants of this flame-sculpted landscape as the ecosystem cycles through living and dying in delicate balance. I walked headlong into my grief and fear when I entered Cold Canyon in December 2015, and I walked through it again in 2020. Only by turning toward fire and knowing this place deeply could I understand its full power and potential. Choosing to engage has changed everything for me and has the ability to do so for us all.

acorn woodpeckers
crossing from one
side to the other

So many
honeybees on
the mustard

2 pipevine swallowtails
in flowering elderberry

wiry snapdragon
Antirrhinum
    vexillo-calyculatum

next to the mustard

CONCLUSION
The Newt's Way

It is May 2021. It has been nine months since the 2020 Markley Fire and nearly six years since the 2015 Wragg Fire. I lock my car, loop my binoculars around my neck, and pull my sketchbook and pen out of my pack. It is midmorning and in the high sixties, warming quickly. Much has changed since I first visited Cold Canyon after the Markley Fire last October. The ash is less obvious, and many places are covered in the yellowed stalks of nonnative annual grasses that grew up quickly after the fire and have since dried for the summer. Trees and shrubs have been resprouting, so there is more green in the canyon bottom and the hillsides.

I walk onto the trail, my brisk pace halted almost immediately by late-spring flowers and active, buzzing pollinators. An outpouring of honeybees is enjoying the wild mustard, two nonnative species taking advantage of the open, sunny postfire spaces. Native flowers enjoy this spot too—wiry snapdragon, elegant Clarkia, and twining snake-lily. And since I'm stopped, drawing these colorful hubs of activity, I spend a moment watching the Nuttall's and acorn woodpeckers flashing overhead. They seem to spend a lot of time crossing from one side of the canyon to the other, lighting on still-standing charred tree trunks on both sides.

In some ways the canyon feels familiar, very much the way it looked when I first started to study it the winter after the Wragg Fire. Burned, but full of life and activity, with plenty of organisms that find nothing amiss in this greatly altered tableau. But in other ways, it is completely alien. There are far fewer tree skeletons this time, as the ones that were left after the first fire burned up completely this time. It is also much less green than it was the May after the Wragg Fire. I'm not sure whether shrub resprouting has decreased, but I do see less vine growth than in 2016. Climate conditions are different now. We are in another severe drought, with only a couple of wetter years between this drought and the last. It is impossible to separate the effects of drought and fire, but the two combined have had a marked impact.

I walk along, watching the dry, cracked earth beneath my boots, appreciating what I can see and extending my imagination to what lies beyond. I wonder whether the California lilacs will germinate and what happened to the woodrats this time. It takes them a while to recolonize an area, and I do not know how many had done so between the Wragg and Markley Fires. Sometimes as I walk, I probe my feelings about the very different experience I am having now compared to the spring after the Wragg Fire. I find the dull ache that I am never quite without—dread and sadness at what we might be losing and what this portends.

But then I keep walking. Because that is what this project is about. Moving through time along with this ecosystem. The future is uncertain, of course. That is why I am here, and that is why I made the commitment to know this place. Nearly six years in, I find that I am inextricably bound to Cold Canyon because I need to know what comes next. I am invested in the individual plants I have come to know, shrubs and trees that I've watched grow after the fire. I've spent so much time thinking about them—about the leaves and branches I can see and about all of their underground parts that I cannot—that instead of hiking the canyon admiring beautiful scenery, I travel through greeting old friends. After the Markley Fire, many of the plants and animals are gone. But what I know now, and did not in 2016, is that some are not. They are here, some out of sight and some dramatically altered, but here nonetheless, and I can greet them in their new forms too. Roots and burls sending up shoots. Seeds germinating. Wrentits gazing fiercely from the lowest branches of a bay laurel.

I cannot help but continue to come here to watch their lives unfold. Having discovered these deep connections in the ecosystem, I will be walking these hills now and into the future. In much the same way, I am walking in solidarity with the communities I've discovered, scientists, land managers, cultural and

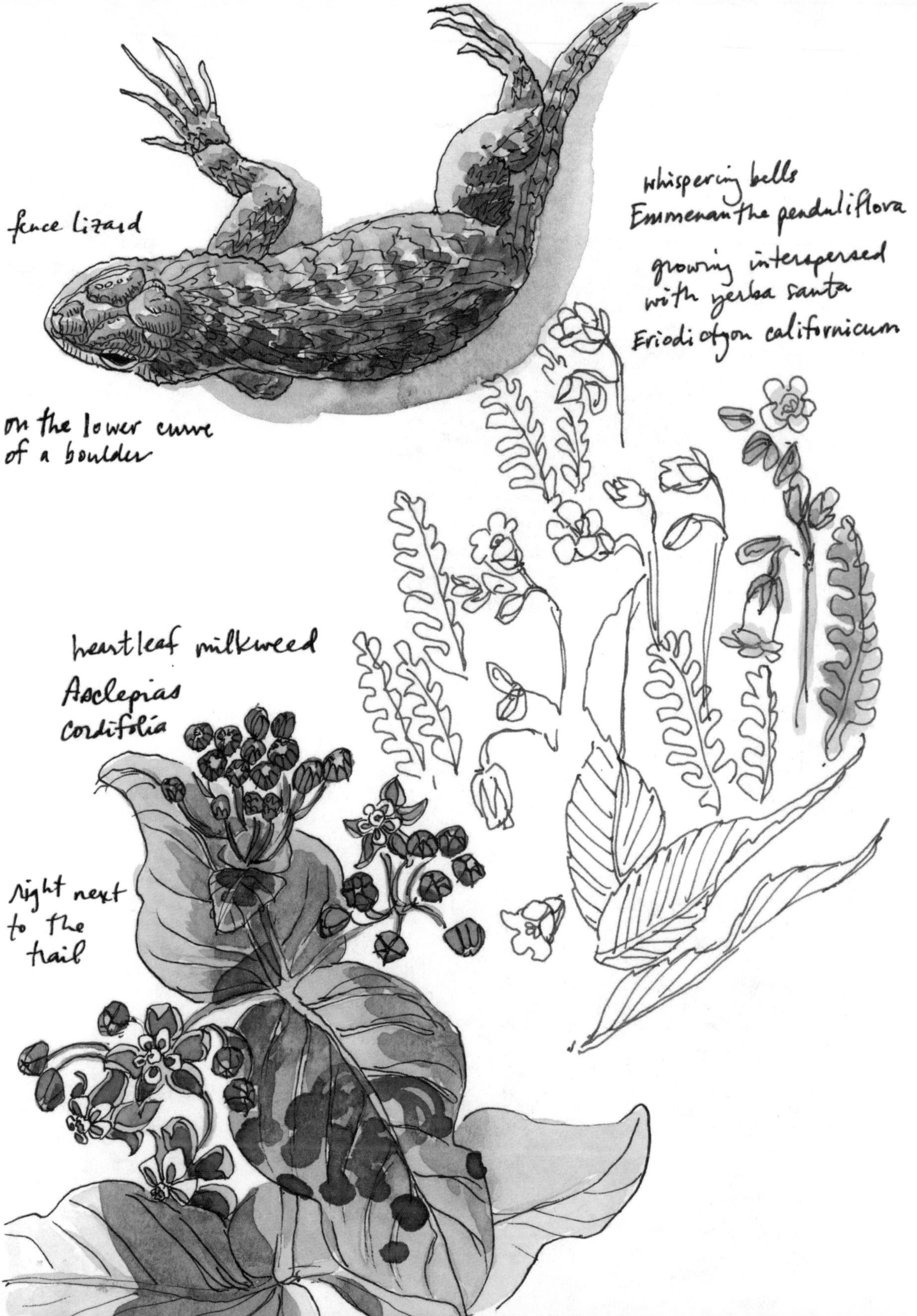

fence lizard

on the lower curve
of a boulder

whispering bells
Emmenanthe penduliflora
growing interspersed
with yerba santa
Eriodictyon californicum

heartleaf milkweed
Asclepias
cordifolia

right next
to the
trail

poison oak
gall mite

Aculops rhois

the last time
I saw this
it was in July
(2016) – is there
a seasonality or
can the galls be
observed year-round?

foothill
penstemon
Penstemon
heterophyllus

pipestem clematis
Clematis lasiantha
climbing through
a toyon

prescribed burning practitioners, all woven together by a shared love for our California landscapes and united in commitment to preserving biodiversity and returning us to healthy fire cycles.

And.

There are whispering bells.

I saw them first in April, quite a few of them, growing along the trail on the east-facing slopes. They glowed in the sunshine as if lit from within. On this May visit, I am walking along the bottom of the canyon, and I find a few small plants in the shade at this time of day. From a distance, especially, they are not a showy wildflower. But up close, the delicate creamy white bells are ethereally beautiful as they hang all in a line along their stalk. If they are here, even in a landscape that still feels like tragedy, there is hope. Hope that they will grow for a couple of generations these next few years, setting enough seeds that they return, again, after the next fire.

Though I always keep in mind the whispering bells and their message, I am at the same time scared of the growing momentum of environmental destruction around me. I am writing this in August in a summer of intense heat waves, with multiple wildfires burning throughout California that have devoured many hundreds of square miles and are still growing. Our severe drought and high temperatures mean that we can count on much more of the same, and worse, in the future. I am thinking about the natural fire cycles that have been lastingly, if not permanently, derailed. I am thinking about time, and the trees whose lives are lived on so much vaster a scale than our own. Once they are gone, it will take them a very long time to return, if they ever do.

I grieve for what might be lost. There are so many mysteries of fire ecology that we have yet to imagine, much less begun to explore. The adaptations we do know about, such as seeds that wait decades to emerge into a recently burned habitat, or beetles that come from many miles around to lay their eggs in dead and dying trees, are surprising and wonderful. And there must be so many more of these stories that we know nothing about. I worry that with fires occurring more fiercely and frequently, many of these wonders will disappear. The loss of those species and relationships is the greatest tragedy, but I am also sad for the loss of knowledge. I don't want to lose the chance to understand a little bit more of the fire cycle. I grieve for all the things that are already gone.

But I also know how much beauty there is to find in things that seem broken. There are always survivors we have overlooked. I do not think that fear and hope are contradictory. Indeed, they are both constant companions on these days of bright, dangerous skies and soaring mercury. I meet my fears head-on by going deeper into the world, not by withdrawing. In a way, I am learning that the two opposing views of fire with which I started this journey are equally true. It is not one or the other. As much as I would like fire to always mean growth and opportunity and joy, now more than ever it also means destruction, grief, and emptiness. But this is an invitation. An opportunity to learn as much as we can about the habitats that are still here while we work to cushion the blows of the great changes already under way—to preserve as much biodiversity as we can in the new ecosystems to come. How we work with or against fire will be vital.

I embarked on this project to immerse myself in a familiar local space—to understand, through close study and closer observation, all I could about wildfire's intimate relationship with the world. I also wanted to record in drawings what I experienced, to share the emotion and the beauty with others. In the process, I learned what it means to walk in a burned and then reburned landscape. Everything around me was a treasure and full of meaning. I saw mystery and loss and promise in every new leaf growing, insect whirring past, and small bird scratching

filling out a small slope at the homestead

warrior's plume
Pedicularis densiflora

little glowing parasites

hemiparasites! they attach to other plants roots when they can

CA polypody
Polypodium californicum

also at the homestead

and growing in a patch of sunlight

in the dirt. But I knew, then and now, that all of this hope depends on habitats experiencing fires that burn patchily and with great variety in heat and size. This is the paradox: fire is vital, but only if it is helping maintain diversity in habitats. And that diversity is best cultivated by fire. California, one of the most richly biodiverse regions in the world, is rapidly losing this diversity, in both habitats and fire. We still have a choice about what our relationship with fire will be, but the door will not be open forever, and the choice is rapidly being made for us.

There is a lot of drama in the way I think about fire. In the way that many Californians today think about fire. And I love the image of the phoenix rising from the still-smoldering ashes of a fire—beauty and grace reborn and climbing triumphantly into the sky. But is this how other organisms experience fire? Maybe. Or perhaps it is more like the quieter image of two California newts walking slowly and deliberately straight into the small oncoming flames of a prescribed fire and emerging on the other side unharmed. I would like to be a newt walking into the flame front, embracing this disruption as a usual part of the cycle, just ordinary life plodding on through the flames.

NOTE 1
Stebbins Cold Canyon
A UC Natural Reserve

The UC Natural Reserve System was established in 1965 to protect California's extraordinarily diverse habitats and make them available for ecological research. The system now includes forty-one Reserves the length and breadth of the state, encompassing nearly all of California's major habitats. As one of the Reserves, Stebbins Cold Canyon is an important sanctuary for habitats that are becoming rarer in California. It is fitting that the Reserve, established in 1979, was named for G. Ledyard Stebbins, at the time professor emeritus in the UC Davis Department of Genetics. A devoted botanist and important contributor to the science of plant evolutionary biology and plant conservation, Stebbins focused especially on the documentation and preservation of rare plants in California.

The Reserves' ecological diversity makes them natural laboratories, where teaching and research support each other in the wild. Scientists use Cold Canyon for research in a variety of disciplines, including ecology, botany, entomology, parasitology, and geology. But what sets Cold Canyon apart from almost all the other Reserves is that it is open to the public. It is a beloved destination, thanks to its accessibility and the unique window it opens into such iconic California habitats as blue oak woodland and chamise chaparral, along with its ridgetop panoramic views.

Dramatically increased recreational use over the past decade has led to high visitor numbers, with over sixty-five thousand people coming to Cold Canyon every year. They come to Cold Canyon to hike, run the trails, photograph the flowers and the vistas, jump the boulders in the creek, and commune with nature. They bring their children, their dogs, and their friends. The population that visits is overwhelmingly local, most driving less than an hour to reach the site, which means that visitors are exploring their own home habitats.

As a research field site open to the public, Cold Canyon offers another kind of transformative experience. In an extension of the Reserve's value beyond recreational opportunities, the public has been invited into the scientific process in a number of citizen science projects over the years. The California Phenology Project brought together researchers and members of the public to observe the timing of plant life cycles—leafing out, flowering, and fruiting. There have also been several City Nature Challenges at Cold Canyon, where volunteers record as many species as they can find over the course of three days. These projects are an invitation to immerse ourselves more fully in our surroundings and deepen our connection to important ecosystems of the California Coast Ranges.

Watson's manroot
Marah watsonii

The Reserve is a rare treasure, shared and shaped jointly by scientists and the public. It is a place where students come on field trips or to conduct research projects. Where scientists have access to public opinions and public participation in projects. Where the public comes to explore and enjoy their natural surroundings. Where those seeking greater engagement find opportunities to participate in citizen science. And where the public has now been able to explore a burned landscape and have their perceptions of wildfire challenged and expanded. It is an inspiring model for engaging all members of the community in observing nature, understanding wildfire, and committing to lifelong stewardship.

NOTE 2
Ecoreportage
Drawing a Changing Landscape

I grew up in Davis and returned to live here again in 2014. At the time, my house was at the northern edge of town, near a long storm-water channel running between the neighborhood and agricultural fields. The channel had recently been revitalized to create a functioning riparian corridor and wildlife habitat. I took to walking along the edge of the channel in the evenings, watching the light fade over the fields, the soft pinks of the sunset reflected in the irrigation water running between the tidy furrows, and I was surprised by the changes I saw in the Central Valley. Davis winters were foggy when I was a kid. Even though the temperatures were never that low, and only some years saw a lot of rainfall, the arrival of the tule fog always emphasized the changing of the seasons and the arrival of winter. Moving back, I discovered that the fog was almost entirely gone. Of course the rain still comes and goes, but the temperatures are noticeably warmer. Concern about the climate has occupied my thoughts and animated my fears since childhood, but these changes felt like a turning point.

Watching the world change around me became more of a preoccupation, and I noted the things that I once took for granted but were no longer certain: weather patterns, seasons, wildfire frequencies and intensities, and the populations and behavior of the plants and animals around me. I felt compelled to chronicle these changes and the signs of human impact on the environment. I started with the things I saw on my evening walks. Water filling the storm-water channel nearly to the brim in wet years and reduced to mosquito-y puddles in dry years. Irrigation pumps and irrigated fields, humming away on hot evenings, delivering water to the dry fields. Smoke on the horizon from the inevitable summer fires. Barn owls flying from the tall trees in neighborhood backyards at dusk out to the fields to hunt—perfect examples of a species making use of the edge habitat between town and country.

I think of what I have been doing as *ecoreportage*: close observation of the environment at a specific location, repeatedly returning over time to build a picture of ecological change—including how humans are affecting the local environment in ways both big and small. I want to know how and why my surroundings came to look the way they do, and I want to understand how they change as I observe them over time. I have come to see this work as a form of journalism, requiring me to understand my subject's past and to ask probing questions about what it looks like now, compiling a detailed picture as I return again and again over the years. I take inspiration for the name from the reportage artists who chronicle human events—social events, protests, emergencies, and military conflicts—in lively, compelling sketches, capturing a sense of the place and the action with visual storytelling.

I document my observations in images and in words. It is nature journaling, but with sustained attention to specific places and how they change over months and years. I draw to let what I see move through my body and out again

IRRIGATED FIELDS

onto the page. The drawings are first and foremost for myself, as important experiences in the moment and as aids to memory. But they are also meant to communicate what I am seeing and feeling, to convey to others the life I see around me, as it is now and as it will be.

Ecoreportage is a way

barn owl heading out over the fields from the
trees along the ditch where the owl boxes are   dusk

to ask where the world is going. My work has opened up an ever-growing list of insights and discoveries. Changes each year in the seasonality of plants and insects. A memorial to things lost, like the dense Central Valley fog of my childhood. Documentation of what I see right now, so I can compare it to what I will find in the future. A record of momentous events—wildfires or storms or migrations. Maps of changes, in the ranges of species or the slow creep of urban sprawl. The slow recovery of species after disease outbreaks—for example, California black walnuts, which have been devastated by the fungus/beetle complex called thousand cankers disease. Or yellow-billed magpies and their sharp decline and partial recovery from West Nile virus.

Climate change is the beating drum beneath all the things I am driven to document. I am fascinated by the human activity I see around me—urban planning practices, agricultural shifts, land management choices, and fire management—and how it impacts the environment. As the effects of climate change escalate, making these connections feels vital to understanding what I see happening around me and communicating it to others.

All close observers of the natural world are in a position to chronicle this inexorable change that marks our present and haunts our future. We all have the tools and experience that come from paying careful attention to our surroundings, and we can use them to document, analyze, and share what is happening in our own neighborhoods and the environments we encounter regularly. We have a great power to become more deeply enmeshed in our world—understanding its past and watching as the present unfolds into the future.

Tools and practices

When I draw in the field, I travel light and am open to everything around me. Drawing what I see forces me to slow down and truly notice all the details and all the additional lives I would have otherwise missed, such as the small green leaf beetle and tiny black thrips on the flowers of mountain mahogany on a bright March morning. I carry a sketchbook and a pen and a limited set of watercolors.

For a sketchbook, I like it to be lightweight, with drawing or mixed-media paper, but nothing as thick as watercolor paper. I do most of my drawing standing or squatting, so the sketchbook needs to be a size and shape comfortable to support on one hand and forearm while drawing with the other.

A pencil is a fantastic tool for sketching in the field. But I use bold black ink most, and I nearly always draw directly in ink when I am nature journaling. I use fountain pens that I can refill with ink, both to reduce the plastic waste of disposable pens and because I love the expressive variable lines I can get from a fountain pen. I like refillable brush pens for the same reason. Drawing in ink with no pencil lines is my favorite way to ensure that I am capturing spontaneous impressions. I always find that the first version of a drawing conveys the most vitality and feeling—and this is what matters most to me.

For color, I sometimes use a few colored pencils, but more often a little box with around six colors of watercolor paint. I use a waterbrush, which holds water in its handle and makes painting in the field extremely easy. When I paint my field observations, I am never trying to accurately reproduce all the details of the subject. Instead, I focus on the overall feeling the colors convey, and use paint to loosely wash reminders of this on the page. And I don't always use color. Sometimes I add color later, at home, based on memory or photographs. Other sketches I leave in black and white, having recorded all the information I need.

Because this is a long-term project and I know that I will want to come back and compare changes over the years, I document my visits in photographs too. There are only so many things I can draw each visit, and photographs allow me to later catalog all the species I observed.

Resources

If you are thinking about starting an ecoreportage project and would like more guidance on nature-journaling tools and techniques, there are many excellent books and references. Here are a few of my favorites.

field sketching supplies

John Muir Laws. *The Laws Guide to Nature Drawing and Journaling*. Berkeley, CA: Heyday, 2016.

Susan Leigh Tomlinson. *How to Keep a Naturalist's Notebook*. Mechanicsburg, PA: Stackpole Books, 2009.

Clare Walker Leslie and Charles E. Roth. *Keeping a Nature Journal: Discover a Whole New Way of Seeing the World around You*. North Adams, MA: Storey Publishing, 2003.

Hannah Hinchman. *A Trail through Leaves: The Journal as a Path to Place*. New York: Norton, 1997.

NOTE 3
Names of Species Discussed in the Text

Plants

Alders, *Alnus* spp.

Arroyo lupine, *Lupinus succulentus*

Bishop pine, *Pinus muricata*

Blue dicks, *Dipterostemon capitatus*

Blue elderberry, *Sambucus nigra* ssp. *caerulea*

Blue oak, *Quercus douglasii*

Blue wildrye, *Elymus glaucus*

Broadleaf cattail, *Typha latifolia*

Bur clover, *Medicago polymorpha*

California bay laurel, *Umbellularia californica*

California black walnut, *Juglans hindsii*

California buckeye, *Aesculus californica*

California fuchsia, *Epilobium canum*

California lilacs, see hairy-leaf ceanothus and wedge-leaf ceanothus

California manroot, *Marah fabacea*

California melic, *Melica californica*

California pipevine, *Aristolochia californica*

California pitcher sage, *Lepechinia calycina*

California spicebush, *Calycanthus occidentalis*

California tea, *Rupertia physodes*

Canyon delphinium, *Delphinium nudicaule*

Chamise, *Adenostoma fasciculatum*

Chaparral currant, *Ribes malvaceum*

Chaparral false bindweed, *Calystegia occidentalis*

Cheatgrass, *Bromus tectorum*

Checker-lily, *Fritillaria affinis*

Chick lupine, *Lupinus microcarpus*

Common manzanita, *Arctostaphylos manzanita*

Coyotebrush, *Baccharis pilularis*

Deergrass, *Muhlenbergia rigens*

Deerweed, *Acmispon glaber*

Douglas fir, *Pseudotsuga menziesii*

Dove's foot geranium, *Geranium molle*

Eastwood manzanita, *Arctostaphylos glandulosa*

Elegant clarkia, *Clarkia unguiculata*

Fernald's iris, *Iris fernaldii*

Fiddleneck, *Amsinckia menziesii*

Foothill delphinium, *Delphinium hesperium*

Four-spot, *Clarkia purpurea*

Fremont cottonwood, *Populus fremontii*

Fremont's star-lily, *Toxicoscordion fremontii*

Golden fairy lantern, *Calochortus amabilis*

Gray pine, *Pinus sabiniana*

Hairy vetch, *Vicia villosa*

Hairy-leaf ceanothus, *Ceanothus oliganthus*

Henderson's shooting star, *Primula hendersonii*

Innocence, *Collinsia heterophylla*

Interior live oak, *Quercus wislizeni*

Ithuriel's spear, *Triteleia laxa*

Knobcone pine, *Pinus attenuata*

Large-leaved hound's tongue, *Cynoglossum grande*

checker-lily
Fritillaria affinis

Lodgepole pine, *Pinus contorta*

Milkmaids, *Cardamine californica*

Miniature lupine, *Lupinus bicolor*

Mountain mahogany, *Cercocarpus betuloides*

Pacific peavine, *Lathyrus vestitus*

Penstemons, *Penstemon* spp.

Phacelias, *Phacelia* spp.

Poison oak, *Toxicodendron diversilobum*

Popcorn flowers, *Plagiobothrys* spp.

Purple needlegrass, *Nassella pulchra*

Purple sanicle, *Sanicula bipinnatifida*

Red ribbons, *Clarkia concinna*

Redstem filaree, *Erodium cicutarium*

Scrub oak, *Quercus berberidifolia*

Seep monkeyflower, *Erythranthe guttata*

Silver bush lupine, *Lupinus albifrons*

Sticky monkeyflower, *Diplacus aurantiacus*

Three-leaf sumac, *Rhus trilobata*

Toyon, *Heteromeles arbutifolia*

Twining snake-lily, *Dichelostemma volubile*

Warrior's plume, *Pedicularis densiflora*

Wavy-leaved soap plant, *Chlorogalum pomeridianum*

Wedge-leaf ceanothus, *Ceanothus cuneatus*

Western redbud, *Cercis occidentalis*

Whispering bells, *Emmenanthe penduliflora*

White foothill delphinium, *Delphinium hesperium* ssp. *pallescens*

Wild oat, *Avena fatua*

Willows, *Salix* spp.

Yellow starthistle, *Centaurea solstitialis*

Yerba santa, *Eriodictyon californicum*

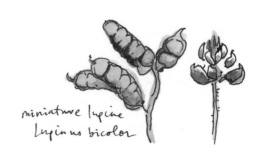

miniature lupine
Lupinus bicolor

Animals

Acorn woodpecker, *Melanerpes formicivorus*

American crow, *Corvus brachyrhynchos*

American kestrel, *Falco sparverius*

American robin, *Turdus migratorius*

Anna's hummingbird, *Calypte anna*

Black-backed woodpecker, *Picoides arcticus*

Black-chinned hummingbird, *Archilochus alexandri*

Black-headed grosbeak, *Pheucticus melanocephalus*

Bobcat, *Lynx rufus*

Brush mouse, *Peromyscus boylii*

Bullock's oriole, *Icterus bullockii*

California carpenter bee, *Xylocopa californica*

California elderberry borer, *Desmocerus californicus*

California mouse, *Peromyscus californicus*

California newt, *Taricha torosa*

California quail, *Callipepla californica*

California slender salamander, *Batrachoseps attenuatus*

California tortoiseshell, *Nymphalis californica*

California towhee, *Melozone crissalis*

Charcoal beetle, *Melanophila consputa*

Cooper's hawk, *Accipiter cooperii*

Coyote, *Canis latrans*

Crystalline gall wasp, *Andricus crystallinus*

Dark-eyed junco, *Junco hyemalis*

Digger bees, *Anthophorini (Apidae)*

Dusky-footed woodrat, *Neotoma fuscipes*

Filbert weevil, *Curculio occidentis*

Filbert worm, *Cydia latiferreana*

Foothill yellow-legged frog, *Rana boylii*

Fox sparrow, *Passerella iliaca*

Great horned owl, *Bubo virginianus*

Gray fox, *Urocyon cinereoargenteus*

Hairy woodpecker, *Leuconotopicus villosus*

Horntails, Siricidae

Leafroller moths, Torticidae

Membrane bees, Colletidae

Mining bees, Andrenidae

Mompha moths, Momphidae

Mountain lion, *Puma concolor*

Mourning cloak, *Nymphalis antiopa*

Mule deer, *Odocoileus hemionus*

Northern flicker, *Colaptes auratus*

Northern pygmy owl, *Glaucidium californicum*

Nuttall's woodpecker, *Dryobates nuttallii*

Oak titmouse, *Baeolophus inornatus*

Owlet moths, Noctuidae

Pacific chorus frog, *Pseudacris regilla*

Pine engraver, *Ips pini*

Pine sawyers, *Monochamus* spp.

Pipevine swallowtail, *Battus philenor*

Protodufourea wasbaueri, *Protodufourea wasbaueri*

Red-breasted sapsucker, *Sphyrapicus ruber*

Ruby-crowned kinglet, *Regulus calendula*

Rufous hummingbird, *Selasphorus rufus*

Sara orangetip, *Anthocharis sara*

Scrub jay, *Aphelocoma californica*

Sonoma chipmunk, *Neotamias sonomae*

Southern alligator lizard, *Elgaria multicarinata*

Spotted owl, *Strix occidentalis*

Spotted towhee, *Pipilo maculatus*

Steller's jay, *Cyanocitta stelleri*

Striped skunk, *Mephitis mephitis*

Sweat bees, Halictidae

Tragidion annulatum, *Tragidion annulatum*

Turkey vulture, *Cathartes aura*

Twirler moths, Gelechiidae

Urchin gall wasp, *Cynips quercusechinus*

Variable checkerspot, *Euphydryas chalcedona*

Verrill's underwing, *Catocala verrilliana*

Western black widow, *Latrodectus hesperus*

Western deer mouse, *Peromyscus sonoriensis*

Western fence lizard, *Sceloporus occidentalis*

Western pond turtle, *Actinemys marmorata*

Western screech owl, *Megascops kennicottii*

Western skink, *Plestiodon skiltonianus*

Western tanager, *Piranga ludoviciana*

Western toad, *Anaxyrus boreas*

White-throated sparrow, *Zonotrichia albicollis*

Wrentit, *Chamaea fasciata*

Verrill's underwing
Catocala verrilliana

Fungi

Hare's foot inkcap, *Coprinopsis lagopus*

Mossy maze polypore, *Cerrena unicolor*

Purplepore bracket fungus, *Trichaptum abietinum*

Turkey tail, *Trametes versicolor*

Yellow fieldcap, *Bolbitius titubans*

Lichens

Beard lichens, *Usnea* spp.

Disk lichens, *Lecidea* spp.

Dog lichens, *Peltigera* spp.

Rosette lichens, *Physcia* spp.

Speckled greenshield lichens, *Flavopunctelia* spp.

Strap lichens, *Ramalina* spp.

Sunburst lichens, *Xanthoria* spp.

Whiskered jelly lichen, *Leptochidium albociliatum*

Bibliography

Agee, James K. *Fire Ecology of Pacific Northwest Forests*. Washington, DC: Island Press, 1993.

Alcock, John. *After the Wildfire: Ten Years of Recovery from the Willow Fire*. Tucson: University of Arizona Press, 2017.

Alexander, John D., Elizabeth J. Williams, Caitlyn R. Gillespie, Sarahy Contreras-Martínez, and Deborah M. Finch. *Effects of Fire and Restoration on Habitats and Populations of Western Hummingbirds: A Literature Review*. General Technical Report RMRS-GTR-408. Fort Collins, CO: US Department of Agriculture, Forest Service, Rocky Mountain Research Station, 2020.

Anderson, M. Kat. *Tending the Wild: Native American Knowledge and the Management of California's Natural Resources*. Berkeley: University of California Press. 2005.

Anderson, M. Kat, and Michael Kauffmann, eds. "California Geophytes." Special issue, *Fremontia* 44, no. 3 (December 2016).

Anderson, Tamara. *Conservation Assessment for the Woodpeckers in the Black Hills National Forest South Dakota and Wyoming*. Custer, SD: US Department of Agriculture, Forest Service, Rocky Mountain Region, 2003.

Bakhshandeh-Savadroodbari, Maryam, Rahim Maleknia, Abbas Banj Shafiei, Mohammad-Reza Zargaran, and Ziaedin Badehian. "The Temporal Effects of Forest Fires on Abundance and Diversity of Oak Gall Wasps (Hymenoptera: Cynipidae)." *North-Western Journal of Zoology* 13, no. 2 (December 2017): 211–19.

Barro, Susan C., and Susan G. Conard. "Fire Effects on California Chaparral Systems: An Overview." *Environment International* 17, nos. 2 and 3 (1991): 135–49. https://doi.org/10.1016/0160-4120(91)90096-9.

Battey, Christopher J. "Ecological Release of the Anna's Hummingbird during a Northern Range Expansion." *American Naturalist* 194, no. 3 (September 2019): 306–15. https://doi.org/10.1086/704249.

Bond, Monica L., Rodney B. Siegel, Richard L. Hutto, Victoria A. Saab, and Stephen A. Shunk. "A New Forest Fire Paradigm: The Need for High-Severity Fires." *Wildlife Professional*, Winter 2012, 46–49.

Bruns, Thomas D., Jacqueline Baar, Paul Grogan, Thomas R. Horton, Annette M. Kretzer, Dirk Redecker, Jenny Tan, and D. Lee Taylor. "Community Dynamics of Ectomycorrhizal Fungi following the Vision Fire." In *Vision Fire—Lessons Learned from the 1995 Fire*, 31–39. US Department of Interior, National Park Service, Point Reyes National Seashore, 1996. https://www.nps.gov/pore/learn/management/upload/firemanagement_visionfire_lessonslearned.pdf.

Bunyard, Britt A. "A Tripartite Relationship between a Woodrot Fungus, a Wood-boring Sawfly, and the Giant Ichneumonid Wasp." *FUNGI* 8, no. 1 (Spring 2015): 14–20. https://www.fungimag.com/spring-2015-articles/Woodrot%20Fungus%20LR.pdf.

Carle, David. *Introduction to Fire in California*. Berkeley: University of California Press, 2008.

Covert-Bratland, Kristin A., William M. Block, and Tad C. Theimer. "Hairy Woodpecker Winter Ecology in Ponderosa Pine Forests Representing Different Ages since Wildfire." *Journal of Wildlife Management* 70, no. 5 (November 2006): 1379–92. http://www.jstor.org/stable/4128059.

Cronin, James T., George Melika, and Warren G. Abrahamson. "Time-since Fire and Cynipid Gall Wasp Assemblages on Oaks." *Biodiversity and Conservation* 29, no. 4 (March 2020): 1177–1203. https://doi.org/10.1007/s10531-020-01930-w.

Diffendorfer, Jay, Genie M. Fleming, Scott Tremor, Wayne Spencer, and Jan L. Beyers. "The Role of Fire Severity, Distance from Fire Perimeter and Vegetation on Post-Fire Recovery of Small-Mammal Communities in Chaparral." *International Journal of Wildland Fire* 21 (2012): 436–48.

Eversman, Sharon, and Diana Horton. "Recolonization of Burned Substrates by Lichens and Mosses in Yellowstone National Park." *Northwest Science* 78, no. 2 (March 2004): 85–92.

Force, Don C. *Ecology of Insects in California Chaparral*. Research Paper PSW-201. Berkeley, CA: US Department of Agriculture, Forest Service, Pacific Southwest Research Station, 1990.

Fryer, Janet L. "Quercus douglasii." In *Fire Effects Information System* [Online]. US Department of Agriculture, Forest Service, Rocky Mountain Research Station, Fire Sciences Laboratory, 2007. https://www.feis-crs.org/feis/.

Greene, Correigh, and Mikaela Huntzinger, eds. *The Natural History of Stebbins Cold Canyon Reserve*. 2nd ed. University of California Natural Reserve System, 2004.

Guo, Qinfeng. "Early Post-Fire Succession in California Chaparral: Changes in Diversity, Density, Cover and Biomass." *Ecological Research* 16, no. 3 (2001): 471–85. https://doi.org/10.1046/j.1440-1703.2001.00410.x.

Haggerty, Patricia K. "Damage and Recovery in Southern Sierra Nevada Foothill Oak Woodland after a Severe Ground Fire." *Madroño* 41, no. 3 (1994): 185–98. http://www.jstor.org/stable/41425015.

———. *Fire Effects in Blue Oak Woodland*. General Technical Report PSW-126. US Department of Agriculture, Forest Service, Pacific Southwest Research Station, 1991.

Hanlon, Tara Sióbhan. "Stebbins Cold Canyon Reserve: Master Trail Plan." Senior undergraduate thesis project, University of California, Davis, 2010. https://humanecology.ucdavis.edu/sites/g/files/dgvnsk161/files/inline-files/THanlon.pdf.

Harris, Lucas, and Alan H. Taylor. "Previous Burns and Topography Limit and Reinforce Fire Severity in a Large Wildfire." *Ecosphere* 8, no. 11 (2017). https://doi.org/10.1002/ECS2.2019.

Hass, Bob, and Glen Holstein, eds. "California's Prairies and Grasslands." Special issues, *Fremontia* 39, nos. 2 and 3 (May/September 2011).

He, Tianhua, Byron B. Lamont, and Juli G. Pausas. "Fire as a Key Driver of Earth's Biodiversity." *Biological Reviews* 94, no. 6 (July 2019): 1983–2010. https://doi.org/10.1111/brv.12544.

Holmes, Katherine A., Kari E. Veblen, Truman P. Young, and Alison M. Berry. *California Oaks and Fire: A Review and Case Study*. General Technical Report PSW-GTR-217. US Department of Agriculture, Forest Service, Pacific Southwest Research Station, 2008.

Hossack, Blake R., and David S. Pilliod. "Amphibian Responses to Wildfire in the Western United States: Emerging Patterns from Short-Term Studies." *Fire Ecology* 7, no. 2 (August 2011): 129–44. https://doi.org/10.4996/fireecology .0702129.

Howard, Janet L. "Pinus sabiniana." In *Fire Effects Information System* [Online]. US Department of Agriculture, Forest Service, Rocky Mountain Research Station, Fire Sciences Laboratory, 1992. https://www.feis-crs.org/feis/.

Innes, Robin J., Dirk H. Van Vuren, Douglas A. Kelt, Michael L. Johnson, James A. Wilson, and Peter A. Stine. "Habitat Associations of Dusky-footed Woodrats (*Neotoma fuscipes*) in Mixed-Conifer Forest of the Northern Sierra Nevada." *Journal of Mammalogy* 88, no. 6 (December 2007): 1523–31. https://doi .org/10.1644/07-MAMM-A-002R.1.

Kelly, Luke T., and Lluís Brotons. "Using Fire to Promote Biodiversity: Biodiversity Can Benefit from Fires Tailored to Suit Particular Ecosystems and Species." *Science* 355, no. 6331 (March 2017): 1264–65. https://doi.org/10.1126/science .aam7672.

Loverin, John K., Andrew N. Stillman, Rodney B. Siegel, Robert L. Wilkerson, Matthew Johnson, and Morgan W. Tingley. "Nestling Provisioning Behavior of Black-backed Woodpeckers in Post-Fire Forest." *Journal of Field Ornithology* 92, no. 3 (July 2021): 273–83. http://dx.doi.org/10.1111/jofo.12371.

McCreary, Douglas D. *Fire in California's Oak Woodlands*. University of California Integrated Hardwood Range Management Program, June 2004. https://ucanr .edu/sites/fire/files/288191.pdf.

Mendelsohn, Mark B., Cheryl S. Brehme, Carlton J. Rochester, Drew C. Stokes, Stacie A. Hathaway, and Robert N. Fisher. "Responses in Bird Communities to Wildland Fires in Southern California." *Fire Ecology* 4, no. 2 (December 2008): 63–82. https://doi.org/10.4996/fireecology.0402063.

Miller, Jesse E. D., Heather T. Root, and Hugh D. Safford. "Altered Fire Regimes Cause Long-Term Lichen Diversity Losses." *Global Change Biology* 24, no. 10 (October 2018): 4909–18. https://doi.org/10.1111/gcb.14393.

Miller, Jesse E. D., and Hugh D. Safford. "Are Plant Community Responses to Wildfire Contingent upon Historical Disturbance Regimes?" *Global Ecology and Biogeography* 29, no. 10 (October 2020): 1621–33. https://doi.org/10.1111/geb.13115.

Mooney, Harold, and Erika Zavaleta. *Ecosystems of California*. Oakland: University of California Press, 2016.

National Wildfire Coordinating Group. *Guide to Wildland Fire Origin and Cause Determination*. April 2016. https://www.nwcg.gov/sites/default/files/publications/pms412.pdf.

Neary, Daniel G., Kevin C. Ryan, and Leonard F. DeBano, eds. *Wildland Fire in Ecosystems: Effects of Fire on Soils and Water*. General Technical Report RMRS-GTR-42-vol.4. Ogden, UT: US Department of Agriculture, Forest Service, Rocky Mountain Research Station, 2005 (rev. 2008).

Pascoe, Emily L., Benjamin T. Plourde, Andrés M. López-Perez, and Janet E. Foley. "Response of Small Mammal and Tick Communities to a Catastrophic Wildfire and Implications for Tick-Borne Pathogens." *Journal of Vector Ecology* 45, no. 2 (December 2020): 269–84. https://doi.org/10.1111/jvec.12398.

Pausas, Juli G., Byron B. Lamont, Susana Paula, Beatriz Appezzato-da-Glória, and Alessandra Fidelis. "Unearthing Belowground Bud Banks in Fire-Prone Ecosystems." *New Phytologist* 217, no. 4 (March 2018): 1435–48.

Powell, Jerry A. "Recovery of Lepidoptera (Moths and Butterflies) following a Wildfire at Inverness Ridge in Central Coastal California." In *Vision Fire—Lessons Learned from the 1995 Fire*, 21–32. US Department of Interior, National Park Service, Point Reyes National Seashore, 1996. https://www.nps.gov/pore/learn/management/upload/firemanagement_visionfire_lessonslearned.pdf.

Pyne, Stephen J. *California: A Fire Survey*. Tucson: University of Arizona Press, 2016.

Quinn, Ronald D., and Sterling Keeley. *Introduction to California Chaparral*. Berkeley: University of California Press, 2006.

Raudabaugh, Daniel B., P. Brandon Matheny, Karen W. Hughes, Teresa Iturriaga, Malcolm Sargent, and Andrew N. Miller. "Where Are They Hiding? Testing the Body Snatchers Hypothesis in Pyrophilous Fungi." *Fungal Ecology* 43 (February 2020). https://doi.org/10.1016/j.funeco.2019.100870.

Ray, Chris, Daniel R. Cluck, Robert L. Wilkerson, Rodney B. Siegel, Angela M. White, Gina L. Tarbill, Sara C. Sawyer, and Christine Howell. "Patterns of Woodboring Beetle Activity Following Fires and Bark Beetle Outbreaks in Montane Forests of California, USA." *Fire Ecology* 15, no. 21 (July 2019). https://doi.org/10.1186/s42408-019-0040-1.

Schiff, Nathan M., Steven A. Valley, James R. LaBonte, and David R. Smith. *Guide to the Siricid Woodwasps of North America*. Morgantown, WV: US Department of Agriculture, Forest Service, Forest Health Technology Enterprise Team, 2006.

Schmitz, Helmut, and Herbert Bousack. "Modelling a Historic Oil-Tank Fire Allows an Estimation of the Sensitivity of the Infrared Receptors in Pyrophilous *Melanophila* Beetles." *PLoS ONE* 7, no. 5 (2012): e37627. https://doi.org/10.1371/journal.pone.0037627.

Schofield, Lynn N., Stephanie A. Eyes, Rodney B. Siegel, and Sarah L. Stock. "Habitat Selection by Spotted Owls after a Megafire in Yosemite National Park." *Forest Ecology and Management* 478 (December 2020): 118511. https://doi.org/10.1016/j.foreco.2020.118511.

Sharnoff, Stephen. *A Field Guide to California Lichens*. New Haven, CT: Yale University Press, 2014.

Siegel, Rodney B., Monica L. Bond, Christine A. Howell, Sarah C. Sawyer, and Diana L. Craig, eds. "A Conservation Strategy for the Black-backed Woodpecker (*Picoides arcticus*) in California – Version 2.0." Institute for Bird Populations and California Partners in Flight. Point Reyes Station, California, February 2018. https://www.birdpop.org/docs/pubs/Siegel_et_al_2018_BBWO_Cons_Strat_V2.pdf.

Sowards, Laura A., Helmut Schmitz, David W. Tomlin, Rajesh R. Naik, and Morley O. Stone. "Characterization of Beetle *Melanophila acuminata* (Coleoptera: Buprestidae) Infrared Pit Organs by High-Performance Liquid Chromatography/ Mass Spectrometry, Scanning Electron Microscope, and Fourier Transform-Infrared Spectroscopy." *Annals of the Entomology Society of America* 94, no. 5 (2001): 686–94. http://dx.doi.org/10.1603/0013-8746(2001)094[0686:COBMAC] 2.0.CO;2

Stahle, David W., Daniel Griffin, David M. Meko, Matthew D. Therrell, Jesse R. Edmondson, Malcolm K. Cleaveland, Laura N. Stahle, Dorian J. Burnette, John T. Abatzoglou, Kelly T. Redmond, Michael D. Dettinger, and Daniel R. Cayan. "The Ancient Blue Oak Woodlands of California: Longevity and Hydroclimatic History." *Earth Interactions* 17, no. 12 (August 2013): 1–23. https://doi .org/10.1175/2013EI000518.1.

Steel, Zachary L., Brandon M. Collins, David B. Sapsis, and Scott L. Stephens. "Quantifying Pyrodiversity and Its Drivers." *Proceedings of the Royal Society B* 288, no. 1948 (April 2021). https://doi.org/10.1098/rspb.2020.3202.

Steel, Zachary L., Hugh D. Safford, and Joshua H. Viers. "The Fire Frequency-Severity Relationship and the Legacy of Fire Suppression in California Forests." *Ecosphere* 6, no. 1, article 8 (January 2015): 1–23. https://doi.org/10.1890/ES14 -00224.1.

Stillman, Andrew N., Teresa J. Lorenz, Philip C. Fischer, Rodney B. Siegel, Robert L. Wilkerson, Mathew Johnson, and Morgan W. Tingley. "Juvenile Survival of a Burned Forest Specialist in Response to Variation in Fire Characteristics." *Journal of Animal Ecology* 90, no. 5 (May 2021): 1317–27. https://doi .org/10.1111/1365-2656.13456.

Stillman, Andrew N., Rodney B. Siegel, Robert L. Wilkerson, Mathew Johnson, and Morgan W. Tingley. "Age-Dependent Habitat Relationships of a Burned Forest Specialist Emphasise the Role of Pyrodiversity in Fire Management." *Journal of Applied Ecology* 56, no. 4 (April 2019): 880–90. https://doi.org/10.1111/1365 -2664.13328.

Stromberg, Mark R. "*Taricha torosa* (California Newt) Response to Fire." *Herpetological Review* 28, no. 2 (1997): 82–83.

Swiecki, Tedmund J., and Elizabeth Bernhardt. *Effects of Fire on Naturally Occurring Blue Oak (Quercus douglasii) Saplings*. General Technical Report PSW-GTR-184. US Department of Agriculture, Forest Service, Pacific Southwest Research Station, 2002.

Swift, Ian, and Ann M. Ray. A Review of the Genus *Tragidion* Audinet-Serville, 1834 (Coleoptera: Cerambycidae: Cerambycinae: Trachyderini). *Zootaxa* 1892, no. 1 (October 2008). https://doi.org/10.11646/zootaxa.1892.1.1.

Syphard, Alexandra D., Teresa J. Brennan, and Jon E. Keeley. "Chaparral Landscape Conversion in Southern California." In *Valuing Chaparral: Ecological, Socio-Economic, and Management Perspectives*, edited by Emma C. Underwood, Hugh D. Stafford, Nicole A. Molinari, and Jon E. Keeley, 323–46. Springer Series on Environmental Management. New York: Springer, 2018.

Uzun, Habibullah, Randy A. Dahlgren, Christopher Olivares, Cagri Utku Erdem, Tanju Karanfil, and Alex T. Chow. "Two Years of Post-Wildfire Impacts on Dissolved Organic Matter, Nitrogen, and Precursors of Disinfection By-Products in California Stream Waters." *Water Research* 181 (August 2020). http://doi.org/10.1016/j.watres.2020.115891.

van Mantgem, Elizabeth F., Jon E. Keeley, and Marti Witter. "Faunal Responses to Fire in Chaparral and Sage Scrub in California, USA." *Fire Ecology* 11, no. 3 (December 2015): 128–48. https://doi.org/10.4996/fireecology.1103128.

van Wagtendonk, Jan W., Neil G. Sugihara, Scott L. Stephens, Andrea E. Thode, Kevin E. Shaffer, and Jo Ann Fites-Kaufman, eds. *Fire in California's Ecosystems*. Oakland: University of California Press, 2018.

Walker, Ryan B., Jonathan D. Coop, Sean A. Parks, and Laura Trader. "Fire Regimes Approaching Historic Norms Reduce Wildfire-Facilitated Conversion from Forest to Non-Forest." *Ecosphere* 9, no. 4 (April 2018). https://doi.org/10.1002/ecs2.2182.

Watts, Andrea, Jane E. Smith, Ariel D. Cowan, and Ari Jumpponen. "The Recovery of Soil Fungi following a Fire." *Science Findings* 207. US Department of Agriculture, Forest Service, Pacific Northwest Research Station, 2018.

Weill, Alexandra M., Lauren M. Watson, and Andrew M. Latimer. "Walking through a 'Phoenix Landscape': Hiker Surveys Reveal Nuanced Perceptions of Wildfire Effects." *International Journal of Wildland Fire* 29, no. 7 (2020): 561–71. https://www.nwfirescience.org/sites/default/files/publications/Weill%20et%20al.pdf.

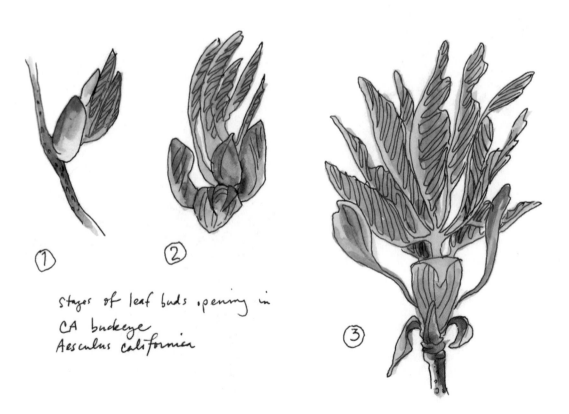

stages of leaf buds opening in
CA buckeye
Aesculus californica

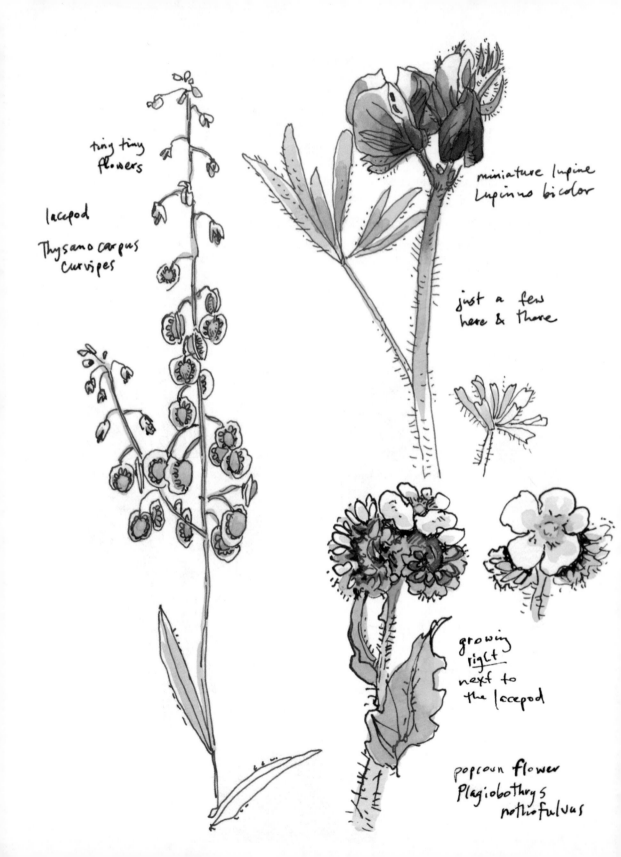

tiny tiny
flowers

lacepod

Thysanocarpus
curvipes

miniature lupine
Lupinus bicolor

just a few
here & there

growing
right
next to
the lacepod

popcorn flower
Plagiobothrys
nothofulvus

Acknowledgments

This journey began as a solo quest, but was infinitely enriched by all of the people I met along the way. They have made this project deeper and more connected than I ever imagined.

I owe the existence of this book to John Muir Laws, whose enthusiasm for my sketchbooks and interest in this project led me to Heyday, and whose support means more than I can say. My thanks also go to Steve Wasserman at Heyday for his belief in the book and its potential. Marthine Satris has been a deeply insightful editor, deftly helping shape the book's final form. I am also grateful for excellent storytelling advice from Gayle Wattawa at a crucial moment, Emily Grossman's grant-writing expertise, Michele Jones for skillful copyediting, and Ashley Ingram for molding the words and images into a beautiful and cohesive book. I thank the Moore Family Foundation for supporting the production of this book.

The UC Natural Reserve System has shown unfailing support for this work, especially Jeffrey Clary, Sarah Oktay, and Paul Havemann. It is always such a pleasure to run into Paul Havemann along the trail on a weekday morning and exchange stories about what we've seen that day and how things are looking after the fires.

When I had only just started visiting and documenting Cold Canyon after the Wragg Fire, John DeBenedictis was kind enough to allow me to tag along on a moth-collecting visit at dusk, and to share his insights stretching back to just after the previous fire, nearly thirty years before. Janet Foley discussed mammals in the canyon, especially dusky-footed woodrats, and the research her team was doing after the fire.

Later in the project, Lynn Schofield offered many valuable insights into the work she and colleagues have been doing with bird populations in burned areas.

I contacted Mark Stromberg to ask about his astonishing observations of California newts in fire, and was thrilled to learn so much more about all of his experiences with fire in a range of Western habitats, as well as his thoughts about cultural attitudes toward fire and its place in the West.

Jesse Miller and Jes Coyle generously allowed me to observe a small piece of their research into the implications of fire for lichens. I am looking forward to following the results of their research as it unfolds over the next few years. So too the work of Ashley Grupenhoff, who, along with studying fire ecology more generally, is working on monitoring the impacts of prescribed fire statewide.

Miriam Morrill, an important friend and collaborator, is doing inspiring work using her extensive experience as a fire specialist along with her artistic skills to connect the worlds of nature journaling and fire safety and awareness. The trip she organized for nature journalers to participate in a Klamath TREX (prescribed fire training exchange) was a life-changing view into prescribed and cultural burning, and I am grateful for everyone who made it possible for us to be there: Jeremy Bailey (the Nature Conservancy), Erika Terence and Will Harling (Mid Klamath Watershed Council), Bill Tripp (Karuk Tribe), Margo Robbins (Cultural Fire Management Council, Yurok Tribe) and Frank Lake (US Forest Service, Yurok and Karuk Tribes).

Closer to home, the Cache Creek Conservancy's Tending and Gathering Garden has an inspiring cultural burning program, and I am grateful to Zachary Emerson and the members of the TGG Steering Committee for allowing me to observe the burning and participate in some of the site preparation and postfire work.

Growing up hiking with my family was central to my concept of myself and what is most important in the world. So my love and gratitude to my sister, Katie Bea—Lizard Spotter—guaranteed to see lizards long before anyone else did. To my father, Daryl Carlson—Mule Deer—we often spotted only his tail far ahead on the trail. And to my mother, Susan Carlson—Plant Watcher—always bringing up the rear, calling us back to share some beautiful or noteworthy find. I will also always be grateful for the important lesson in perspective that my grandfather, David Prendergast, taught me—he was an entomologist and encouraged me to consider the world from an insect's point of view. And for the staunch interest and support of Bill and Alison Rukeyser for this project, beginning long before I knew it would become a book.

Finally, and most important, I thank Isaac Rukeyser for being a constant source of curiosity, creativity, and ideas, and being a model for living a rich and fulfilling life, full of interests. And Jacob Rukeyser for believing in my writing, always being willing to talk through ideas, skillfully helping shape narrative, and being an editor with an eye for rich imagery and lively detail. You are both truly my favorite storytellers and favorite mammals on the planet.

spice bush
Calycanthus
occidentalis

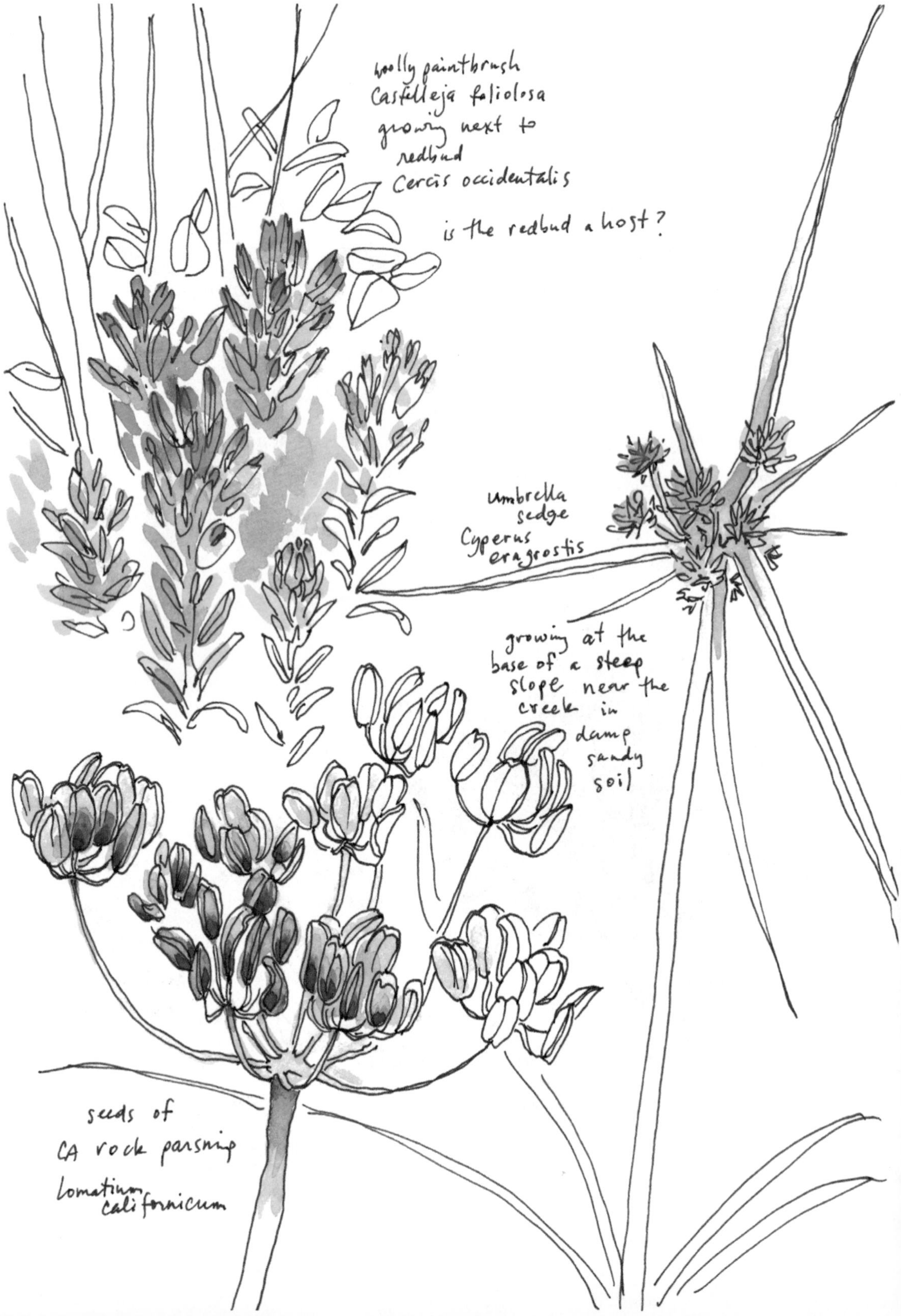

woolly paintbrush
Castilleja foliolosa
growing next to
redbud
Cercis occidentalis

is the redbud a host?

umbrella
sedge
Cyperus
eragrostis

growing at the
base of a steep
slope near the
creek in
damp
sandy
soil

seeds of
CA rock parsnip
Lomatium
californicum

About the Author

Photo by James Scott

Robin Lee Carlson is a natural science writer and illustrator. After studying evolutionary biology at UC Santa Cruz and the University of Chicago, she spent many years working on stream habitat restoration projects in California. She is most interested in how landscapes and ecological communities change over time, especially ecosystem dynamics after disruption. Her artwork is always grounded in observing and documenting the world around her as it unfolds. Visit her website at robinleecarlson.com.

A Note on Type

Freight is a humanist-style typeface created by California-born type designer Joshua Darden and released through Phil's Fonts in 2005. With five families (including with and without serifs) and more than one hundred character styles, the typeface fits a broad range of aesthetics and uses. Freight balances visual appeal and reader comfort, adapting well to both small and large amounts of text.